CRITICAL
INSIGHTS

The Hero's Quest

CRITICAL INSIGHTS

The Hero's Quest

Editors
Bernard Schweizer
Long Island University
Robert A. Segal
University of Aberdeen, Scotland

SALEM PRESS
A Division of EBSCO Publishing
Ipswich, Massachusetts

Cover Photo: Dante and Virgil by Eugene Delacroix.
© Alfredo Dagli Orti/The Art Archive/Corbis

Editor's text © 2013 by Bernard Schweizer and Robert A. Segal

∞ The paper used in these volumes conforms to the American National Standard
for Permanence of Paper for Printed Library Materials, Z39.48-1992 (R1997).

Library of Congress Cataloging-in-Publication Data
The Hero's Quest / editors, Bernard Schweizer, Robert Segal.
  p. cm. -- (Critical insights)
 Includes bibliographical references and index.
 ISBN 978-1-4298-3737-8 (hardcover) -- ISBN 978-1-4298-3785-9 (ebook)
 1. Heroes in literature. 2. Quests (Expeditions) in literature. 3. Epic literature-
-History and criticism. I. Schweizer, Bernard, 1962- II. Segal, Robert Alan.
 PN56.5.H45H53 2013
 809'.93352--dc23
                          2012017995

PRINTED IN THE UNITED STATES OF AMERICA

Contents _____

Critical Contexts

Critical Readings

Resources

About This Volume

Bernard Schweizer

Not all heroes undertake quests, and not all quests are heroic, but in myth and in literature, heroism and quests are often connected. Both heroism and the quest push boundaries. Questing pioneers, for instance, often cross geographical thresholds as their journeys lead them into lands beyond the boundaries of known territories and charted seas. Quest narratives often verge on the supernatural or transcend into the magic realm. Questers regularly go to the limits of physical endurance as they are required to muster extraordinary efforts to complete their task. These adventurers frequently transcend psychological or mental boundaries as well as face their fears, aspirations, and desires that are lodged deeply within the unconscious realm of their psyches. Cognitive limits are also expanded since heroic travelers throw themselves at the mercy of cosmic imponderables or confront undreamed of worldly situations. Heroes test boundaries of an ethical kind, too, as they weigh the individual versus the collective good when facing questions of justice and considering the wisdom of sacrifice. Finally, literary quests tend to offer new ways of storytelling, stretching the reader's endurance through texts of epic length and confronting them with startling creative innovations.

Looking at themes as fundamental as heroism and the quest means taking a long and broad view of things. It is not enough to limit oneself to the mythical expressions of the hero's quest in oral traditions. It is not enough to consider the heroic quest in canonical epics only. It is not enough to pursue the modifications of heroes and quests in modern and even postmodern literatures exclusively. All of these varieties must be studied. The varieties of genres, which range from fragment to travelogue (and every point in between), must be studied.

Although striving to be inclusive in the range of national literatures covered in individual essays, this volume is limited to what is normally identified as "Western literature," with discussions of heroic quests in ancient Persian, Greek and Roman, medieval French, Italian, and

Anglo-Saxon, as well as in modern Anglo-American texts. This volume focuses wholly on literary, textual narratives and does not study movies, oral stories, or computer games.

The essay topics are arranged chronologically from some of the oldest known heroic quests in the Western tradition to some of the most recent instances. Thematically, an array of quests and questers is covered. The epic quest, the chivalric quest, the spiritual quest, the bildungsroman, the philosophical quest, the modernist quest, the fantasy quest, and the traveler's quest are all explored in this volume. In this sense, the undergraduate reader is given an overview of the heroic quest in as broad and in as specific a manner as possible.

The first four chapters in this volume provide an introduction since most quest narratives can be considered from the following four perspectives:

1. A reception history of the theme. (Robert Segal offers an overview of the most influential theories of hero myths: those of Otto Rank, Joseph Campbell, and Lord Raglan.)

2. A specific approach to quest. (Eric Ziolkowski reads Wolfram from Eschenbach's *Parzival* through the lens of Søren Kierkegaard's linear progression of the quest from the aesthetic to the ethical to the religious stage, a view that contrasts to Joseph Campbell's differently patterned monomyth.)

3. The changes that the theme has undergone over time. (Jeremy Downes illustrates the evolution of the quest motif from pictorial representations of prehistoric hunting scenes to the canonical epics of Western literature to modern uses of the theme by authors as diverse as Jane Austen and T. S. Eliot.)

4. A comparative approach. (Michael Bell compares Joseph Conrad's *Heart of Darkness* with D. H. Lawrence's *The Man Who Died*, two modernist texts that are "informed by modern anthropological, psychological, and philosophical understanding" and offers critiques of these works that not only engage, but radically overturn fundamental values of their culture.)

The nine remaining essays explore major heroic quest stories in Western literature. Beginning with the great epics, the foundational texts of the quest motif, the quest may be the journey to the monster's den, the trip to the Underworld, the voyage home, the search for immortality, or the founding of a civilization. Classics such as *The Epic of Gilgamesh, The Odyssey*, and *The Aeneid* evince these most fundamental aspects of the traditional quest.

Katherine King discusses at once the search for immortality, the quest as an instrument of political legitimation, and the role of storytelling in establishing individual worth in the two foundational quest narratives of the Western tradition: *Gilgamesh* and *The Odyssey*. As she puts it, "Both heroes learn painfully that physical immortality and humanity are incompatible categories, but Odysseus chooses humanity willingly, while Gilgamesh is forced into tragic acceptance."

Eric Sandberg looks at the ambivalent nature of Aeneas's heroism in *The Aeneid*. Although often breezily characterized as the founder of a future world empire, a dashing warrior, and a bold adventurer, Aeneas turns out to be an unconventional hero who mainly does the bidding of the gods, whose heroism partly consists in resisting a powerful death wish, and who is inclined toward melancholy. Rather than giving us a super-human hero, Virgil is actually presenting us with a fate-buffeted, proto-existentialist, and at times despairing Aeneas who fittingly reflects the turmoil that had preceded the establishment of Augustus's Principate and his uncertainty over Rome's future.

James Kelley situates *Beowulf* in both its literary and its cultural contexts. Echoing another essay in this collection, Robert Evan's chapter on *Moby-Dick*, Kelley sees the quest as a multiple rather than a unitary undertaking. Hence, while elements of mythologist Joseph Campbell's monomyth (or hero's journey) can doubtlessly be found in *Beowulf*, the work, like any other narrative, harbors its own distinctive brand of heroism. The question of the hero's transformation, so central both to Campbell's theory and to our conventional understanding of the meaning of heroism, is called into question by the third section of

Beowulf, where, in the battle with the dragon, pride and irresponsibility threaten to undercut the hero's coming into his own as a mature leader of his people.

No overview of heroic quests would be complete without consideration of the medieval chivalric quest. Anthony Adams discusses *Sir Gawain and the Green Knight*. He sees the story as presenting the tension between a didactic Christian element and a war-like masculine ethos. As so often emerges with the works examined in this volume, Sir Gawain's quest appears to challenge rather than to confirm conventional expectations of what heroism is. As Adams pointedly explains in his conclusion, "*Sir Gawain and the Green Knight* presents readers with a flawed but keenly appealing hero on a quest that questions the value and composition of such heroism." *Sir Gawain and the Green Knight* turns the reader's attention gradually away from any political objective to the pursuit of meaning in a shifting and ultimately uncertain world of competing sets of rules.

In his essay on Dante's *Divine Comedy*, Matthew Bolton explores what is a classic religious quest. In Dante's hands, the quest motif is wrested from its pre-Christian, "pagan" implications in Homer and Virgil and is redirected to asserting Christian ideas of heroism. Dante misses no opportunity to portray the Christian's quest for God's kingdom and the poet's quest for fame as the only true forms of heroism. Dante, who aspires to embody both kinds of heroism himself, replaces worldly conquests and rewards with salvation and artistic acclaim.

Robert Evans discusses what is arguably the greatest American quest narrative: *Moby-Dick*. He demonstrates Melville's ingenious method of balancing the destructive spiritual quest and paranoid pursuit of Ahab with a range of secondary quests of a more constructive nature. Here the quest serves not a single dominant passion but rather as an almost ubiquitous impulse that manifests itself in multiple ways—commercial, social, and military—in the context of seafaring.

Two essays in this volume explore the contribution of fairy tale motifs to quest narratives. In fact, conventions and plot elements from fairy tales have informed both the bildungsroman—that quintessential nineteenth-century genre of the hero's maturation—and the twentieth-century genre of the fantasy novel. Using *Jane Eyre* and *Great Expectations* as examples, Victoria Williams demonstrates how the quest motif was adapted in the nineteenth century to reflect the process of securing an identity. She also shows how elements from popular fairy tales were employed to heighten the quest-like structure of this process. There turns out to have been a difference in the maturation process between male and female characters. "Jane Eyre reveals that the female protagonist must undergo a much more convoluted path to maturity than the male hero" in *Great Expectations*.

The other contributor who explores fairy-tale elements in modern quest narratives is Stephen Potts. Beginning with a brief discussion of Frank L. Baum's *The Wizard of Oz*, Potts works out the basic plot of the fantasy quest, a plot that progresses from crossing a threshold, receiving supernatural aid, confronting death, and ultimately undergoing a personal transformation that leads to mature adulthood. Potts shows how these elements are also found, with different emphases, in two other popular works of twentieth-century fantasy: J. R. R. Tolkien's *The Hobbit* and Philip Pullman's trilogy, *His Dark Materials*. The pattern identified by Potts is independent of the religious overtones of the stories themselves, overtones that are Christian in the case of Tolkien, humanist in the case of Baum, and anti-Christian in the case of Pullman.

Finally, Simon Cooke examines travel writing, an age-old vehicle for quest narratives. He focuses on Bruce Chatwin's instant classic, *In Patagonia*, which has proved to be a highly influential prototype of the postmodern travelogue. Although Chatwin ironically undercuts his own pretenses to being a quester after a postmodern kind of "fleece," he does in fact contribute to a new kind of questing. The contemporary quest is no longer for wealth, conquest, or discovery but rather for a state of mind, for a heightened awareness of the connectedness of the world that is able to connect both the past to the present as well as connect the present to a global, ecological awareness.

On the Hero's Quest

Robert A. Segal

We are sometimes told that there are no longer any heroes. It is said that we live in a skeptical age where even the most acclaimed figures are invariably exposed as flawed. It is lamented that if true heroes once existed, today we are left with mere humans, some better than others but none so elevated as to be worthy of the name *hero*.

Yet just as often we are told the opposite: that the term *hero* has been stretched so wide that today seemingly everyone is a hero. To quote from Gregory Kendrick's *The Heroic Ideal* (2010), "At the beginning of the twenty-first century, hero and heroism are ubiquitous words applied to all kinds of people and every manner of action. Heroes are Congressional Medal of Honor recipients, Hollywood celebrities, unconventional schlumps, and fictional comic book characters; and heroism encompasses everything from selfless acts of courage to the assuaging of public boredom" (5).

Both positions are exaggerated. On the one hand, there are still heroes, and lots of them. On the other hand, new and contemporary notions of heroism have arisen. These new notions supplement rather than replace traditional ones.

The study of heroism raises many issues. Are heroes human or divine? Can heroes be living as well as dead? Can there be female as well as male heroes? Can there be young as well as adult heroes? Can heroes be commoners as well as aristocrats or royalty? Are heroes born or made? Can heroism be self-serving, or must a hero serve others?

The basic question is, what must persons do to win the title hero? The most common answer, though hardly the only one, is that a hero must undertake a quest. What the quest is for and whether it must even be achieved varies among authorities on heroism. The authority who most tightly ties heroism to a quest is the American mythographer Joseph Campbell (1904–87), author of, most famously, *The Hero with a Thousand Faces* (1949). For Campbell, whose approach will be considered in full in the next chapter, a quest means a literal journey from home to a new world and then back. Literally, the journey is outward, from one place to another. Symbolically, the journey is inward, from one part of the mind (ordinary consciousness) to another part (the unconscious) and then back. Campbell presents a common plot, or pattern, for all hero myths that depict heroism as a journey. The outward pattern is meant to track a symbolic, psychological journey.

Campbell was at the time largely a follower of the psychologist C. G. Jung, who was Freud's strongest rival in the field of depth psychology. For Campbell, the physical journey is meant as a metaphor for the mental journey that Jung calls that of the "second half" of life, from adulthood on. For Freud, by contrast, heroism involves no journey. By no coincidence Campbell is by far the theorist cited most often by contributors to this volume, focusing as the volume does on heroism as a quest. But not all approaches to heroism concentrate on any quest, let alone on a journey. And not all those who apply Campbell to myths of heroism as a journey go beyond the outer journey to the inner one.

The notion of heroism is perhaps as old as humanity, but the classic modern starting point for the study of the subject is the book *On Heroes, Hero-Worship, and the Heroic in History* (1841) by the Scottish man of letters Thomas Carlyle (1795–1881). The stereotype of the century in which Carlyle lived was that great events were believed to be the work of individuals. By contrast, the stereotype of the twentieth century is that great events are assumed to stem from impersonal forces, even in the face of seemingly "game-changing" leaders like Hitler, Stalin, Roosevelt, Churchill, and Mao. While Carlyle is taken as the exemplar of the nineteenth-century view, he was actually writing in defense of heroes as key to events: "I am well aware that in these days Hero-worship, the thing I call Hero-worship, professes to have gone out, and finally ceased" (12).

In *On Heroes* Carlyle presents eleven figures, grouped into six categories: the hero as divinity (Odin), the hero as prophet (Mahomet, or Mohammed), the hero as poet (Dante, Shakespeare), the hero as priest (Martin Luther, John Knox), the hero as man of letters (Samuel Johnson, Jean-Jacques Rousseau, Robert Burns), and the hero as king (Oliver Cromwell, Napoleon).

On the first page of his book Carlyle offers the most famous expression of the "Great Man" view of history:

> For, as I take it, Universal History, the history of what man has accomplished in this world, is at bottom the History of the Great Men who have worked here. They were the leaders of men, these great ones; the modelers, patterns, and in a wide sense creators, of whatsoever the general mass of men contrived to do or to attain; all things that we see standing accomplished in the world are properly the outer material result, the practical realization and embodiment, of Thoughts that dwelt in the Great Men sent into the world: the soul of the whole world's history, it may justly be considered, were the history of these (1).

For Carlyle, heroes are saviors: "In all epochs of the world's history, we shall find the Great Man to have been the indispensable savior of his epoch, the lightning, without which the fuel never would have burnt" (13). But how they accomplish what they do varies with their talents. If the heroism of all can be said to involve a quest, the quest need not involve a journey and can be for fame, for wealth, for power, or for salvation. Still, all of Carlyle's heroes sought to direct the proverbial course of history.

Yet Carlyle is not claiming that heroes can fully determine events. For him, heroes are as much at the mercy of history as in control of history. It is for all their insight into the course of society that Carlyle lauds them. Unlike ordinary humans, who mistake appearance for reality, heroes see beyond appearance to reality: "A Hero, as I repeat, has this first distinction, which indeed we may call first and last, the Alpha and Omega of his whole Heroism, [t]hat he looks through the shews of things into *things*" (55).

Furthermore, the period dictates the category of hero that is needed and that is possible. The hero as divinity could only have arisen in a prescientific age, presupposing as it does the "pagan" belief in the immanence of divinity in the physical world and in humanity. While there have long been kings, Carlyle, writing at a time when monarchs still reigned in Europe, deems kings distinctly modern heroes, for they are needed to overcome the wide modern divide between the spiritual and the physical realms. By contrast, the hero as poet can arise in any age. Still, heroes of thought as well as of action can save society, and Carlyle was writing to inspire men of letters to enlist their disparate talents to do so.

A fellow nineteenth-century advocate of heroism was the German philosopher Friedrich Nietzsche (1844–1900). In *Thus Spoke Zarathustra* (1884–85), Nietzsche espouses the emergence of the hero he calls the *übermensch*, or "overman," a term sometimes translated as "superman." The overman is very different from any of Carlyle's heroes. First, the overman has yet to appear, though Nietzsche singles out Socrates, Jesus, Caesar, Leonardo, Michelangelo, Shakespeare, Goethe, and Napoleon as foreshadowing him. Second, the overman is a personal, not a social, hero. He transforms himself, not society. His quest is personal. He transforms himself by rejecting conventions of all kinds, especially of morality based on religion. He chooses—wills— his own morality and judges it himself. He is a nihilist, not a savior.

For both Nietzsche and Carlyle, heroes are exceptional persons. There are few of them, and they are deservedly famous. For Campbell, by contrast, anyone can be a hero. Any adult can undertake the psychological journey from everyday consciousness to the unconscious and back. The journey is not easy, and success is hardly guaranteed. In fact, Campbell gives almost as many examples of failed heroes as of successful ones. And a hero can fail at any place along the way. But heroism for Campbell, as for Jung, is intended for all. Heroism means the fulfillment of human nature. Nietzsche and Carlyle confine heroism to a status attainable by only a few whose feat is so extraordinary as to make them almost more than human.

Nietzsche's influence lay more in the twentieth century than in the nineteenth. In the nineteenth century, Carlyle was the more influential. Yet he was scarcely without critics. His most vitriolic contemporary opponent was the pioneering English sociologist Herbert Spencer (1820–1903), who, in *The Study of Sociology* (1873), rejects as primitive, childish, romantic, and unscientific the claim that individuals make history. For Spencer, it is social conditions that make history. Sociology, not biography, is the key to understanding history. Great men are at most the immediate causes of great changes, but they are themselves the product, not the cause, of social change. In Spencer's famous phrase, "Before he [the great man] can re-make his society, his society must make him" (35). Any would-be quest by a hero would for Spencer be putting the cart before the horse.

The twentieth century spurred even stronger skepticism toward the role of heroes. The classic twentieth-century critique of heroism was *A Century of Hero-Worship* (1944), by Eric Bentley, an English-born literary and drama critic. Bentley attacks what he calls "heroic vitalism" for its antidemocratic outlook.

There have, however, been defenses of heroism. In *The Hero in History* (1943) the American philosopher Sidney Hook argues for a reasonable middle ground between crediting heroes with everything, which he takes Carlyle to be doing, and crediting them with nothing, which Spencer is doing. Hook confines himself to heroes of action.

On the one hand, Hook concedes that movements like the Renaissance, the Reformation, and the industrial revolution were more than the handiwork of great men. Similarly, he concedes that no one could have prevented World War I.

On the other hand, Hook asserts that individuals can make a difference. He credits Hitler with taking advantage of the situation in Weimar Germany to gain power. He credits Lenin with bringing about the Russian Revolution, whatever the existing situation. He refuses to attribute events simply to the times. In his admiration for the ability of individuals to make a difference, he is closer to Carlyle than to Spencer. Carlyle himself ties heroes to circumstances.

Yet Carlyle goes further than Hook in declaring that heroes are "worshiped": "in all times and places, the Hero has been worshipped" (15). He cannot mean literally worshiped, for all but one of his eleven heroes are human. The exception is Odin, and Carlyle attributes the posthumous deification of Odin to the loss of records that would have preserved his human status: "Why, in thirty or forty years, were there no books, any great man would grow *mythic*, the contemporaries who had seen him, being once all dead" (25–26). Once records began to survive, no more divine heroes emerged: "in the history of the world there will not again be any man, never so great, whom his fellowmen will take for a god" (42).

At the same time, Carlyle calls his heroes "mythic" and uses the term interchangeably with "divine": "were there no books, any great man would grow *mythic*." Hero myths are stories about heroes raised to gods—gods in effect, even if formally still humans. Heroism does not demote gods to humans but rather elevates humans to gods. For ordinary humans, the divide between humans and gods remains, but heroes are heroes because they surmount it.

Heroism transforms humans into virtual gods by conferring on them divine qualities, though usually just one quality each. The qualities can be physical attributes—strength, looks, size—or intangible ones—intelligence, integrity, drive. The difference between humans and gods may be of kind. Unlike humans, gods can fly, can change shape, and live forever. More often the difference is of degree: gods are bigger, stronger, sexier, and smarter than humans. Yet so great is the difference even of degree that it still puts heroism beyond the aspirations of ordinary persons.

Carlyle maintains that some kinds of heroes fit only certain periods. Surely he is right. It is hard to imagine an aristocratic hero like

Don Juan fitting the twentieth century. Other heroes do survive either because their appeal continues or because they are protean enough to adapt to the times.

In the twentieth century, as in prior centuries, not only have traditional heroes been transformed, but also new kinds of heroes have arisen. If particularly nineteenth-century heroes were the romantic hero (Lord Byron's Childe Harold) and the bourgeois hero (Gustave Flaubert's Emma Bovary), particularly twentieth-century heroes are the ordinary person as hero (Arthur Miller's Willy Loman), the comic hero (Philip Roth's Alexander Portnoy), the schlemiel as hero (I. B. Singer's Gimpel the Fool), and the absurd hero (Samuel Beckett's Vladimir and Estragon). From the standpoint of the nineteenth century, twentieth-century heroes are antiheroes.

Anything but divine, the contemporary hero is all too human—mortal, powerless, amoral. The present-day hero is often lowly even within the human community—more the outsider than the insider, more the loser than the winner, more the villain than the savior. The contemporary hero is not a once-great figure who has fallen, such as Oedipus, but a figure who never rises. Not Oedipus but Sisyphus typifies present-day heroism. As presented by Albert Camus, Sisyphus is still to be heralded, but for never giving up. Persistence replaces success; survival replaces achievement. Old-fashioned heroic virtues like courage and duty give way to new ones like irony and detachment.

Contemporary heroism is different from the heroism espoused by Campbell. For Campbell, everyone has the capacity to become a hero, but the hero must still achieve a goal, and that goal involves a quest, not to mention a journey. The "democratic" nature of heroism does not make a hero an antihero. Heroism for Campbell remains a feat, no matter how open heroism is to all.

It might seem farfetched to link contemporary antiheroism to a quest, but persistence and survival can themselves be deemed goals. Still, because contemporary heroes scarcely reach the stature of gods, their stories do not constitute myths.

Yet it would surely be going too far to maintain that traditional heroism has died out. Contemporary heroes in sports, entertainment, business, and politics are admired for their success, not for their mere endurance, and the acclaim conferred on them often reaches the same divine plateau as in past eras. The most sensible view would be that alongside the traditional notion of heroism as success has emerged the new notion of heroism as sheer "keeping going," as in the conventional contemporary reading of Don Quixote.

Heroes can be celebrated even when their historicity is questioned. Jesus remains a model for even those Christians who doubt that he performed all the miracles attributed to him. Even a fictional Oedipus can be a tragic hero for twentieth-century Westerners.

Outright indisputably fictional figures can be heroic. Take Sherlock Holmes and James Bond. They are treated as if real (see Saler). They can even upstage real heroes exactly because they harbor no offscreen vices that must be discounted. Holmes and Bond hold the same status for adults as fairy-tale figures do for children. The title of a popular book sums up the point: *The 101 Most Influential People Who Never Lived* (Lazar, Kaplan, and Salter 2006).

In his *Did the Greeks Believe in Their Myths?* (1988) French classicist Paul Veyne begins with this question: "Did the Greeks believe in their mythology? The answer is difficult, for 'believe' means so many things" (1). Veyne grants that "not everyone believed that Minos, after his death, continued being a judge in Hell or that Theseus fought the Minotaur" (1). But he contends that "in the minds of the Greeks," Theseus and in some form Minos "had, nonetheless, existed" (1). Despite what we today might think, few Greeks dismissed altogether the truth of hero myths.

Furthermore, in ancient times the line between the historical and the mythical fluctuated. Initially, heroes were placed in a prior, sacred, "once upon a time"—a time distinct from the present, where heroes were no longer to be found. Later, the supernatural element was removed in order to make the historicity of heroes more persuasive. But they remained real heroes, and the elimination of the supernatural only reinforced their historicity. Veyne declares that from the fifth century BCE to the fourth century AD, "absolutely no one, Christians included, ever expressed the slightest doubt concerning the historicity of Aeneas, Romulus, Theseus, Heracles, Achilles, or even Dionysus" (42).

Opposite to Veyne stands the English folklorist Lord Raglan, author of *The Hero* (1936). He demands a clear-cut divide between history and myth. His proof that heroes are mythic is that they are not historical. For him, there is nothing in between. Setting the biographies of indisputably historical heroes like Alexander the Great and Napoleon against the biographies of "mythic" heroes like Theseus and King Arthur, he asserts that the kinds of events that supposedly occur in the lives of mythic heroes find no counterpart in the lives of historical ones. This disparity is intended to prove that mythic heroes are "merely" mythic.

For example, the hero of "tradition," or of myth, never wins a battle. He leads no army. By contrast, "the warrior kings of history, whether civilized or barbarian, have won their renown as leaders" (194). Whenever mythic heroes do fight, theirs are "single combats against other kings, or against giants, dragons, or celebrated animals" (194).

But it is in fact not so easy to sift out the historical from the mythical. A traditional kind of hero might have lived but be credited with unrealistic deeds or attributes. A brave soldier might become fearless; a kindly soul might become saintly. The magnifications need not even be taken at face value. Americans can want to believe that George Washington was utterly truthful without fully accepting it. Brits may still want very much to think that Princess Diana was wholly selfless without quite accepting the claim. Heroism permits and even requires make-believe.

Of all present-day heroes, the ones closest to gods are Hollywood stars. They seem to bypass the status of heroes and become gods outright. A-listers are "idolized" and "worshiped." As "stars," they reside in heaven, not on earth.

Unlike other kinds of celebrities, such as sports stars and rock stars, Hollywood stars, like gods, are rarely seen in person. Also, unlike other kinds of celebrities, they, like gods, take on disguises—their roles. In film, they, like gods, can do all kinds of things that celebrities who perform in person cannot. And in a movie theater they are gargantuan in size. Like gods, they are greater than ordinary folks in degree, not kind. Like gods, they are superhuman not in every respect but in a single, dominant respect, one that varies from figure to figure. On screen, merely human virtues get magnified into superhuman ones: strength becomes omnipotence, bravery becomes fearlessness, beauty becomes incandescence, kindliness becomes saintliness, and wisdom becomes omniscience.

Although some might argue that while gods remain gods in both private and public, film stars are in fact mere mortals offscreen. Many fans, however, make no distinction between the onscreen star and the offscreen human. Actors are assumed to be playing themselves no matter the role, and fans are often dismayed to learn that in "real life" their favorite actors fall short of the characters they play. Additionally, gay Hollywood actors often choose to keep their sexual preference secret lest they no longer be cast in "straight" roles.

It might understandably be argued that even if film stars are god-like in their attributes, they cannot, like gods, affect the physical world, yet film stars and other celebrities are assumed to have power greater than that of heads of states or of traditional religious leaders. Here they become heroes, and they have almost as much influence as traditional heroes. Like traditional heroes, they have goals and can be said to be involved in quests.

Against this argument, it might sensibly be observed that nobody believes the hype. No one believes that Hollywood stars are really different from you and me. They may have more discretionary income, but they face the same obstacles and tribulations as the rest of us. What sells better than an "unauthorized" biography of a star—a biography that brings a *star* down to *earth*? But this hard-nosed view of fans is the naive one. Fans continue to "idolize" and "worship" stars, not in ignorance of their flaws but in defiance of them. It is not that fans don't know better. It is that they don't want to know better, or else don't care. Yet the devotion of fans is not mindless. As with George Washington and Princess Diana, so with film stars: the devotion is done knowingly. It is make-believe, not credulity. Hero worship does not require the refusal to acknowledge any evidence to the contrary. It requires the refusal to let the evidence get in the way. Contemporary heroism, and perhaps heroism any time, involves fantasy as well as fact.

Works Cited

Bentley, Eric. *A Century of Hero-Worship: A Study of the Idea of Heroism in Carlyle and Nietzsche*. 2nd ed. Boston: Beacon, 1957.

Campbell, Joseph. *The Hero with a Thousand Faces*. 2nd ed. Princeton, NJ: Princeton UP, 1968.

Carlyle, Thomas. *The Works of Thomas Carlyle: On Heroes, Hero-Worship, and the Heroic in History*. Ed. Henry Duff Traill. London: Chapman and Hall, 1897.

Hook, Sidney. *The Hero in History*. Boston: Beacon, 1955.

Kendrick, M. Gregory. *The Heroic Ideal: Western Archetypes from the Greeks to the Present*. Jefferson, NC: McFarland, 2010.

Lazar, Allan, Dan Karlan, and Jeremy Salter. *The 101 Most Influential People Who Never Lived*. New York: Harper, 2006.

Lord Raglan. *The Hero: A Study in Tradition, Myth, and Drama*. London: Methuen, 1936.

Nietzsche, Friedrich. *Thus Spoke Zarathustra*. Trans. Walter Kaufmann. New York: Viking, 1966.

Saler, Michael. "'Clap If You Believe in Sherlock Holmes': Mass Culture and the Re-enchantment of Modernity, c. 1890–c. 1940." *The Historical Journal* 46:3 (2003): 599–622.

Spencer, Herbert. *The Study of Sociology*. New York: Appleton, 1874.

Veyne, Paul. *Did the Greeks Believe in Their Myths?* Trans. Paula Wissing. Chicago: U of Chicago P, 1988.

CRITICAL CONTEXTS

Theories of Myth

Robert A. Segal

There is no uniform definition of myth. For some authorities, myth need not even take the form of a story, as might be assumed, but can instead be a belief or a conviction. For other authorities, myth, if a story, need not take place in the past but can take place in the present or the future. It can take place on earth, in heaven, or in space. For yet other authorities, the characters in myth need not be gods but can alternatively be humans or even animals. What happens in myth is open-ended. Myth need not, for example, be about the creation of something but can instead be about the destruction of something or be about an event within an existing family, society, or cosmos.

There are many kinds of myths—among them creation myths, myths of paradise, flood myths, myths of nations and of races, and myths of the future. One other category of myths is hero myths. Here, too, nothing is uniform. For some authorities, heroes, while most often human, can also be divine. Animals, especially ones called tricksters, can be heroic as well. For other authorities, heroes can be ordinary as well as extraordinary persons. Sometimes anyone can be a hero, which is not to say that anyone automatically is a hero. There can be child heroes as well as adult heroes. Heroes can come from any class. And heroes can come from either gender.

Heroism itself can take varying forms including heroism in the form of a quest, which means a journey. The journey can be outward or inward. One may have to cross the globe, or one may be able to sit at home. Heroism as a journey is the approach taken by, above all, Joseph Campbell, whose views will be compared with those of other leading authorities on myth.

A myth can be studied either by itself, in isolation from other myths, or in comparison with other myths. "Theories" of myth compare myths with one another, indeed with all others. Theories are generalizations about myth. They claim to know the answers to the main questions

---

about any myth: What is its origin, what is its function, and what is its subject matter? The answer is the same for any myth.[1]

Origin of myth means why and how myth arises. The origin proposed by a theory is recurrent rather than historical. The origin refers not to the time and place of the first appearance of myth, such as the Garden of Eden, but to why and how myth arises whenever and wherever it does. The answer to the "why" of origin is not a location but a need, which antedates myth and which myth is created to fulfill. What the need is varies from theory to theory. It can range from the brute need for food to the sublime need for meaningfulness in life.

The "how" of origin refers to the means by which myth arises. For example, a theory may contend that even with the need for hunger, a myth will not arise without a group. Or a theory may contend that even with a need for explanation of the physical world, a myth will not arise unless there exists the belief in god. Some theories ignore the how of origin.

Function means why and how myth lasts. Like the origin, the function is recurrent. The why of the function is the flip side of the why of the origin: Whatever need explains the creation of myth explains also the continuation of myth. The how is the means by which myth lasts. For example, a theory may assert that myth lasts only as long as it is tied to a ritual or to a group.

Most theories of myth come from the social sciences—from anthropology, economics, psychology, political science, and sociology. Social scientific theories tend to focus on origin and function. It is not that social scientists confine themselves to behavior and ignore texts. It is that they tend to emphasize why and how texts are created and read (or heard) and not what texts say. In one sense of an admittedly confusing pair of terms, the social scientific focus is on the *explanation* rather than the *interpretation* of myth.[2]

By contrast, theories of myth from the humanities—art, literature, philosophy, and religious studies—focus on the *interpretation* of myth, which is to say on the content. The key issues are: Is myth to be read symbolically rather than literally? If so, what is being symbolized? Must myth be a story? If so, of what kind? What recurrent themes or patterns appear in myth?

Some theories seek both to explain and to interpret myth. For example, the theories of Sigmund Freud and C. G. Jung not only identify who creates and uses myth and why, but also offer full glossaries for reading myth, for translating the literal meaning into a psychological one.

Myth and Literature

What is the connection between myth and literature? The perpetuation of myth in literature is the most obvious connection. Courses in literature often trace ancient classical or biblical myths through Western literature. Specific figures and events are usually traced—for example, the figure of Prometheus and the return home to Ithaca of Odysseus (Ulysses). Also popular is the tracing of mythic categories, such as that of the hero or of the trickster. Ancient myths have been read literally, read symbolically, rearranged, and even rewritten.

Freud used the figure Oedipus and Jung the term Electra to name the most fundamental human drives. Freud took from others the figure Narcissus to name self-love. Further psychological maladies that take their names from mythological characters are nymphomania, which has as its male counterpart the far less well-known satyriasis, and the Pygmalion effect, which means the effect that others' expectations, positive or negative, have on persons.

The survival of classical, or pagan, mythology in the West is much more impressive than the survival of biblical mythology: Classical mythology has survived the death of the religion of which it was originally a part, whereas biblical mythology has been sustained by the nearly monolithic presence of Christianity. Classical mythology has been preserved by the culture that killed off classical religion.[3] Until recently, the very connotation of the term *paganism* was negative.

Deeper than the perpetuation in literature of mythic figures, events, and categories has been the perpetuation of mythic themes. In his famous essay "On the Teaching of Modern Literature," the celebrated American literary critic Lionel Trilling asserted that "the characteristic element of modern literature . . . is the bitter line of hostility to civilization which runs through it" (3).

Trilling attributes this theme to Nietzsche and Freud but most of all to the pioneering Scottish anthropologist J. G. Frazer: "I asked myself what books of the age just preceding ours had most influenced our literature. . . . It was virtually inevitable that the first work that should have sprung to mind was Sir James Frazer's *The Golden Bough*. Anyone who thinks about modern literature in a systematic way takes for granted the great part played in it by myth, and especially by those examples of myth which tell us about gods dying and being reborn . . ." (Trilling 14). Where Frazer is conventionally read as scorning myth and religion as outdated "primitive" counterparts to science, itself exclusively modern, Trilling reads him as celebrating the "primitivism" that scientific modernity has lost: "Scientific though his purpose was, Frazer had the effect of validating those old modes of experiencing the world which modern men, beginning with the Romantics, have sought to revive in order to escape from positivism and common sense" (Trilling 17). For Trilling, Frazer espouses primitivism *against* civilization, and the heart of primitivism is myth.

In *The Literary Impact of* The Golden Bough, American literary critic John Vickery, spurred by Trilling, traces the influence of Frazer's key mythic themes on the chief modernists in English literature: Yeats, Eliot, Lawrence, and Joyce. The titles of Vickery's chapters make clear his focus on Frazer—for example, "William Butler Yeats: The Tragic Hero as Dying God" and "James Joyce: *Ulysses* and the Human Scapegoat." For both Vickery and Trilling, modern literature rejects the modern in favor of the primitivism depicted by Frazer. The influence of myth on literature has thus been the influence of *theories* of myth on literature.

Myth as Story versus Myth as Science

If one way that myth influences literature is by the carrying over to literature of mythic figures, events, categories, and themes, another way is by tying myth to story rather than to science.[4]

A topic in the study of myth as frequent as that of myth and literature is that of myth and science. Here "science" means natural rather than social science. It means biology, chemistry, and physics. If one can generalize, the nineteenth century viewed myth as the primitive counterpart to science, which was assumed to be exclusively or at least largely modern. Myth was taken to arise and to serve to explain all physical events. In origin and function, myth was identical with science. The difference was in the explanation. Where the mythic explanation attributes events to decisions by gods or to the condition of gods, the scientific explanation attributes events to impersonal processes, processes taking the form of laws.

This nineteenth-century position is epitomized by the pioneering English anthropologist E. B. Tylor, for whom myth is an explanation as an end in itself, and by Frazer, for whom the explanation is a means to the securing of food. For Tylor, myth is the primitive counterpart to theoretical science. For Frazer, myth is the primitive counterpart to applied science.

If one can generalize further, the twentieth century viewed myth as anything but the primitive counterpart to science, itself still considered largely modern. Myth, it was assumed, differs from science in either subject matter or function. Either myth is not about the physical world, or myth is not an explanation or a manipulation of the physical world. Myth is instead about society, the mind, or the place of humans in the physical world. Or myth arises and functions to unify society, to facilitate the experience of the unconscious, or to express the place of humans in the world. Bronislaw Malinowski, Rudolf Bultmann, Hans Jonas, Hans Blumenberg, and Freud and Jung typify the twentieth-century approach to myth, and so do Trilling and Vickery in their reading of Frazer.

Theories from political science see myth as ideology, which can take the form of a conviction or a credo without any accompanying story. But most theories take myth to be a story. They differ over the significance of myth as story. The "structuralist" approach to myth pioneered by the French anthropologist Claude Lévi-Strauss spurns the linear, progressive unfolding of the plot in favor of the sheer repetition of the opposing elements of the structure.

Neither Tylor nor Frazer would deny that a myth is a story. But they consider myth a causal explanation of events in the physical world that simply takes the form of a story. Literary considerations are ignored. (The twentieth-century focus on models and metaphors in science long postdates Tylor and Frazer.) Because myth for Tylor and Frazer is intended to explain regular events, it can be rephrased as a law. Whenever the sun rises, it rises because the sun god has chosen to mount his chariot, to which the sun is attached, and to drive it across the sky, and always for the same reason.

Antithetical to Tylor stands the German philosopher Hans Blumenberg, author of *Work on Myth*. Blumenberg rejects what he would call Tylor's Enlightenment view of myth on the grounds that myth continues to exist in modernity. The survival of living myth in the wake of science supposedly proves that, contrary to Tylor (and Frazer), its function was never scientific.

Blumenberg denies that myth is explanatory. Rather than explaining, myth tells stories. Furthermore, within a myth, anything can derive from anything else in which case there must be scant interest in accurate derivation and therefore in derivation itself: "When anything can be derived from anything, then there just is no explaining, and no demand for explanation. One just tells stories" (Blumenberg 127).

For Tylor, myth is an explanation that incidentally takes the form of a story. For Blumenberg, myth is a story and therefore not an explanation.

Hero Myths, Male and Female

There are many categories of myth. Hero myths are perhaps the most popular. The study of hero myths goes back to ancient times. The most important modern theorists of hero myths have been the Viennese psychoanalyst Otto Rank (1884–1939), the American mythographer Joseph Campbell (1904–87), and the English folklorist Lord Raglan (1885–1964). Rank later broke bitterly with Freud, but when he wrote the original edition of *The Myth of the Birth of the Hero* (1909), he was a Freudian disciple and at one point was heir apparent.[5] Campbell was never a full-fledged Jungian, but he wrote *The Hero with a Thousand Faces* (1949) as a kindred soul of Jung.[6] Raglan wrote *The Hero* (1936) as a follower, if also at times a critic, of Frazer.[7]

Otto Rank

Freudians analyze all kinds of myths but often turn other kinds of myths into hero myths. Rank himself turns birth and survival into heroic feats and is typically Freudian is his restriction of heroes to males. Freudians point to creation myths that credit the feat of giving birth to the world to males.[8]

Rank's pattern, for heroism, which he applies to over thirty hero myths, falls within what Jungians call the "first half of life": birth, childhood, adolescence, and young adulthood. Heroism here means growing up and becoming independent of one's parents and mastering one's instincts:

> The hero is the child of most distinguished parents, usually the son of a king. His origin is preceded by difficulties, such as continence, or prolonged barrenness, or secret intercourse of the parents due to external prohibition or obstacles. During or before the pregnancy, there is a prophecy, in the form of a dream or oracle, cautioning against his birth, and usually threatening danger to the father (or his representative). As a rule, he is surrendered to the water, in a box. He is then saved by animals, or by lowly people (shepherds), and is suckled by a female animal or by an humble

woman. After he has grown up, he finds his distinguished parents, in a highly versatile fashion. He takes his revenge on his father, on the one hand, and is acknowledged, on the other. Finally he achieves rank and honors. (Rank et al. 57)

Literally (consciously) the hero can be legendary or historical like Oedipus. He is heroic because he wins a throne or other title. (Rank's pattern stops there. Oedipus' life thereafter does not count.) He is a victim of either his parents or, ultimately, fate.

Symbolically (unconsciously) the hero is heroic because he has the courage and nerve to kill his father, not because he dares to win a throne. The cause is not revenge but sexual frustration. The father has refused to surrender his wife, who is the real object of the son's efforts: "[A]s a rule the deepest, generally unconscious root of the dislike of the son for the father, or of two brothers for each other, is referable to the competition for the tender devotion and love of the mother" (Rank et al. 74). The true meaning of the hero myth is too difficult to face and is therefore suppressed by the concocted story, which makes the father, not the son, the culprit. The pattern is simply "the excuse, as it were, for the hostile feelings which the child harbors against his father, and which in this fiction are projected against [i.e., onto] the father" (Rank et al. 68–69). The hero's incestuous goal is perceived instead as power. Most of all, who the hero is becomes a third party—the named hero—rather than either the creator of the myth or anyone stirred by it. The myth maker or reader is able to identify with the named hero and celebrate vicariously the hero's triumph. Myth is really autobiography, and the myth maker or reader is the real hero of it.

Although the myth concludes with the hero's literal attainment, usually of a throne, the hero is also gaining a symbolic mate as well. The myth then seems to adequately fulfill the goal of the first half of life. The opposite, however, is the case: Rather than achieving independence and detachment from one's parents, the wish fulfilled results in the most intense of possible relationships with one's parents, that of parricide, incest, and even rape. The wish fulfilled is that of a child of three to five, and the fantasy is the fulfillment of the Oedipal wish to kill one's father in order to have sex with one's mother. Although symbolic rather than literal, the myth provides fulfillment of a kind.

Rank never explains why the apparent conflict is over the throne. But that conscious motive surely need not skew hero myths toward males. The fight for the English throne between Elizabeth I and Mary, Queen of Scots, was as lethal as that between any males. Nevertheless, Rank confines hero myths to males. *The Incest Theme in Literature and Legend* is even more Oedipal than *The Myth of the Birth of the Hero* and is more strikingly so even after his break with Freud, beginning with *The Trauma of Birth*.

Where in *The Myth of the Birth of the Hero* the father is the culprit for opposing birth, in *The Trauma of Birth* the mother becomes the culprit for giving birth. Oedipus's blinding of himself upon discovering that he has committed incest represents not guilt for his Oedipal deeds but "a return into the darkness of the mother's womb" (Rank 43).

With Rank begins the change of focus among psychoanalysts from the Oedipal stage to the pre-Oedipal one. Now the key relationship is not that between father and son but that between mother and child of either sex. The father allies himself with the mother rather than, as in the Oedipal stage, vice versa.

Joseph Campbell

Joseph Campbell was never a straightforward "Jungian," though commonly called one.[9] Still, Campbell stands close to Jung and stands closest in *The Hero with a Thousand Faces*, which remains the classical Jungian analysis of hero myths.

Where for Freud and Rank heroism is limited to the first half of life, for Jung it involves the second half even more. For Freud and Rank, heroism involves relations with parents and instincts. For Jung, heroism in even the first half of life involves, in addition, relations with the unconscious. One must detach oneself from not only parents and anti-social instincts, but even more from the unconscious. The forging of consciousness is considered a supremely heroic feat—one as imperative for females as for males.

The goal of the uniquely Jungian second half of life is, for males and females alike, also consciousness, but now consciousness of the distinctively Jungian, or collective, unconscious rather than of the external world. One must return to the unconscious from which one has ineluctably become severed, which is also Campbell's metaphor of a journey.

For Rank, heroism consists of killing the hero's father. The journey from the place where the hero grew up back to his real home is merely logistical and is hardly central to heroism. For Campbell, heroism is a journey—from the familiar to an unfamiliar world. But the aim is not to sever one's ties to the external world. On the contrary, the aim is to return to the external world. In Jungian terms, the ideal is a balance between consciousness of the external world and consciousness of the unconscious. The aim of the second half of life is to supplement, not to reject, the achievements of the first half.

Just as classically Freudian problems involve the failure to establish oneself in the outer world in the form of working and loving, so distinctively Jungian problems involve the failure to reestablish oneself in the inner world in relation to the unconscious. Freudian problems stem from excessive attachment to the world of childhood; Jungian problems stem from excessive attachment to the world one enters upon breaking free of the childhood world: the external world. To be disconnected from the internal world is to feel empty and lost.

Jung allows for heroism in both halves of life by females as well as by males.[10] Yet the image that he uses to characterize heroism in both halves is that of a mother and her son. For Freud and Rank, both Freudian and post-Freudian, the mother is one's actual mother. For Jung, the mother is a symbol of one's unconsciousness and is called the Great Mother or the Terrible Mother. For Freud and Rank, the son means a male. For Jung, the son is a symbol of everyone's ego consciousness, or consciousness of the external world, which is to say consciousness of the external world as separate from oneself: "the mother corresponds to the collective unconscious and the son to consciousness" (Jung, *Symbols* 259). In the first half of life the son seeks to break free of the mother and become independent of her. In the second half of life the son, now independent, seeks to return to the mother to reconnect with her and in turn to return to ordinary consciousness to form the self. Jung compares this two-part process with the course of the sun: from sunrise to sunset and back to sunrise (see Jung, *Symbols* 171).

Jung calls the accomplishment of the tasks of both halves of life heroic because of the difficulty involved. In the first half the son is as tempted to remain with the mother as the mother is to keep him with her. Breaking free of her requires courage and will. In the second half the son is as tempted never to leave the mother again as the mother is not to let him go again. Managing to resist her allure also demands discipline and determination.

Jung associates masculinity with consciousness, ego, and culture and associates femininity with the unconscious, egolessness, and instincts. Still, the goal is not the replacement of femininity by masculinity but rather the harmonizing of the two. But it is the ego, symbolized by the son, which accomplishes this task. Psychological development is the work of one's—anyone's—masculine side.

Jung bases his key analysis of hero myths in *Symbols of Transformation* on the fantasies of an American, not a patient of his, whose pseudonym was "Frank Miller." Yet Frank Miller was actually a woman, so that for Jung, heroism as symbolically male comes from a female's fantasies.[11]

Where Jung allows for heroism in both halves of life, Erich Neumann, above all in *The Origins and History of Consciousness*, focuses on heroism in the first half of life.[12] Following Jung, whose outright disciple he was, Neumann characterizes the course of psychological development as one of continuing heroism—with each stage posing a Herculean-like task. Also following Jung, Neumann characterizes heroism for all as symbolically masculine, and he associates masculinity with consciousness, ego, and culture and associates femininity with the unconscious, egolessness, and instincts.

In contrast to Neumann and to Rank, Campbell in *The Hero with a Thousand Faces* confines himself to heroism in the second half of life. Campbell's pattern begins where Rank's ends: with the adult hero ensconced at home. Rank's hero must be young enough for his father still to be reigning. Campbell's hero must be no younger than the age at which Rank's hero myth therefore ends: young adulthood. Alas, some of Campbell's own examples are of child heroes, but they violate his scheme according to which heroes must be willing to leave behind all that they have accomplished at home. Child heroes violate even more Campbell's Jungian meaning whereby heroes must be fully developed egos ready to encounter the unconscious from which they have long been separated. Campbell's heroes should then be in the second half of life. Campbell does acknowledge heroism in the first half of life and even cites Rank's monograph, but he himself demotes youthful heroism to mere preparation for adult heroism.

Rank's hero must be the son of royal or at least titled parents. Campbell's need not be. Campbell's pattern dictates human heroes, even though many of his heroes are divine. Rank's pattern, by contrast, allows for divine as well as human heroes. Most important, Campbell's heroes, unlike Rank's, can be female or male.

Where Rank's hero returns to his birthplace, Campbell's marches forth to a strange, new world, the world of the gods. The hero should hail from the human world exactly to be able to experience the distinctiveness of the divine one.

Where Rank's hero returns home to encounter his father and mother, Campbell's hero leaves home to encounter a male and a female god who are or should be neither his parents nor a couple. Because the goddess is not the hero's mother, sex with her does not constitute incest. Despite appearances, the hero's relationship to the male god is for Campbell no less positive and so no less non-Oedipal.

When Campbell writes that myths "reveal the benign self-giving aspect of the archetypal father," he is using the term in its Jungian sense (Campbell 139–40). For Freudians, gods symbolize parents. For Jungians, gods symbolize father and mother archetypes, which are components of the hero's personality. The hero's relationship to these gods symbolizes not, as for Freud and Rank, a son's relationship to other persons—his parents—but the relationship of one side of anyone's personality, the ego, to another side, the person's unconscious. Jung reinterprets the incest taboo as intended not to keep an adult male from acting out a yearning for sex with his mother but to keep anyone's ego consciousness from dissolving back into unconsciousness (see Jung, *Symbols* 235–36, 255, 259, 271, 417–18).

For Jung and Campbell, myth originates and functions not, as for Freud and the Freudian Rank, to satisfy neurotic urges that have been repressed, but to express normal sides of the personality that have never had a chance at realization.

By identifying himself with the hero of a myth, Rank's myth maker or reader vicariously lives out in his mind an adventure that, if ever directly fulfilled, would be acted out on his parents themselves. While also identifying oneself with the hero of a myth, Campbell's myth maker or reader vicariously lives out an adventure that even when directly fulfilled would still be taking place in the mind because parts of the mind are what are being encountered.

Because Campbell enlists myths of female heroes as often as those of male ones—his opening example is that of the Grimm's "The Princess and the Frog"—it seems odd to deem Campbell's heroes exclusively male. Yet Campbell actually restricts heroism to males once the three-part heroic journey moves from the stage of departure to the stage of initiation. Without notice, Campbell abruptly narrows his range to male ones. While, to be sure, he does include female heroes in the first subsection of the stage of initiation, or the "road of trials," once he gets to the heart of initiation—the encounter with the god and the goddess—most of his heroes are male, for Campbell still cites some female examples, even though they clearly are not "meeting with the goddess," facing "woman as the temptress," or achieving "atonement with the father."

Straight-laced Campbell, it can be taken for granted, never envisions other than heterosexual relations with the goddess, and even the reconciliation with the male god, which is what Campbell means by "atonement with the father," assumes a male hero. In short, Campbell could effortlessly have widened the substages of stage two to allow for encounters on the part of either female or male heroes. But he does not.

Understandably, then, others have offered a feminine counterpart to what they take to be Campbell's exclusively masculine brand of heroism. Carol Pearson and Katherine Pope write in *The Female Hero in American and British Literature*: "The great works on the hero—such as Joseph Campbell's *The Hero with a Thousand Faces*, Dorothy Norman's *The Hero: Myth/Image/Symbol*, and Lord Raglan's *The Hero: A Study in Tradition, Myth and Drama*—all begin with the assumption that the hero is male" (vii). Pearson writes in *The Hero Within*, "The great books on the hero, such as Joseph Campbell's *The Hero with a Thousand Faces*, assumed either that the hero was male or that male heroism and female heroism were essentially the same" (xx).[13] Pearson and Pope grant that Campbell declares at the outset that the hero may be either male or female, but they lament that he "then proceeds to discuss the heroic pattern as male and to define the female characters as goddesses, temptresses, and earth mothers" (4). They fault Jung as well on the same grounds (see Pearson and Pope 4).

In *The Hero Within,* Pearson follows Campbell in deeming the heart of heroism a journey, but she proposes six archetypes, or roles, that male and female heroes follow in different orders and with different emphases. The traditional male progresses from Orphan to Warrior to Wanderer to Martyr to Magician. The traditional female moves from Orphan to Martyr to Wanderer to Warrior to Magician. Furthermore, most contemporary men's values "are very much defined by the Warrior ethic" (Pearson, *Hero Within* 9). By contrast, most contemporary women either are Martyrs or "have moved quickly through the Wanderer and Warrior stages and are beginning to experiment with being Magicians" (9).

In the processing of proposing a new heroic journey to counter the male proclivity of Campbell's heroism, Pearson abandons Campbell's Jungian approach. The roles she delineates are not innate predispositions, as for Jung, but choices. Her "archetypes" are more Sartrean; they are chosen identities.

Lord Raglan

Lord Raglan's brand of myth-ritualism derives ultimately from Frazer: Myth provides the script for ritual. Frazer presents two versions of the myth and ritual scenario. In one version the king merely plays the part of the god of vegetation in the annual dramatization of the myth of the death and rebirth of the god. In the version used by Raglan,[14] the king is himself divine with the soul of the god of vegetation residing in his body. As the physical state of the king goes, so goes that of the god and in turn that of vegetation. The king is killed at the first sign of weakness or at the end of a fixed term so short as to minimize the chance of illness or death in office. The king is immediately replaced and the soul of the god immediately transferred to the successor's body.

Frazer's key examples of gods of vegetation are male: Adonis (Greek) (or Tammuz [Babylonian]), Attis (Syrian), Osiris (Egyptian), and Dionysus (Greek)—and also Jesus. Frazer does acknowledge that "a great Mother Goddess, . . . the personification of all the reproductive energies of nature, was worshipped under different names but with a substantial similarity of myth and ritual by many peoples of Western Asia" (*The Golden Bough*, 385). But for him the male god of vegetation is more important, and in the first version of myth-ritualism it is primarily the myths of male gods that are ritually enacted to revive vegetation. Frazer's fullest female counterpart to Adonis, Attis, Osiris, and Dionysus is Persephone.

For Frazer, the king may in effect be a hero to his community, but Raglan labels him one. Like Rank and Campbell, Raglan turns a theory of myth in general into a theory of hero myths in particular. Also like them, he introduces his own detailed hero pattern, which he applies to twenty-two hero myths.

In contrast to Rank's and Campbell's patterns, Raglan's covers both halves of life:

1. The hero's mother is a royal virgin;
2. His father is a king, and
3. Often a near relative of his mother, but
4. The circumstances of his conception are unusual, and
5. He is also reputed to be the son of a god.
6. At birth an attempt is made, usually by his father or his maternal grandfather, to kill him, but
7. He is spirited away, and
8. Reared by foster-parents in a far country.
9. We are told nothing of his childhood, but
10. On reaching manhood he returns or goes to his future kingdom.
11. After a victory over the king and/or a giant, dragon, or wild beast,
12. He marries a princess, often the daughter of his predecessor, and
13. Becomes king.
14. For a time he reigns uneventfully, and
15. Prescribes laws, but
16. Later he loses favor with the gods and/or his subjects, and
17. Is driven from the throne and city, after which
18. He meets with a mysterious death,
19. Often at the top of a hill.

20. His children, if any, do not succeed him.

21. His body is not buried, but nevertheless

22. He has one or more holy sepulchres. (Rank et al. 138)

Clearly, parts one through thirteen correspond roughly to Rank's entire scheme, though Raglan himself never read Rank. The victory that gives the hero the throne is not, however, Oedipal, for the vanquished is not necessarily his father, and his father may not even be the one who originally sought the future hero's death at birth. Parts fourteen through twenty-two do not correspond at all to Campbell's scheme. The hero's exile is loosely akin to the hero's journey, but heroism takes the form of self-sacrifice and not of a journey, which is at most secondary. Moreover, for Raglan there is no return. For Rank, the heart of the hero pattern is gaining kingship or other title. For Raglan, the heart is losing kingship. Wherever Campbell's heroes are kings, the heart is their "sabbatical" journey while king.

For Raglan, kingship ties the myth to the ritual: What for Raglan is the core of the myth, the toppling of the king, corresponds to the undeniable core of the ritual: the killing of the king. The myth, which describes the life of a past hero, is less the script for the ritual, as in Frazer's first version, than the inspiration for the ritual of killing the incumbent king. The myth is intended to spur the incumbent to submit to the ritual and thereby be a hero to his subjects.

For Raglan, kingship also ties the hero to the god: Heroes are kings, and kings are gods. True, the hero must die and must therefore be literally a mere mortal, but the hero's death accomplishes a superhuman feat: It ensures the revival of vegetation and thereby the survival of the kingdom. Raglan's heroes have the power to affect the physical world, even if only by dying. They are the saviors of their subjects. Somehow queens cannot do the same.

Raglan's preoccupation with kingship obviously dictates male heroes. Mary Ann Jezewski's proposing a female hero pattern for Raglan is not nearly so damning as Pearson's proposing one for Campbell since Raglan, unlike Campbell, never presumes to be considering other than male heroes. Jezewski breaks with Raglan in not insisting that female heroes either rule or be removed before they die. But then Jezewski severs the link between hero and god. Moreover, she limits herself to the mythic pattern and so ignores any link to ritual. What she offers is a whittled-down version of Raglan. The price she pays for a female hero, à la Raglan, is the elimination of the heart of Raglan's theory. Her attempt to "feminize" Raglan's theory shows how male-centered his is.

In sum, the payoff of the theories of Rank, Campbell, and Raglan is that they discover similarities among hero myths worldwide. Differences are not denied, just downplayed. More important, the theories both explain and interpret the similarities they uncover. The limitation of the theories is that they in fact apply to only certain kinds of hero myths.

Of these three theorists, the most popular has been Campbell. The reason may be the common association of heroism with a quest, of which a journey is the most concrete expression. The reason may also be the broader range of heroes permitted by Campbell for whom heroes can be female as well as male and common as well as royal or aristocratic. And despite his seeming restrictions, Campbell allows for divine as well as human heroes and for young as well as adult ones.

Campbell is by far the most frequently cited authority in this volume. Some of the chapters use only Campbell's heroic pattern. Others use the Jungian meaning that that pattern is supposed to symbolize. But all of the chapters equate heroism with a quest, and most equate a quest with a journey, which, for Rank and Raglan, is at most incidental rather than central.

Notes

1. On theories of myth, see Segal, *Theorizing* and *Short Introduction*.
2. On these confusing terms, see Segal, *Explaining*.
3. On the preservation of classical mythology, see Bush, *Renaissance* and *Romantic*; Seznec; and Bull.

4. A third way of linking myth to literature is deriving literature from myth. On the mythic origin of literature, see Segal, *Ritual* 9–11, 191–303.

5. Citations are to the reprint in Rank.

6. Citations are to the second edition, Campbell 1968.

7. Citations are to the reprint of part 2 in Rank.

8. See Dundes.

9. On the differences between Campbell and Jung, see Segal, *Joseph Campbell*, chapter 12.

10. For Jung's interpretation of heroism in both halves of life, see Jung *Symbols*, 171–444; and *Archetypes*,151–81.

11. On Frank Miller, see *Shamdasani.*

12. See Neumann, *Origins* 131–256; *Great Mother* 203–08.

13. On female Jungian heroes, see Covington.

14. See Raglan, *Hero* 89–136; *Death*; *Origins*, especially chapters 9 and10.

Works Cited

Blumenberg, Hans. *Work on Myth*. Trans. Robert M. Wallace. Cambridge, MA: MIT Press, 1985.

Bull, Malcolm. *The Mirror of the Gods*. London: Allen Lane, 2005.

Bultmann, Rudolf. "New Testament and Mythology." *Kerygma and Myth: A Theological Debate*. Ed. Hans-Werner Bartsch. Trans. Reginald H. Fuller. Vol. I. London: S.P.C.K, 1953. 1–44.

Bush, Douglas. *Mythology and the Renaissance Tradition in English Poetry*. Minneapolis: U of Minnesota P, 1932.

_____. *Mythology and the Romantic Tradition in English Poetry*. Cambridge, MA: Harvard UP, 1937.

Campbell, Joseph. *The Hero with a Thousand Faces*. Princeton, NJ: Princeton UP, 1968.

Covington, Coline. "In Search of the Heroine." *Journal of Analytical Psychology* 34.3 (1989): 243–54.

Dundes, Alan. "Earth-Diver: Creation of the Mythopoeic Male." *American Anthropologist* 64.5 (1962): 1032–51.

Frazer, James George. *The Golden Bough*. Abr. ed. London: Macmillan, 1922.

Jezewski, Mary Ann. "Traits of the Female Hero: The Application of Raglan's Concept of Hero Trait Patterning." *New York Folklore* 10. 1–2 (1984): 55–73.

Jonas, Hans. *The Gnostic Religion: The Message of the Alien God and the Beginnings of Christianity*. 2nd ed. Boston: Beacon, 1963.

Jung, C. G. *The Collected Works of C. G. Jung: The Archetypes and the Collective Unconscious*. 2nd ed. Eds. Sir Herbert Read et al. Trans. R. F. C. Hull. Vol. 9.1. Princeton, NJ: Princeton UP, 1968.

_____. *The Collected Works of C. G. Jung: Symbols of Transformation.* 2nd ed. Eds. Sir Herbert Read et al. Trans. R. F. C. Hull et al. Vol. 5. Princeton, NJ: Princeton UP, 1967.

Malinowski, Bronislaw K. "Myth in Primitive Psychology." *Magic, Science and Religion and Other Essays.* Ed. Robert Redfield. Garden City, NY: Doubleday, 1954. 93–148.

Neumann, Erich. *The Great Mother: An Analysis of the Archetype.* 2nd ed. Trans. Ralph Manheim. Princeton, NJ: Princeton UP, 1972.

_____. *The Origins and History of Consciousness.* Trans. R. F. C. Hull. Princeton, NJ: Princeton UP, 1970.

Pearson, Carol S. *Awakening the Heroes Within: Twelve Archetypes to Help Us Find Ourselves and Transform Our World.* San Francisco: Harper, 1991.

_____. *The Hero Within: Six Archetypes We Live By.* Exp. ed. San Francisco: Harper, 1989.

Pearson, Carol, and Katherine Pope. *The Female Hero in American and British Literature.* New York: Bowker, 1981.

Raglan, Lord. *Death and Rebirth: A Study in Comparative Religion.* London: Watts, 1945.

_____. *The Hero: A Study in Tradition and Myth.* London: Methuen, 1936.

_____. *The Origins of Religion.* London: Watts, 1949.

Rank, Otto. *The Incest Theme in Literature and Legend: Fundamentals of a Psychology of Literary Creation.* Trans. Gregory C. Richter. Baltimore: Johns Hopkins UP, 1992.

_____. *The Trauma of Birth.* London: Kegan Paul, 1929.

Rank, Otto, Lord Raglan, and Alan Dundes. *In Quest of the Hero.* Princeton, NJ: Princeton UP, 1990.

Segal, Robert A. *Explaining and Interpreting Religion: Essays on the Issue.* New York: Lang, 1992.

_____. *Joseph Campbell: An Introduction.* Rev. ed. New York: Meridian, 1997.

_____. *The Myth and Ritual Theory: An Anthology.* Malden, MA: Blackwell, 1998.

_____. *Myth: A Very Short Introduction.* New York: Oxford UP, 2004.

_____. *Theorizing About Myth.* Amherst: U of Massachusetts P, 1999.

Seznec, Jean. *The Survival of the Pagan Gods: The Mythological Tradition and Its Place in Renaissance Humanism and Art.* New York: Pantheon, 1953.

Shamdasani, Sonu. "A Woman Called Frank." *Spring: A Journal of Archetype and Culture* 50 (1990): 26–56.

Trilling, Lionel. "On the Teaching of Modern Literature." *Beyond Culture: Essays on Literature and Learning.* New York: Viking, 1968. 3–30.

Tylor, Edward Burnett. *Primitive Culture.* 5th ed. 2 vols. New York: Harper, 1958.

Vickery, John B. *The Literary Impact of* The Golden Bough. Princeton, NJ: Princeton UP, 1971.

Wolfram's *Parzival* Considered through a Kierkegaardian Lens

Eric Ziolkowski

No work in world literature more conspicuously epitomizes the theme
of the hero's quest than the courtly epic poem *Parzival*, which was composed about 1200–10 and was written by Wolfram von Eschenbach (ca.
1170–ca. 1220). In 1836, the German poet and critic Heinrich Heine
ranked *Parzival* among "the most magnificent works of the Middle
Ages" (7); in our own time, Joseph Campbell pronounced Wolfram
"the greatest poet of the Middle Ages" (*Flight* 208). Yet to most native English speakers, neither Wolfram nor *Parzival* is well known,
if known at all. Outside German departments and medieval studies
programs in colleges and universities, few native English speakers
today have heard of Wolfram, and acquaintance with his masterpiece
is limited mainly to opera lovers familiar with the adaptation of it in
Richard Wagner's music drama *Parsifal* (libretto 1877; score and pre-
mière 1882). Indeed, while the English-speaking world remains generally ignorant of medieval literature (Germanic or otherwise) in which
Parzival is a central classic, most modern German readers, untrained
in Wolfram's Middle High German, can read him only in modern German translation.

Despite these linguistic and cultural barriers, however, the fact remains that *Parzival* revolves around, and crucially serves to perpetu-
ate, one of the most popular and enduring themes in Western literature,
a theme that crystallized in a symbolic image: "the Grail" (Old French:
graal; Middle High German: *grâl*), or, commonly, "the Holy Grail,"
whose actual form varies from a cup or chalice (supposed by some to
be either the one from which Jesus drank at the Last Supper or the one
that received his blood from the Cross) to some other dish or a stone.
The theme emerged in the late twelfth century, putatively in the unfinished romance *Perceval* or *Le Conte du graal* (Story of the Grail) by the
French poet Chrétien de Troyes (ca. 1140–ca. 1191), which Wolfram

retells and completes, professedly drawing upon the account by one Kyot "laschantiure" ("the singer" or "the enchanter"), an "author" Wolfram probably invented. The Grail theme thenceforth persisted as a recurrent preoccupation of chivalric romances with a religious gist and attraction. As Romanian historian and philosopher Mircea Eliade (1907–86) points out, the entire cycle of Arthurian romances, of which the Perceval/Parzival tales comprise a part, is filled with motifs and scenarios of initiation (although Eliade does not identify initiation with quest in the same way that Campbell does),[1] and the widespread popularity of these stories in the Middle Ages "seems proof to us that such adventures met a profound need of medieval people" (Eliade, *History* 105). Today, despite its memorably hilarious subjection to satire in the popular film *Monty Python and the Holy Grail* (dir. Terry Gilliam/ Terry Jones, 1975), the Holy Grail remains "a metaphor for spiritual salvation and the goal of a quest by the elect" (Kahane/Kahane 3649).

Given the prevalence of mysteries, challenges, duels, ordeals, and other initiatory elements in *Parzival*, together with the tripartite formula of separation–initiation–return underlying the definitively *circular* "monomyth" of the hero posited by Campbell (*Hero* 30 and 245, where the formula is schematized with a circle), it is not surprising that Campbell should construe Wolfram's poem, at least in passing, within the monomythic framework (see *Creative Mythology* 480).[2] In the present essay, however, despite a pattern of individual repetitions inherent in Wolfram's plot, I shall suggest that the overall trajectory of the hero's quest in *Parzival* is *linear*, and therefore that a more suitable critical lens through which to interpret it is the structure of three successive stages of existence expounded by the (fictive) "authors" of the voluminous pseudonymous writings of the Danish philosopher, theologian, and literary artist Søren Kierkegaard (1813–55). Conventionally regarded as the progenitor of modern existentialism, Kierkegaard developed a view of the hero as a type that is radically different from Campbell's view.[3] As I have noted elsewhere, Kierkegaard owned a copy of *Parzival* but seems to have never read it.

Elaborated mostly through the "voices" of Kierkegaard's numerous oddly named pseudonyms ("A," "B," Judge William, Johannes de Silentio, Vigilius Haufniensis, etc.), each of whom expresses a different existential viewpoint, the linear progression of Kierkegaard's "stages on life's way" can be summed up as follows. (Here, following somewhat the outline of these stages in Taylor 76–78, we must reduce a vast, almost unfathomably complex, nuanced, multivolume account to its barest minimal structure.) The development of each individual self begins in the *aesthetic* stage of existence, which divides into two poles: the immediate pole, dominated by erotic desire, epitomized by Don Juan, and the reflective pole, epitomized by Faust, which naturally conflicts with immediacy. In this stage, the individual self remains only an inchoate possibility, caught up either in potentially infinite desire or infinite reflection. The next stage, the *ethical*, can be entered only by choice, exemplified by the decision to marry, and it is here that the individual first acquires authentic selfhood, as the self can only be defined by the choices it makes. Determined by the self's commitment to universally obligatory rules, the ethical is transitional toward the third and last stage, the *religious*. Like the aesthetic, the religious divides into two poles. "Religiousness A," the religiousness of immanence, whose hallmark is the sense of guilt, occurs even in paganism. "Religiousness B," distinguished by its consciousness of sin, is the uniquely Christian religiousness of transcendence. Entry to the religious, where the person becomes completed and fulfilled as a "single individual," is achieved through faith, a leap-like movement epitomized by the biblical Abraham, the "knight of faith," entailing a "teleological suspension of the ethical" (Kierkegaard, *Fear* 66)—as when Abraham suspends the universal norm against filicide in order to obey God's command to sacrifice his own son (Gen. 22).

Pertinent to our aim of considering *Parzival* through a Kierkegaardian lens is an observation by Mircea Eliade regarding the "corruption" of myths. "A myth," he says, "may degenerate into an epic legend, a ballad or a romance, or survive only in the attenuated form of 'superstitions,' customs, nostalgias, and so on; for all this, it loses neither its essence nor its significance. . . . The 'trials,' sufferings, and journeyings of the candidate for initiation survived in the tales of the sufferings and obstacles undergone by heroes of epic or drama before they gained their end" (Eliade, *Patterns* 431). To illustrate the point, Eliade parenthetically cites Wagner's Parsifal, together with Ulysses (Odysseus), Aeneas, certain protagonists of Shakespeare, and Faust. Although such characters' "trials" and "sufferings" do not all occur on the same "initiatory plane," "typologically, the wanderings of Ulysses, or the search for the Holy Grail, are echoed in the great novels of the nineteenth century, to say nothing of paperback novels, the archaic origins of whose plots are not hard to trace" (431). This comment suggestively broaches a matter related to our task. To be sure, there are theoretical lengths to which many are unwilling to accompany Eliade, as when he proceeds to link the mythic Achilles with the actual Kierkegaard on the basis of their shared avoidance of marriage in favor of the hope for immortality, to suggest that "patterns . . . from the distant past never disappear" but always retain the possibility of returning "to life," even in "modern consciousness" (Eliade, *Patterns* 432). This linkage is premised upon Eliade's quasi-Jungian theory of archetypes as timeless, universal paradigms of human behavior that surface first in myth, and then "degenerate" through stages of "corruption" in epics, ballads, romances, novels, films, and other artistic media—a theory crystallized in his assumption that "man . . . is forever the prisoner of his own archetypal intuitions" (433). It is to be assumed instead that the thematic and conceptual commonalities we shall explore between the plot of *Parzival* and the existential stages charted in Kierkegaard's writings reflect that Wolfram and Kierkegaard shared a historical bond with the same Western Christian tradition (especially as shaped by St. Augustine in the late fourth and early fifth centuries), no matter how divergent Kierkegaard's nineteenth-century Danish Lutheran roots might seem from Wolfram's medieval Germanic Christian context. Had Kierkegaard read *Parzival*, he would have found it to foreshadow crucial aspects, including the very structure, of his existential thinking, even though Parzival as a quester-hero may not ultimately fit the mold of a Kierkegaardian knight of faith.

Parzival opens with the surprising announcement that its hero, lauded as a steely, courageous, "dauntless man, though laggard in discretion," "sweet balm to woman's eyes, yet woman's heart's disease," and "shunner of all wrongdoing," is as yet "unborn to this story" (Wolfram 16). The first two of the poem's sixteen books tell not of Parzival but of his father, Gahmuret of Anjou. In Gahmuret, whose story is almost entirely Wolfram's (not Chrétien's) creation, we meet a worthy embodiment of Kierkegaard's initial, aesthetic stage, the one associated with paganism. He exhibits all the restlessness of a Don Juan bound by desire within this stage of immediacy and the erotic. A gallant, nominally Christian knight, part fairy by descent, he seeks out adventures in non-Christian "Eastern" lands, where he meets and weds the Moorish queen Belacane. Yet his marriage is only a momentary deceit, and, unlike the choice to enter matrimony in Part 2 of Kierkegaard's *Either/Or*, it does not signify passage from the aesthetic stage to the ethical. Driven by his inborn passion, Gahmuret abandons Belacane, leaving her pregnant. Later, "fated by his fairy blood to love or sue for love" (Wolfram 58), he marries Herzeloyde, Queen of Waleis and Norgals, on the condition that she never chaperone him. "For if my sorrows ever leave me," he warns, "I should like to go out jousting. If you will not let me go to tournaments I have not forgotten my own trick, how once before I gave my wife the slip" (59). By the time she gives birth to their son Parzival, Gahmuret has returned to the East and been slain.

Given the determinant roles that heredity and context play in the aesthetic stage where the individual lacks spiritual direction, it seems natural that when Parzival is introduced as a youth in book 3, he seems a pure aesthete, displaying traits inherited from his father. Pampered in the forest by his mournful widowed mother who withdrew there to raise him in ignorance of human ways, society, and knighthood, he feels his breast tighten one day in response to the sweet sound of birds singing. This incident, the first indication that Parzival is "the victim of amorous desire to which his race was heir" (Wolfram 71), might from *Either/Or*'s perspective confirm his entrapment in the "musical erotic" phase of the aesthetic, where "music is the demonic" (Kierkegaard, *Either/Or* 1:65).

This is not to suggest that Parzival is demonic; on the contrary, he is a "simple," "backward" lad, "dull of understanding" (Wolfram 80, 83, 242). Moreover, in Wolfram's and Kierkegaard's view, this young fool, "not yet grown to years of discretion" (Wolfram 141), would be fully subject to the taint of original sin, the sinfulness that he and all other humans have "inherited" from Adam and Eve. Although a youth, he is childlike in the sense in which Kierkegaard's Johannes Climacus distinguishes the child from the adult as a "sinner without the consciousness of sin" (Kierkegaard, *Postscript* 1. 592). Aesthetically ignorant of good and evil, Parzival proves as firmly bound to the immediate desires as was his father. When he happens to encounter four knights in the woods, he regards them as divine because their brightly shining armor matches the description Herzeloyde offered when he once asked her what God is: "He Who took on a shape in the likeness of Man is brighter than the sun" (Wolfram 71–72). After they tell him about their profession, Parzival leaves his mother to become a knight, but only after she has dressed him up in fool's clothing and given him a set of instructions to follow.

Metaphorically, Kierkegaard's Johannes de Silentio speaks of madness as the "fool's costume" to be calmly donned by the Abrahamic individual, that is, one who will suspend normal ethical considerations in order to heed a divine calling, as Abraham did when commanded to sacrifice Isaac. All that matters, says Johannes de Silentio, is that such a person still understands inwardly that a single, concentrated "look to heaven" can indicate "that he has been true to his love" (Kierkegaard, *Fear* 49). Yet Herzeloyde's intention in attiring Parzival as a fool has nothing to do with encouraging him to look to heaven or to remain true to any love; on the contrary, Herzeloyde hopes that his ridiculous-looking garb will cause Parzival to be derided by other people, and hence prompt him to give up his quest and to return to her. This scheme, together with Herzeloyde's instructions, will have the effect of impeding Parzival's development out of the aesthetic stage, into the ethical.

As we shall see, Herzeloyde's instructions, and two more sets of counsels that Parzival will later receive from two other mentors, correspond respectively to Kierkegaard's three stages of existence. These sets of instructions roughly reflect the "state of nature," the "rule of law," and the "state of grace" (Poag 71). Thus Parzival's passage from the aesthetic (compare nature) into the ethical (compare law) will be prompted by his reception of the second set of instructions, and his at least partial passage from the ethical into the religious (compare grace) will be aided by his reception of the third set of counsels.

Taken to heart by Parzival, Herzeloyde's instructions have disastrous consequences, for they only reinforce his natural impulses and desires that stem from what Kierkegaard would view as his existence in instinctual, unreflective immediacy. Herzeloyde instructed her son to greet everyone he meets, and so he does this, foolishly and indiscriminately, always adding like an imbecile: "That's what my mother told me" (Wolfram 77, 80ff.). Additionally, she advised him that to win good fortune, he should accept the ring of a chaste and good lady, and he should kiss and embrace her without hesitation. This too he does at the first opportunity, in a scene that unfolds like a parody of the seduction rehearsed by the aesthetic "author" of "The Seducer's Diary" in Part 1 of Kierkegaard's *Either/Or*. In this case, however, the "seducer" is a young simpleton who knows nothing of sex, and his "victim," whom he does not actually—nor ever intended—to seduce or to rape, but roughly hugs, kisses, and robs of her ring and brooch, is the beautiful duchess Jeschute, who mistakes him for a page who has lost his sanity. Yet Herzeloyde also exhorted him to subjugate King Lähelin, usurper of her lands and oppressor of her people. Accordingly, in his ignorance and by ignoble means, Parzival slays the noble knight Ither, who, unbeknownst to Parzival, is related to him by blood, but whom he mistakes for Lähelin. Parzival next commits an impulsive act of desecration, stripping Ither's corpse of the beautiful red armor he has coveted since he first saw it and donning it now as his own.

Like the death of his mother, which he does not know of but which resulted from her heartbreak over his leaving her (hence her name Herzeloyde, meaning "heartache"), Parzival's murder of a blood relative is a disaster for which he will be later held accountable after he progresses from the aesthetic stage into the ethical. From a Kierkegaardian viewpoint, this progression seems presaged during his serendipitous encounter with a cousin of his, the beautiful Sigune, of whom he has no prior knowledge but who now reveals to him his name and family history—both of which Kierkegaard would deem requisite for anyone hoping to choose his or her own individual self, the *sine qua non* of ethical existence. In the words of Kierkegaard's Judge William, the individual entering the ethical "discovers that the self he chooses has a boundless multiplicity within itself inasmuch as it has a history, a history in which he acknowledges identity within himself" (Kierkegaard, *Either/Or* 2. 216).

Ironically, the instructions Herzeloyde gave to keep Parzival bound within aesthetic immediacy include one that enables him to enter the ethical: If a wise gray-haired man offers to teach him good manners, Parzival must obey him. After visiting the palace of King Arthur, who finds him charming but too coarse yet to be knighted, Parzival is admitted into the castle of Gurnemanz, a kindly old prince who matches Herzeloyde's description of the man whose advice Parzival should heed. Despite Parzival's lack of refinement, Gurnemanz recognizes the youth as a scion of noble forebears. So he invites him to stay and begins to initiate him to the ways of knighthood. After having him remove his fool's clothes, which, emblematic of his aesthetic existence, he had continued wearing under his armor, Gurnemanz has him bathed and given elegant attire worthy of a knight. Next, he takes him to Mass and teaches him "to make his offering and cross himself and so punish the Devil" (Wolfram 95). After this first exposure to formal worship, meant to implant in him a sense of ethical responsibility to the absolute (i.e., God), Parzival is urged to sever his emotional tie with his mother: "You speak like a child," Gurnemanz tells him. "Why do you not stop talking of your mother and turn your mind to other things? Keep to my advice, it will save you from wrong-doing" (95).

Gurnemanz proceeds to draw the youth out of the aesthetic stage and into the ethical. Indoctrinating him in chivalric ethics, Gurnemanz instructs him to cultivate a sense of shame, to show kindness and generosity to the needy, to be discreet in financial affairs, to practice moderation, to refrain from asking many questions, to show mercy to defeated foes, to maintain personal hygiene, to be manly and cheerful, to hold ladies in high esteem, and to pursue courtly love. These teachings transform Parzival from a wild fool into a cultivated, ethical knight. Yet he also proves a worthy son of the aesthetical Gahmuret through the strength and spirit he displays while mastering the arts of combat in which Gurnemanz also trains him.

Consistent both with Kierkegaard's insight that humans separate themselves from nature through their ability to choose to live ethically and with Judge William's use of the choice to marry to symbolize ethical duty (see Kierkegaard, *Either/Or* 2. 245), the entry of Parzival into ethical existence coincides with his initial contemplation of nuptial commitment. However, Parzival does something remarkably similar to Kierkegaard, who, in 1841, suddenly broke off his engagement with his fiancée Regine Olsen and fled Copenhagen for Berlin. Parzival, when positioned to wed Gurnemanz's lovely daughter Liaze, abruptly departs, promising that if he ever wins fame as a knight, he will return to ask for her. This promise proves false. Parzival soon marries a different woman, Queen Condwiramurs of Brobarz, whose city he frees from siege by a wicked king, thereby establishing his own reputation as a knight. (The like-father-like-son aspect of this is obvious, as Parzival's actions recall Gahmuret's abandonment of Belecane.)

Like Chrétien's Perceval, Wolfram's Parzival proves so naïve about matters of sex that he fails—out of ignorance, not physical incapacity—

to consummate his marriage on his first two nights in bed with his wife. Nonetheless, Parzival's ethical existence seems confirmed from a Kierkegaardian perspective by the fact that Parzival, unlike his late philandering father, remains always faithful to his wife. His absorption of Gurnemanz's ethics is further reflected in the mercy he henceforth shows to vanquished foes (see Wolfram 115). Yet his service on behalf of the chivalric-ethical absolute soon proves insufficient to qualify him fully for existence in the religious stage of existence.

How and why does Parzival never fully enter the religious stage? After his marriage, he departs one morning with the aim of visiting his mother and seeking adventure. "Destined now to suffer great anguish" (Wolfram 120), he comes seemingly by chance to Munsalvaesche, the castle of the Holy Grail, and commits his greatest blunder there. A large, sorrowful company in the castle wines and dines him and even allows him to see the Grail. Yet Parzival adheres so strictly to Gurnemanz's instruction not to ask questions that he refrains from inquiring after the affliction of his host, the crippled Grail king Anfortas, a man of whose identity and significance he is unaware. Had he simply asked the afflicted ruler what ailed him, Parzival would have healed him, restored joy to the castle, and succeeded him as custodian of the Grail. Although it will eventually be revealed that Parzival is destined by personal virtues, family descent, and divine assignment to achieve all these ends, neither he nor the reader knows this at present, and we are left to surmise that bad fortune led him to the castle before he was meant to go there. Because his ethical training, together with his ignorance and indiscretion, caused him not to ask the question, this pivotal episode might confirm the conviction of Kierkegaard's Climacus that the ethicist's effort to satisfy the requirement of the eternal (which is symbolized in *Parzival* by the Grail) must inevitably lead to recognition of the futility of that effort.

Another motif congruent with Kierkegaard's concerns is Parzival's fateful silence in Anfortas's presence. For Kierkegaard, who wrote much on silence and its manifold implications, Parzival's silence would seem problematic because it was not rooted in inwardness (one of Kierkegaard's favorite terms for connoting subjective experience), as all authentic silence must be. Instead, Parzival's failure to ask the compassionate question, resulting from his simple-minded adherence to the ethical protocol of restraint in speech, might be aptly explained by a comment by one of Kierkegaard's chief religious pseudonyms, Anti-Climacus. According to Anti-Climacus, the individual who succumbs to social conformity suffers from a form of despair, "find[ing] it too hazardous to be himself and far easier and safer to be like the others, to become a copy" (*Sickness* 34). Such dejection is rarely discernible, and even when it is detected, it is not commonly recognized as despair because to all appearances, social conformity, despite the hidden despair that accompanies it, makes life comfortable. This is why there are so many proverbs extolling the superior value of silence:

> For example, we say that one regrets ten times for having spoken to once for having kept silent—and why? Because the external fact of having spoken can involve one in difficulties, since it is an actuality. But to have kept silent! And yet this is the most dangerous of all. For by maintaining silence, a person is thrown wholly upon himself; here actuality does not come to his aid by punishing him, by heaping the consequences of his speaking upon him. No, in this respect it is easy to keep silent. But the person who knows what is genuinely appalling fears most of all any mistake, any sin that takes an inward turn and leaves no outward trace. (*Sickness* 34)

Parzival's silence does prove "most dangerous," but not the way Anti-Climacus imagined. To adapt Anti-Climacus's terms, Parzival's silence is as much an outward "actuality" as any speaking might be, inasmuch as his silence signals to everyone present, and to others who later learn of his silence, that Parzival has not attained the maturity and discretion he needs to fulfill his destiny. To be sure, Parzival's silence amounts to a "sin that takes an inward turn," leading him to the brink of inward despair. But this "sin" of silence leaves an "outward trace," and he is punished by the actual consequences of his silence.

The morning after his blunder, Parzival awakes to find Munsalvaesche deserted, and as he departs, he is cursed by a lone page for his failure the night before. Henceforth, a number of overriding Kierkegaardian themes emerge. Above all, the theme of "repetition" calls to mind Kierkegaard's little book (1843) of that title, ascribed to the pseudonym Constantin Constantius. Repetition, Constantin explains, is in modern philosophy what recollection was for the Greeks. Just as the Greeks construed knowing as recollecting, so modern philosophy construes life as repetition (see Kierkegaard, *Repetition* 131). In *Parzival*, instances of repetition that reverse earlier disastrous acts become crucial in the denouement of events furnishing the hero opportunities to atone for his past blunders and ultimately to return to Munsalvaesche for a second chance.

The initial repetition occurs through Parzival's second encounter with Sigune. After informing him that Anfortas is his mother's brother, Sigune curses Parzival for the same reason the page did. When she then pronounces Parzival "dead" as far as his fortune goes (Wolfram 135), he promises to make amends. Anticipating Kierkegaard's view of atonement as "the most profound expression of repetition" (*Repetition* 313), Parzival's atonement will entail three providentially arranged repetitions that enable him to atone for his three major sins. First, when he is about to vanquish an unrecognized opponent in a duel, Parzival learns that the man is his kinsman Gawan. Throwing down his sword, Parzival avoids repeating his earlier sin of causing his own mother's death. Next, following another victory in combat, this time over a fearsome monarch, Parzival's earlier murder of Ither is made up for when a miraculous breakage of his sword (the one he stole from Ither's corpse) prevents him from unwittingly slaying another kinsman in battle, this time his half-brother Feirefiz (Gahmuret's son by Belacane). Finally, when providence leads him back to Munsalvaesche, he asks Anfortas the question, thus atoning for his earlier silence and thereby healing the old man and earning for himself the guardianship of the Grail.

This series of atonements-through-repetition was anticipated much earlier, as soon as he departed from Sigune after vowing to atone. He met up again with Jeschute, the woman he had earlier assaulted. Weeping forlornly, clad only in a tattered shift, and riding an emaciated nag, she was following her husband Duke Orilus, who had dismissed her as his wife on the conviction that she had committed adultery with the man who had taken her ring. Parzival, now learning of her plight, subdued (but refrained from killing) Orilus in battle, and then, to restore her honor, accompanied them to a hermit's cell. There, he revealed Jeschute's innocence to Orilus, confessed his own guilt in having robbed her jewelry, and persuaded Orilus to accept her back as spouse.

Between that episode and the later series of atoning repetitions, Parzival has to struggle through and overcome the same sort of self-destructive despair that obsesses Kierkegaard's Anti-Climacus. After repairing the damage he caused to the marriage of Jeschute and Orilus, he experiences another repetition: he finds his way back to King Arthur, who now admits him as a knight of the Round Table. Soon afterwards, however, the sorceress and Grail messenger Cundrie arrives and publicly curses him, and Parzival departs in shame. He even renounces God, whom he now regards in the same way that a knight would view a disloyal king. "Alas, what is God?" he asks himself. "Were He all-powerful—were God active in His almightiness—he would not have brought us to such shame! Ever since I knew of Grace I have been [God's] humble servitor. But now I will quit His service!" (Wolfram 172). One is here reminded of Anti-Climacus's reflection:

> When the sinner despairs of the forgiveness of sins, it is almost as if he walked right up to God and said, "No, there is no forgiveness of sins, it is impossible," and it looks like close combat. Yet to be able to say this and for it to be heard, a person must become qualitatively distanced from God. (Kierkegaard, *Sickness* 114)

Parzival wanders in despair for four and a half years before being providentially guided to the hermit Trevrizent, another of his maternal uncles. Here too the force of repetition is manifest, as Parzival has been led to Trevrizent only after having met up with Sigune once again, and then later having recognized Trevrizent's dwelling as the same spot where he long ago reconciled Orilus to Jeschute (see Wolfram 233; compare 141–42). That event, we recall, anticipated Parzival's long, still incomplete atonement process. During his third encounter with Sigune, she forgave him, perceiving that he had forfeited happiness in the years since his blunder with Anfortas.

As Parzival's final tutor, Trevrizent will supplement Gurnemanz's earlier ethical instructions with teachings of a religious sort, which Wolfram and Kierkegaard alike, as believing Christians, would have regarded as higher than exclusively aesthetic or ethical teachings. How do we sense that Parzival has exhausted the ethical stage and is prepared for the religious? As if auguring Climacus's identification of "the totality of guilt-consciousness" (Kierkegaard, *Postscript* 1:560) as the most edifying aspect of religiousness A, Parzival greets Trevrizent by declaring: "Sir, guide me now: I am a sinner" (Wolfram 233). Trevrizent imparts to Parzival three main kinds of knowledge. First, learning of Parzival's resentment of God, he urges that one must always trust in God and be "unswervingly constant towards Him, since God Himself is perfect constancy," and that "he that atones for his sins serves Him for His noble favour" (236, 238). Second, learning of and ultimately forgiving Parzival's sins (including the responsibility for Herzeloyde's death, of which Parzival only now learns), Trevrizent expounds the doctrine of original sin and the history behind the falls of Lucifer and Adam. Third, Trevrizent reveals to Parzival the secrets of the Grail, including an explanation of what it is: a divinely empowered stone of purest essence that sustains everlastingly the lives of all who look upon it. He also discloses the cause of Anfortas's suffering: a wound from a poisoned lance through the scrotum, sustained as divine punishment for a youthful indiscretion. Finally, Trevrizent makes known to Parzival how Anfortas is to be saved (that is, by posing the compassionate question), as well as Parzival's relation to the Grail family whose headship he is destined to assume.

Parzival will not complete his maturation until he follows Trevrizent's exhortation to do penance and in effect undoes his sins through the aforementioned series of redemptive repetitions. These occur in books 14–16 and culminate with Parzival's asking Anfortas the question of what ailed him. Only then, fulfilling Kierkegaard's and Anti-Climacus's definition of "reduplication," does Parzival come "to be what [he] says" (Kierkegaard, *Journals and Papers* 6:37, entry 6224) and "to exist in what [he] understands" (Kierkegaard, *Practice* 134)—that is, not only to reflect upon, to understand, or perhaps even to speak of the religious ideals he has been taught, but actually to incorporate them within his existence so as to, in effect, *live* them.[4]

Parzival's success could only be achieved through his atonement-by-suffering, and it is only through the resulting spiritual maturation that he has been prepared to grasp this fact. As Kierkegaard points out, the "natural man" would never think of desiring to suffer: "The most profound change must first take place before a person can believe this secret of sufferings. He must first be gripped by and then be willing to learn from the only one who went out into the world with the purpose of willing to suffer, with the choice of willing to suffer and with insistence upon it" (Kierkegaard, *Upbuilding Discourses* 250). This lesson about Christ's voluntary suffering and death was taught to Parzival by an aged knight, Gabenis, who then directed Parzival to Trevrizent, informing him that the latter would advise him, allot penance to him, and remove his sins: "Where was greater loyalty seen than that shown by God for our sakes when they hung Him on the Cross? . . . He bartered His noble life in death in order to redeem our debt, in that Mankind was damned and destined to Hell for our sins" (Wolfram 229).

A crucial question remains: Is Parzival, in approaching or entering the religious stage, able to be equaled with the Kierkegaardian knight of faith?

Although Parzival tries to adhere to the universal (that is, the ethical) during his career as knight, his destiny as Grail king is singular and requires that he breach his understanding of ethical protocol to ask Anfortas the necessary question. Parzival engages in nothing analogous to the knight of faith's suspension of ethical obligations, epitomized by the readiness of Abraham to sacrifice his own son. Parzival does resemble Abraham in his divine election and, eventually, his absolute devotion to what Climacus would call the absolute *telos* (end, goal), materially embodied in the Grail. Yet the first of these affinities must be qualified at once. Unlike Abraham, Parzival is never directly called by God, although he has been divinely assigned to the Grail. Unlike Abraham's call, to which the future patriarch alone was initially privy (Gen. 12), the secret that "no man can win the Gral other than one who is acknowledged in Heaven as destined for it" (Wolfram 239) is not revealed to Parzival alone.

The second commonality proves more stubbornly suggestive because Parzival, like Abraham, related himself to the absolute *telos* by undergoing what Johannes de Silentio calls an "ordeal." In the episode of the intended-but-ultimately-interrupted sacrifice of Isaac, which Johannes de Silentio dwells upon, Abraham departed from his wife without uttering a word in order to fulfill his divinely assigned filicidal task. Analogously, Parzival left behind his beloved wife, who, unbeknownst to him at the time, turns out to have been pregnant with twin sons. Then he remains away from her until he obtains the Grail. Like Abraham, Parzival subordinates family to Grail in his hierarchy of values. "My deepest distress is for the Gral," he tells Trevrizent. "After that it is for my wife" (Wolfram 239).

Again, however, Wolfram's "fool" never exhibits an Abrahamic suspension of the ethical. So, though a knight, he never becomes a Kierkegaardian knight of faith. Nonetheless, the apparent failure of Kierkegaard to read *Parzival* seems highly regrettable: He missed encountering a medieval hero whose spiritual quest and existential development, when considered through the lens of Kierkegaard's oeuvre, closely anticipate the stages it traces on life's way.

Reiterating the earlier claim, the Kierkegaardian lens through which we have interpreted *Parzival* has allowed us to view its hero as proceeding *linearly* through three main stages of development (aesthetic, ethical, and religious). Does it follow, then, that we must necessarily privilege this reading of the quest pattern over others? Specifically, does a linear, Kierkegaardian reading of *Parzival* render moot a circular reading such as with Campbell's monomyth? Not necessarily: Different interpretations of a story or literary text can be equally "true," or at least they can both be true to varying degrees in relation to one another. What Clifford Geertz wrote of cultural-anthropological interpretations holds equally true of literary interpretations, namely: "They are, thus, fictions; fictions, in the sense that they are 'something made,' 'something fashioned'—in the original meaning of [the Latin root-word] *fictiō*—not that they are false, unfactual, or merely 'as if' thought experiments" (15).

Something approximating the circular, monomythic pattern is of course discernible in the story of Parzival, not only through its cyclic patterns of repetition that we discussed, but also inasmuch as it begins with his removal (*separation*) from his paradisiacal life with his mother in the wilderness; proceeds with his long, liminal period of ordeals and wanderings (*initiation*), which comprise the vast preponderance of the narrative, including his first, disastrous visit to Munsalvaesche; and ends with his finding his way back to, and being incorporated into the royal company of, Munsalvaesche (*return*). Nonetheless, his return to the Grail Castle, and, indeed, his accession to its throne, is not a return to his original life with his mother (now dead), and this fact alone betrays a significant divergence from the monomythic pattern.

No less so than Campbell, Kierkegaard was keenly aware of the potentially weighty bearing that the relationship between the human being and society might have upon his or her spiritual or religious development, and Kierkegaard, as much so as Campbell, would have likely noted that the story of Parzival is framed by his *separation from* his mother's social company and *return to* the social company of the Grail Castle. Yet, for Kierkegaard, in contrast to Campbell, *initiation* (in Parzival's case, to a Christian religious life) is existentially an individual affair, and existence itself represents a liminal condition from beginning to end (inasmuch as all human beings, in the Christian view, remain separated from God throughout their lives). He tended to be wary of society in general, and his concern with its influences upon its individual members finds expression mainly through criticisms, as when he protests what he calls the "leveling" of the individual in contemporary society, lamenting that "the age of heroes is past" (Kierkegaard, *Two Ages* 87). Kierkegaard's Anti-Climacus thus seeks to clarify the distinction between the "crowd" (or "rabble"), which he associates with the Aristotelian category of "the animal" (Kierkegaard, *Sickness* 118), and the single individual, who, unlike all other animal species, "is more than the species" (121fn.).

In construing the single individual as an existent being whose self-realization can ultimately be achieved only through a linear development apart from external social factors and, instead, in a direct relationship with God, Kierkegaard furnishes a critical lens that allows for a reading of *Parzival* that provides us a more penetrating insight than does Campbell's cyclic monomyth into the medieval Christian assumptions that underlie Wolfram's text, especially regarding the essentially sinful nature of human beings and their reliance on divine providence for salvation.

Notes

1. For Campbell, the hero's quest itself constitutes an initiation (i.e., the second stage of Campbell's monomyth). In contrast, Eliade distinguishes three categories of initiation, only the third of which in certain cases entails a quest: (1) puberty initiations to adulthood; (2) rites for entry into a secret society; and (3) initiations to a mystical or shamanic status, which can come about as a consequence either of "a personal decision to acquire religious power (*the process*

called *'the quest'*)" or "through vocation ('the call')" (*Rites and Symbols* 2–3; emphasis added; see also 87, 96).

2. It is important to note that the notions of heroism Campbell presents in *The Hero with a Thousand Faces* (1949) and in *Creative Mythology* (1968) differ and are hardly compatible. In the former, earlier work, the hero goes on a journey and returns, but returns *transformed*. The circle exists only inasmuch as the hero returns, and the stories of all heroes universally conform to this same pattern— hence Campbell's appropriation of James Joyce's term "monomyth." In *Creative Mythology*, Campbell abandons the monomyth almost entirely (with the exception of the *Parzival* allusion just cited, and also p. 362), and distinguishes notions of heroism according to cultures and historical periods. He now views Wolfram and Wolfram's contemporary, Gottfried von Strassburg, the author of *Tristan* (left incomplete at Gottfried's death, ca. 1210), as the progenitors of a distinctly modern form of heroism leading directly, via Richard Wagner, to the two twentieth-century novelists Thomas Mann and James Joyce. For references, see Note 3.

3. Unlike Campbell, Kierkegaard distinguished religious paragons such as Abraham and Jesus qualitatively from the hero figure, exalting Jesus as a unique "prototype" who requires not only admiration but, instead, imitation. Further, Kierkegaard's pseudonym Johannes de Silentio exalts Abraham and the knight of faith above tragic or even "Church-related" heroes (see Kierkegaard, *Fear* 33, 57, 65, 74–81). Moreover, whereas Campbell (*Hero* 4) suggested that Sigmund Freud, Carl Gustav Jung, and their followers had irrefutably demonstrated that mythic heroes "survive into modern times," Kierkegaard thought that his own age lacked heroes because individuals in modern society have all been reduced to the same low level where heroism is impossible. Finally, Kierkegaard and Campbell held different views of the relationship between literary heroes and the texts they appear in. Campbell came to view Parzival as a modern (*sic*) hero, seeing him, like all modern literary heroes, as the subject of his creator (Wolfram), not of the hero's text (*Parzival*) (see Campbell, *Creative Mythology* 6–7, 38; Segal 61 65). In contrast, Kierkegaard, while regarding Wolfram as epitomizing a medieval duality between spirit ("higher") and flesh ("lower"), never hesitated to second-guess or even to challenge the characterizations of heroes, plots, and other dimensions of literary classics by authors as revered as Shakespeare and Cervantes, and he anticipated the early twentieth-century Spanish philosopher Miguel de Unamuno in judging Cervantes to be inferior to Cervantes's novel *Don Quixote*. Hence, Kierkegaard would have had no trouble assessing *Parzival* and its hero apart from their creator Wolfram.

4. "Reduplication" (from the Latin, *reduplicatus* [doubled again, redoubled, reduplicated], the past participle of the verb *reduplicare*) is one of the most crucial terms in Kierkegaard's and his pseudonyms' vocabulary. As Taylor (49–50) explains, reduplication is for Kierkegaard "the actualization of possibilities," and hence, "another way of indicating the process by which an individual strives to embody in his life that which he has understood. It is another way of point to the

fact that, for an existing individual, religious truth is subjectivity." (In the last clause, Taylor is quoting Johannes Climacus's famous thesis from Kierkegaard's *Concluding Unscientific Postscript* (1846), "truth is subjectivity" (1:189; see also 21, 192–94, 196ff.).

Works Cited

Campbell, Joseph. *The Flight of the Wild Gander: Explorations in the Mythological Dimension*. New York: HarperPerennial, 1990.

_____. *The Hero with a Thousand Faces*. New York: Meridian, 1956.

_____. *The Masks of God: Creative Mythology.* Vol. 4. New York: Viking, 1968.

Chrétien de Troyes. *Perceval, or the Story of the Grail*. Trans. Ruth Harwood Cline. Athens: U of Georgia P, 1985.

Eliade, Mircea. *A History of Religious Ideas: From Muhammad to the Age of Reforms*. Vol. 3. Trans. Alf Hiltebeitel and Diane Apostolos-Cappadona. Chicago: U of Chicago P, 1985.

_____. *Patterns in Comparative Religion*. Trans. Rosemary Sheed. New York: Meridian, 1974.

_____. *Rites and Symbols of Initiation: The Mysteries of Birth and Rebirth*. Trans. Willard R. Trask. Woodstock, CT: Spring, 1994.

Geertz, Clifford. *The Interpretation of Cultures: Selected Essays*. New York: Basic Books, 1973.

Heine, Heinrich. "The Romantic School." *The Romantic School and Other Essays*. Ed. Jost Hermand and Robert C. Holub. Trans. Helen Mustard. New York: Continuum, 1985. 1–127.

Kahane, Henry, and Renée Kahane. "Grail, The." *The Encyclopedia of Religion*. 2nd ed. Ed. Lindsay Jones. Vol. 6. Detroit: Macmillan, 2005. 3649–53.

Kierkegaard, Søren. *Concluding Unscientific Postscript to* Philosophical Fragments. Ed. and trans. Howard V. Hong and Edna H. Hong. Princeton, NJ: Princeton UP, 1992.

_____. *Either/Or*. Ed. and trans. Howard V. Hong and Edna H. Hong. 2 vols. Princeton, NJ: Princeton UP, 1987.

_____. *Fear and Trembling* and *Repetition*. Ed. and trans. Howard V. Hong and Edna H. Hong. Princeton, NJ: Princeton UP, 1983.

_____. *Practice in Christianity*. Ed. and trans. Howard V. Hong and Edna H. Hong. Princeton, NJ: Princeton UP, 1991.

_____. *The Sickness unto Death: A Christian Psychological Exposition for Upbuilding and Awakening*. Ed. and trans. Howard V. Hong and Edna H. Hong. Princeton, NJ: Princeton UP, 1980.

_____. *Søren Kierkegaard's Journals and Papers*. Ed. and trans. Howard V. Hong, Edna H. Hong, and Gregor Malantschuk. Bloomington: Indiana UP, 1967–78.

_____. *Two Ages: The Age of Revolution and the Present Age. A Literary Review*. Ed. and trans. Howard V. Hong and Edna H. Hong. Princeton, NJ: Princeton UP, 1978.

_____. *Upbuilding Discourses in Various Spirits*. Ed. and trans. Howard V. Hong and Edna H. Hong. Princeton, NJ: Princeton UP, 1993.

Poag, James F. *Wolfram von Eschenbach*. New York: Twayne, 1972.

Segal, Robert A. *Joseph Campbell: An Introduction*. New York: Garland, 1987.

Taylor, Mark C. *Kierkegaard's Pseudonymous Authorship: A Study of Time and the Self*. Princeton, NJ: Princeton UP, 1975.

Wolfram von Eschenbach. *Parzival*. Trans. A. T. Hatto. New York: Penguin, 1980.

Ziolkowski, Eric J. *The Literary Kierkegaard*. Evanston, IL: Northwestern UP, 2011.

Romancing the Quest: Quest Narratives in Changing Contexts _____

Jeremy M. Downes

The Question of Quests

The similarity of the terms *quest* and *question* is not accidental. Both words take root in the Latin verb *quaerere,* meaning "to search," or "to inquire." The words lie at the heart of human exploration and human research—in our need to move beyond our current understanding, our current communities—in order to find some object of desire: a loved one, a remedy, a solution, an answer. Of course, this form of human activity, and the *narration* of this activity, goes back much farther than Latin. Indeed, we assume it goes back to the origin of human communities and human language itself, leading some scholars to think of humans as the story-telling animal, *homo narrans.* The way we describe the earliest forms of human community (and the few remaining traditional societies like them in the contemporary world) as "hunters and gatherers" already suggests the centrality of the quest, defined most simply as the process of venturing forth, transformation, and return.[1] Hunting and gathering are both predicated on a departure from the community location; a foray into a less familiar region in search of the desired plant, animal, or other object; the transformative encounter with the desired object; and the successful or unsuccessful return to the community. When much of one's daily activity revolves around quest-like activities, it is hardly surprising that one's narratives, whether told at the fireside or painted on a cave wall, both echo and build on that structure.

At the other end of the human timeline, we still find ourselves almost as deeply enmeshed in the structure of the quest. Whether we are formulating a thesis statement, seeking a cure for disease, or—at the most mundane level—going to the grocery store for bread and milk, we engage in quests of a kind. Contemporary narratives, too, elaborate on this ancient narrative structure of venturing, transformation, and return. Massively multiplayer online role-playing games (MMORPGs), like the popular *World of Warcraft*, structure the player's experience of the virtual world primarily through quests, using floating yellow exclamation marks and question marks to guide the player through a complex, evolving narrative experience.

This discussion strives to suggest some of the major historical and cultural contexts that produce quest narratives. It also explores many of the transformations, or at least the shifts in emphasis, that take place in those narratives as we move through human history. While the basic structure of the quest narrative—venturing, transformation, return—may be common to all humans, it is also fairly obvious that the personal experience of a *World of Warcraft* quest line (mediated through an online avatar, and based in high-tech programming), is going to be very different from the communal experience of listening to a skilled bard performing Beowulf's battle with Grendel or the homecoming of Odysseus. The technological differences over these thousands of years are tremendous and carry with them substantial changes in worldview as well as in material circumstances; these changes inevitably accompany changes in the heroic figures involved, as well as within the quest narrative itself.[2]

Hunters and Gatherers

As previously mentioned, the daily activities of hunting and gathering societies lend themselves to narrative organization built on the quest. But the very commonness of this activity means that artistic representations thereof—stories or paintings, for example—are likely to go beyond the most mundane.[3] The 17,000-year-old Lascaux cave paintings, for example, record over 600 animal images—but there are no images of reindeer, the most commonly hunted animal; similarly, there are no images of vegetation, which would have played a large role in day-to-day living (Curtis 96–97). This kind of distinction is easy to illustrate in our own lives: "What I did today" or "my trip to the grocery store" may be important at the family dinner table, but it typically has limited interest as *story* unless developed into something much more significant. That is, the stories that get developed and passed down or recorded are most often involved with greater themes, with rites of passage, with migrations, with events and issues of significance for the larger community. Thus in Lascaux, we witness the loving care devoted to the painting of the great aurochs in the Hall of the Bulls, which suggests the community's respect for the aurochs, a rare species and challenging to hunt. There are, of course, various interpretations of the images at Lascaux. Are these records of great hunts? Or are they rehearsals, relying on a kind of sympathetic magic, painted to invoke a great hunt? It is hard to say with any certainty, but of course there's no reason that such records—like any other repeated oral narrative—cannot work in both ways: We repeat cheers at a football game, invocations at public ceremonies, or prayers during worship, and each individual performance looks backward as well as forward—backward to the cultural tradition and forward to the culture's continuing future, working both as echo and as prophecy. The aurochs paintings, in particular, have also been connected by scholars with astronomical phenomena, enlarging their possible significance well beyond the single hunt to a meditation on the changing seasons and the constant stars (Rappenglück 1–5).

More recent examples of the connection between the individual and the cosmic through quest narrative can be found in Native American "vision quests" or in the Australian aboriginal "walkabout." Both of these rites of passage have been so popularized and Westernized that it's hard to know their earlier significance, but they signify periods of isolation from the community, during which a boy ventures the paths of his ancestors in order to become a man, entering the spiritual world (or the "dreaming") and following the topographic "songlines" or "myth-lines" of the community (Kane 64–65). Newly identified with one of the cultural heroes or totems of the community, the boy is initiated into adulthood, taking up adult responsibilities. Popularized versions for Western audiences lay stress on the uniqueness of the boy's developing identity, but traditional cultures focus at least as much on the import of the quest for the whole community. As one version of the central Warlpiri initiation story puts it, "It is because of this that we have all become one family and one country, all from the same dreaming, because of those who were all brothers and sisters, our relatives. They were all sitting around the boy ready for the ceremony" (Nungarrayi 87). The boy's initiation into manhood, though it may seem to us an individual quest, resonates throughout the family, the community, and their history, constituting a reenactment of ancestral and heroic travels in the physical and spiritual world of the people. The development of individual identity is simultaneously a redevelopment and affirmation of the identity of the community and its cosmos as a whole.

The Domesticated Quest

We began with hunters and gatherers, thinking of them as nomadic and seminomadic peoples who follow the seasonal migrations of the animals they rely on and who chart their existence through an oral mapping of the landscape (or less often, through paintings and petroglyphs). What happens to the quest, however, as settled communities emerge; as agriculture and domestication develop; as power and technology develop in towns and cities; and as social institutions like kingship, law, and religion establish themselves?

Our earliest recorded narratives show a marked reliance on the quest, even though we imagine a less immediate need for such a structure. But the pattern is rather different. In the oral narratives of settled peoples, the heart of social exchange and communal meaning is more sharply delineated such as is seen in the city of Uruk in *The Epic of Gilgamesh*, or Troy in *The Iliad*, or (much later) the great hall of Heorot in *Beowulf*.[4] Quests are associated with the gods themselves or with warriors directly related to the divine. In a crucial narrative for most agricultural peoples, the cycle of the seasons is elaborated into a tale of death and rebirth. The plants in the field are harvested or die; seed is planted in the earth, and the plants are reborn. Human sexuality is deeply interwoven with these quests for rebirth; often the quest for rebirth is developed as a romantic, erotic narrative, culminating in the *hieros gamos,* or sacred marriage, which allows the renewed fertility of the earth after the barren months of the year. Around 2000 BCE, for example, in one of our earliest recorded narratives, Inanna, the great Sumerian goddess of love and war, is portrayed as descending into the land of the dead and returning to renew the creative powers of the earth. In the seventh century BCE, in the *Homeric Hymn to Demeter*, the Greek goddess Persephone is stolen away to the underworld; her mother Demeter's grief brings the world into wintry barrenness until a compromise is reached, and the seasons are established. (Early agricultural quests such as these are easily seen as the prototype for the many more familiar quests to the underworld in Western literature, whether in the *The Odyssey*, in *The Aeneid*, or even in contemporary video games such as *Doom.*)

But the best-known narratives that emerge from early settled cultures are those of the divine warrior-kings. Best known of all is *The Epic of Gilgamesh,* which records at first the hero's brutal kingship over Uruk, but then records the transformation of that brutality through his friendship with Enkidu, a man of the wilds created by the gods specifically to oppose Gilgamesh's arrogant behavior. The epic is built of multiple quests: Enkidu's exile from nature and his transformation into a civilized human being, which culminates in his confrontation and subsequent friendship with Gilgamesh; the partners' quests and confrontations with the immortals as Gilgamesh and Enkidu turn their energy outward to seek the great guardian of the Cedar Forest. But the quest most often focused on in discussion of the poem is Gilgamesh's failed quest for immortality after the death of Enkidu. The great loss of his friend leads him to seek a remedy beyond the bounds of human existence and beyond the realm of human civilization. The ultimate failure of the quest, and Gilgamesh's resigned return to Uruk, reveal a few things that prove crucial to our understanding of the quest narrative in traditional, principally oral, societies.

First, a quest does not have to be successful in order to be transformative; Gilgamesh does not gain immortality, but he does gain profound wisdom of the place of humans in the world and new insight into the cultural past when he learns the great Mesopotamian flood story from an actual survivor, Utnapishtim (whose name means "He who has found life"). Gilgamesh returns home to Uruk sadder but wiser.

Second, and perhaps more important for the structure of other quests, is the relationship between the heroic figure and the communal, social framework. The power of Gilgamesh, as an abusive king, is already in conflict with the human community. In company with Enkidu, this power is directed outward, against the gods themselves. In his final quest, Gilgamesh strives to exceed all human limitations but is eventually reconciled to them, and brought back within the human social framework. We see this happening again and again in ancient narratives: cultural heroes threaten the social framework, but the framework is ultimately restored. In *The Iliad*, Achilles' brutality, his harsh, self-centered desire for preeminence, is eventually—through heartbreaking loss and empty vengeance—brought back within the social range of human sympathy in his final interview with King Priam of Troy. Though the hero of the Old English epic *Beowulf* is more restrained, his status as a warrior alone (with the strength of thirty men in his handgrip) places him at the outer limits of the human. And Beowulf's battle with Grendel dramatizes this pressure on the social framework quite well, as the two equally matched combatants wrestle on the floor of the great hall, Heorot:

> And now the timbers trembled and sang,
> a hall-session that harrowed every Dane
> inside the stockade: stumbling in fury,
> the two contenders crashed through the building.
> The hall clattered and hammered, but somehow
> survived the onslaught and kept standing:
> it was handsomely structured, a sturdy frame
> braced with the best of blacksmith's work

inside and out. The story goes
that as the pair struggled, mead-benches were smashed
and sprung off the floor, gold fittings and all.
Before then, no Shielding elder would believe
there was any power or person on earth
capable of wrecking their horn-rigged hall
unless the burning embrace of a fire
engulf it in flame. (*Beowulf* 766–81)

This combat, the first climax of the quest begun when Beowulf set out from Geatland, threatens to destroy the very heart of the Danish community, the great mead hall, which is the home of the king and is connected earlier in the poem with the creation of the universe itself. The communal importance of the building is highlighted through its connection with the frightened audience through mention of the workers involved in its building. It resonates still further with the reminder of how "the story goes," the fact that this is a traditional cultural narrative, and even with the brief hint at the end of that community's eventual destruction through fire. But for now the hall, and the social framework that it represents, still stands, and the "token" of victory—Grendel's arm—is literally worked into the building itself. Beowulf, despite his dangerous qualities, is celebrated, even by his earlier detractor Unferth, and the king suggests his deeper incorporation (through marriage, presumably) within the social framework.

The quest, with its pattern of venturing forth, transformation, and return, is vitally important to narrative structure in oral, traditional societies, as it is in literate societies. But it is by no means the only narrative structure. Even in early narratives, we encounter complex interweavings of other narrative genres: of ritual or debate, of courtship or lament, of labor and creation, of confrontation and battle. The Homeric *Iliad*, for example, is structured primarily through confrontations rather than quests: Achilles versus Agamemnon, Achaeans versus Trojans, Achilles versus Hector, the life of peace versus the life of war.

Furthermore, the opposed cities of war and peace on the famous shield of Achilles act to reinforce this dualistic structural motif. These are conflicts unlike the preliminary trials of a knight errant, and they cannot easily be seen leading to a greater resolution. Despite that predominance of conflict, however, we also find the structure of the quest woven into the larger fabric of the whole: Book 9's unsuccessful embassy of Odysseus, Ajax, and Phoinix as they try to lure Achilles back into the fight; the intertwined night sorties of Book 10; and at the end of the poem, Priam's ultimately successful quest to retrieve his son Hector's body from Achilles. In short, the quest is so basic to our understanding of narrative that we find it almost everywhere, but we should not consider it the only way of understanding narrative.

The Odyssey, in contrast to *The Iliad*, develops as quest narrative *par excellence*. Reading the epic, it often seems like a pattern of concentric quests—the search of Telemachus for his father Odysseus, Odysseus's many small quests to explore just one more island, one more strange people—and all of these embraced within the larger circle of Odysseus's quest to return home after the transformative experiences of the Trojan War. This larger quest, even by itself, is not simple. It contains, of course, the romantic quest of the hero for his beloved Penelope; but at the same time Odysseus seeks his father and his son in a quest to restore the patriarchal lineage of the family, and it is a restoration of kingship, restoring order, piety, and ethical behavior to the deeply troubled island kingdom of Ithaca. *The Odyssey* reminds us that quests are rarely about only one thing and that often it is not just one hero who pursues them.

Writing Down the Quest

The quest narratives discussed thus far have arisen out of traditional societies. The heroes are gods or warriors (or often a bit of both), and their heroic actions are portrayed on a communal, political, and even cosmic scale. Even Odysseus, lover, storyteller, and family man, is primarily a warrior and a king.

But in the quest narratives that emerge after the invention and inte-riorization of alphabetic writing in Greece, a different set of emphases and heroisms gradually surface.[5] Where we once encountered active, externally directed heroes—Gilgamesh "the goring wild bull" or swift-footed Achilles—we now encounter heroes like helpless (*amechanos*) Jason in Apollonius's *Argonautica* or the deeply conflicted, often pas-sive Aeneas of Virgil's *Aeneid*, who seems as much a pawn of the gods as does his lover Dido. In the *Aeneid*, this shift away from an active, externally directed heroism toward a more thoughtful, more delicately inflected heroism becomes part of the quest itself, as Aeneas is forced beyond the Homeric mold into a new, particularly Roman set of virtues. (The potential ironies of such contrasting heroisms are exploited much more fully in later satiric quests such as Cervantes's *Don Quixote.*) Both the *Argonautica* and the *Aeneid* are modeled on the Homeric ep-ics, but they also differ substantially from those oral and traditional poems. Narrative detail becomes much more significant, more care-fully patterned. The concrete, anthropomorphic gods of *The Iliad* shift toward abstract divinities and even more abstract allegories. Most of all, the awareness of other texts, and the deep allusions to them, cre-ate a far more layered, introspective experience for both the characters and the readers. The Golden Fleece of Jason's quest becomes almost an afterthought in comparison to the romantic coupling of Jason and Medea, and this in turn is overshadowed by the couple's later history of domestic strife, witchcraft, and murder, not recorded in the epic but justly famous in Greek drama. *The Aeneid* shows this layering even more fully; every landscape, it seems, is already part of another story, layered with Homeric and mythic history. And at the same time, it is enstoried with the future history of Rome and the Roman Empire. The poem is set, like *The Odyssey*, after the fall of Troy. But Virgil, writ-ing in the first century BCE, chronicles much of the Roman history that leads to Emperor Augustus, whether in the landscape of Evander's home (the future site of Rome), in the pageant of Aeneas' descendants (which he sees in the underworld), or on the glorious shield of Aeneas, anachronistically centered on the Roman victory at Actium in 31 BCE.

In addition to this deliberate layering of narrative, the characters themselves become more complex, showing evidence of an interior life and thought processes not reflected in external action. Emotional responses, skepticism, and internal debates become part of the narrative, sometimes in line with but often directly opposed to the physical, external actions and statements of the narrative. In *The Aeneid*, this division is striking, giving rise to our sense—as the scholar Adam Parry pointed out—of two very different voices in the epic, one the voice of imperial propaganda, the other voice far more subversive, questioning, and resistant to empire.

This self-interrogating dimension and the consequent fragmentation of narrative seems an implicit function of written discourse. We know it ourselves, almost as soon as we learn to write—the way words do not quite fit, the way the "I" on the paper is always different from the "I" doing the writing. Writing allows, too, for a much more systematic, explicit form of argument, and for more complex interweaving of narrative, as we see in a text like Augustine's *Confessions*. And we see this increasingly as we move forward with narratives written in manuscript form. The romances, the *lais,* the saints' lives of medieval Europe, even the great medieval and Renaissance epics show this splintering of heroic focus in quest narratives. We see this notably in two key ways. One of them is the penchant for collecting shorter narratives into larger wholes. A singular tale is not quite sufficient, so we add another, and another, adding up to encyclopedic, often interlocking or interlaced stories of knights, saints, good women, or people in general: Malory's *Mort D'Arthur*, the *Legenda Aurea*, Christine de Pizan's *Book of the City of Ladies*, the *Thousand and One Nights*, Chaucer's *Canterbury Tales*, etc. This phenomenon itself suggests two further things: that the nature of heroism itself is changing—a single character can no longer contain or exhaust the diversity of heroisms. The hero's quest is still in there, but in multiple forms, arising from different communities, seeking different objects. It may be a personal quest rather than public, and this leads us to the second thing: That almost any human being can go on a quest, a pilgrimage, a life-changing adventure. The *Thousand and One Nights* are full of fishermen and merchants, slave girls and wise daughters; Chaucer's pilgrims, too, suggest that *anyone* may go on pilgrimage, and that each may have his or her tale to tell.

A second key index of the splintering or fragmentation of the quest narrative is the increased emphasis on allegorical writing and reading, deeply encouraged by the Christian church's insistence on allegorical readings of the Bible. A systematic allegory—a symbolic narrative—is one that cannot easily exist in an oral setting. But in medieval writing, there is almost always that sense of a spiritual reading lurking behind the literal reading. Dante's *Divine Comedy*, of course, is the best example of this, as we follow a quest that is at once personal and cosmic. Dante the poet writes of his personal odyssey through Hell, Purgatory, and Paradise. Dante the pilgrim, lost in his worldly existence, is brought through a prolonged quest with the help of his lost beloved, Beatrice, and the shade of his guide, the great poet Virgil. But at the same time, Dante the pilgrim exists as an Everyman figure, charting for us the course, in medieval Christian belief, of every soul in its progress toward God. The allegory goes farther than that: Dante is also a figure of Christ, repeating his suffering, his descent and harrowing of hell, his eventual ascent to Paradise. And of course, throughout Dante's travels, the reader is engaged with the countless stories of the dead, whatever their ultimate destination. (Some of these are quests of their own, as in the famous additional episode from the life of Odysseus in Canto 26 of the *Inferno*.) But with this encyclopedic view of the state of souls after death, Dante weaves together in his brilliantly imagined cosmos many aspects of the quest that we've been discussing.

Dante also provides one of the fullest depictions of a newer kind of quest hero. Neither god nor king nor warrior, Dante's wanderer is most obviously the poet himself, recounting a psychological and spiritual journey. More than that, and in a fashion similar to that of Aeneas, the initiation of the quest is less a "venturing forth" than it is an exile. Where Aeneas was forced out of Troy, Dante is a hero already exiled, both metaphorically (in the sense of not fully belonging to the earthly community and seeking a true community in heaven) and literally (as a political exile from Florence during the writing of the poem). This is a significant change from the heroes of oral cultures, who struggle against but are also deeply wound up with the social frameworks of their cultures. Though Odysseus is also, like Dante, a storyteller, he is much more centrally the restorative force of order, in harmony with the gods and good government. This difference in attitude makes a lot of sense, as an oral culture cannot easily sustain a skeptical or critical tradition; those with power are those who tell the stories. With writing, and especially with widespread literacy, even those displaced or exiled from the social framework can tell their stories.

Print and the Proliferation of Quests

It is obvious that the invention of the printing press with movable type works to stress and exaggerate those aspects of heroism and those aspects of the quest narrative just discussed. The tendencies in written narrative toward self-interrogation and fragmentation, toward allusiveness and abstraction, as well as the narrative focus on internal struggles and the particular individual, all of these are intensified by the profound democratization of literacy possible under the aegis of Gutenberg's invention.[6] Some writers go so far as to claim that the Protestant Reformation is the direct result of this technological change, putting vernacular literacy and inexpensive Bibles in the control of individuals. But it is important to remember that many other changes were underway throughout these centuries: The increased commerce and cultural contact allowed and enforced by imperial expansions—those of Rome, of Islam, of European Christendom, of the Mongols—which led to hearing new voices and new stories even as it led to cultural conflict; the development of centers of commerce and the improved fortunes of craft workers and merchants, which led to a weakening of aristocratic privilege and an emerging middle class; the rediscovery and communication of texts from ancient Greece, which led—along with everything else—to the European Renaissance.

Print brings with it a veritable explosion in the number of texts produced, and an immense shift in the diversity of authors and of readers; it also encourages an increasingly private experience of texts, both in writing and in reading them. Though many writers worked to appeal to a large public audience and to influence political powers and events, increasingly the focus was more personal; rather than working toward the cohesion of society, with a nod toward the self, writers worked toward cohesion of the self, often in spite of the social framework. The formation of individual identity, that is, is increasingly seen as being at odds with social expectations. In *Paradise Lost*, John Milton's exiled couple sets out from Eden not with a social or political goal, but with the personal goal of establishing "a paradise within . . . happier farr" (12.587). Aphra Behn's *Oroonoko,* though set on the global stage of colonization, celebrates the maintenance of a sense of self, even within the utterly dehumanizing context of slavery. Jane Austen's *Pride and Prejudice*, though set within the framework of a romantic quest, is simultaneously Elizabeth Bennet's quest to remain an individual: to be married, yes, but to be married without sacrificing all that she is and does.

Three changes deserve special comment at this point. First, the increased diversity of voices and quests in literature after the invention of writing, and the proliferation of voices after the development of print, only gradually included large numbers of women who were rarely educated the same way as men and who were even more rarely encouraged to write.[7] But from the eighteenth century onward, women's writing is a large and growing part of literary production, and women as audiences for literature are perhaps even more important. Second, most women's writing, and most writing for women, was produced in prose and in a form—the novel—that owes its existence to the invention of print. As Rosalind Miles observed, to a great extent the novel *is* "the female form." From the eighteenth through twentieth centuries, the prose novel became the major generic home of the quest narrative, and this has significant effects on the structure of the narrative. A third change is the increasing importance of the romantic quest. While the matter of love emerges early in the history of the quest narrative, it is often frankly subsidiary to the main quest. Over the centuries, however, and especially in the medieval romances, the quest for the beloved threatens to become the archetype of the quest. (What is a knight-errant without his lady fair? What other reason for killing the dragon could there be than to secure a bride?) While this shift in emphasis is closely related to the increasing power of women as writers and as audiences, it is also related to the new focus on the isolated individual, less closely involved with his or her family unit, less closely tied to a particular community.

These three changes—the advent and growth of prose narrative, the ever stronger emphasis of the romantic quest for the right man or woman, and the increased gender diversity of authorship and audience—join forces with the other changes implicit in print. The quest for selfhood, partly through economic power, that marks novels like *Pride and Prejudice, Great Expectations*, or *Wuthering Heights*, or poems like Shelley's *Alastor* or Barrett Browning's *Aurora Leigh*, is often at the same time a romantic quest for that erotic other. The example of *Wuthering Heights,* however, also suggests two newer areas of emphasis for quest narrative.

It is obvious enough that our heroism has shifted remarkably since *The Epic of Gilgamesh* from gods and kings to individual humans more or less like ourselves. But perhaps even more important is noting that the ever-present tension between the heroic figure and his or her social framework has practically inverted itself. Heathcliff in *Wuthering Heights*—a typical Byronic hero—is far more *antihero* than conventional hero; Pushkin's Eugene Onegin, Melville's Captain Ahab, and of course Byron's own tortured heroes fall into the same pattern. Increasingly, our new heroes are outcasts, exiles, misfits of one kind or another, far more so the revolutionary, violent Grendel than the stalwart, orthodox Beowulf.

A second area of emphasis, implicit perhaps in the realism associated with prose fiction, is the new uncertainty imposed on the reading audience. The unreliable narrators of *Wuthering Heights* encourage us—or force us—into adopting shifting perspectives, into pursuing our own quests for meaning—for what really happened and what it really meant—as we try to follow the narrative. Though these kinds of ambiguity are implicit in writing, and we've discussed them briefly in the context of *The Aeneid,* it is principally in these latter centuries that the *reader's* quest for meaning becomes so crucial. Where a poet like Walt Whitman may make this invitation to the reader explicit, literally inviting us to take hold of him and make sense of him as a kind of bosom companion, other writers are not so forthcoming. Reading Joseph Conrad, James Joyce, Virginia Woolf, or William Faulkner often seems like hard work in comparison to other kinds of reading. Unlike our experience of straightforward quest narratives (Jules Verne or Edgar Rice Burroughs, for example) suddenly *we* are the ones putting together the quest, and *we* are the heroic figures being transformed by the experience.

The Reader's Quest

T. S. Eliot's daunting poem, *The Waste Land*, is a good example of the quest a reader must undertake, as it teases its reader again and again with elusive allusions to older quest narratives and other shreds and fragments of meaning. But as quickly as the reader starts to grasp a bit of it—the lurking myth of the sacred marriage, the holy grail that might save the dying king—Eliot shifts his scene, switches languages, breaks his syntax, and the reader is left holding only the shadow of meaning. This is frustrating, but it is also the main point: The reader's enforced experience of trying to make meaning in the poem is like that of the poet trying to find orders of meaning in the world. This quest for meaning and for psychological coherence is not unique to Eliot, but rather is central to Western thought in the alienating, mechanized twentieth century, especially after the horrors of world war. What fragments can we possibly shore against the ruin of older orders of meaning, the loss of faith in religious and governmental institutions? Is the quest structure itself sufficient to give meaning to our experience? *The Waste Land* shows that the old quests have little validity, but the structure itself, whether imposed on the reader or partially articulated in the poem, still seems to hold value for Eliot. In his later *Four Quartets*, he seems to elaborate this seeming inevitability to human questions and human quests:

> We shall not cease from exploration
> And the end of all our exploring
> Will be to arrive where we started
> And know the place for the first time. (Eliot 145)

This increasing emphasis of the reader's responsibility on the role of the audience as actual participants in the quest narrative is important, and develops further in modern and postmodern narrative, and perhaps especially in the hypertext narratives mediated by computer technology.

But I want to go back to those less challenging quest narratives I mentioned because the straightforward quest narratives developed in such novels as Verne's *Twenty Thousand Leagues Under the Sea* or *Journey to the Center of the Earth*, or in Burroughs's *Tarzan of the Apes* or *A Princess of Mars* are also vital to understanding twentieth- and twenty-first-century quest narratives. Broadly appealing, fast-paced narratives with clear-cut heroes and villains, they are early indicators of the proliferation of popular "genre" fiction of all types. Fantasy, science fiction, romance, westerns, detective stories and mysteries, thrillers and horror, formulaic fictions of all kinds rely on the structuring narrative of the quest. Often these are less challenging to read than Eliot or Woolf, and we find them comforting rather than troubling. The worlds they establish may not be familiar, but the rules are clear, and generally the good and the bad are well marked. They satisfy our desire for clarity, order, and meaning in a way that the real world of our experience, as well as more sophisticated literature, does not. Often they are our first experience with being utterly lost in a good book. As with most cinema—the other dominant narrative form of the twentieth century—the audience is more passively engaged. The narrative places us firmly on the side of Harry Potter or Frodo Baggins and keeps us there in the same way that the gaze of the camera keeps us firmly on the side of Luke Skywalker, of Buffy the Vampire Slayer, or of Clarice Starling in *Silence of the Lambs*. We follow along easily, and we easily sympathize with their challenges and perils as they leave their communities, as they transform and mature, and as they integrate into new communities or (often) partnerships.

These reading or viewing experiences are more "passive," but this term seems to obscure the intensity of our emotional investment in movies and in our favorite popular novels. The quest narrative in these appealing tales is powerfully affirmative rather than disturbing; a transformation takes place, but it is transformative mainly in the sense that our desire for an orderly world and our sense of self within that world is confirmed. The more sophisticated, more disturbing quest narratives—these challenge us more directly to change our selves or our world or to understand them in a new way.

Choose Your Quest

Computer programming in the late twentieth century allows a very different form of the quest narrative to develop, shifting from our involvement in the virtual world of the novel to our *virtual presence* in an electronic environment. These new narratives capitalize on our love of genre fiction. We can see early examples of this in the "choose your own adventure" books and in book-oriented role playing games like *Dungeons and Dragons*, but these interactive personal quests develop at great speed as technology takes hold, from text-based games like *Adventure* with its "maze of twisty little passages" to highly visual environments like those of *Myst*, and finally to massive multiplayer environments like the interstellar science fiction setting of *EVE Online* or the medievalesque fantasy setting of *World of Warcraft*. In all of these, but especially in the latest games, the quest is the crucial structuring principle. The avatar who stands in for us in the online world is instructed to explore territory, gain items, gain new abilities; and that avatar transforms him- or herself, moving on to the next level, exploring new areas of the game world, building reputation with the dominant game world factions. Finally—perhaps for the first time in the history of the quest narrative—*we* can be the main character, the hero, the central protagonist.[8] (A key point here is the shifting axis of good and evil; in these games, one can be orc or elf, pirate or paladin; the question of ethical good and evil is relative and hinges on our avatar's virtual background, social affiliations, and in-game activity.) All around us, until we leave the game, until we complete or reach the highest level, the world is full of quests and opportunities for quests. Like most games, and somewhat like the interactive reading experience demanded by difficult literature, it can be frustrating. We have to decide where to go, what the language of the quest-giver really means, how to assemble a group of like-minded adventurers to accomplish the quest, how to face the particular challenges or puzzles. And when our first attempts fail, we have to do it again and again. And yet within the framework of the game, it is rewarding. As players of *Tetris* or *Angry Birds* know well, incremental frustration and reward is the key to any computer game's success. What larger games offer is the experience of being a key part of a larger story, like the deeper sense of involvement we get when a quest narrative is related to our own local or familial environments.

Thus on the one hand, the gaming environment is primarily comfortable and affirming in the same way that popular quest-driven fiction is with a much stronger emphasis on personal fulfillment in the establishment of a heroic self. On the other hand, this affirmation is undermined by the fact that *all* the avatars are special, having encountered the same quests or defeated the same monsters. It is the fundamentally social environment of MMORPGs like *World of Warcraft* that enforces a different set of quests, a set of opportunities and challenges behind the quest-driven structure of the game. While some of these are built into the gaming environment—server firsts, achievements, and special rewards or titles—the more interesting possibilities arise strictly from player interaction, mediated by the technological interface. Opportunities for ambiguity, moral uncertainty, and uncomfortable transformative experiences abound in such a social framework as they do in the real world. The gaming environment becomes a rehearsal of roles and possibilities, an opportunity to experiment with possible selves that is much harder to come by in real life (or in most conventional narrative). The key difference from real life, of course, is that in the game, we can disconnect—*or* we can generate a new avatar and start over.

Conclusion

Starting over is perhaps an understudied aspect of the quest. In the same way that one good question will often lead to only a provisional answer and a whole slew of new questions, so quest narratives—which at first would seem to end so finally—have a way of generating new quests. *The Aeneid*, for example, takes one brief remark about Aeneas from *The Iliad* and spins it out into one of the world's greatest sequels. You finish a paper, but all you can think of are the other possible papers, the questions that leap from answering that first one. The quest narrative, too, is perhaps ultimately cyclic, as with the seasonal cycle, both repetition and rehearsal, echo and prophecy. In the same way, an investigation like this one, which seeks to trace some of the major changes and differences of emphasis in human quest narratives, can only be a beginning.

The basic structure of the quest narrative remains the same—what this chapter has described as a pattern of venturing forth, transformation, and return. Most obviously, drastic shifts in medium take place from oral narrative to written, from printed to electronic, and these changes are key to understanding the other changes in the quest narrative.

First, we see a great deal of change in heroism itself, from gods and warriors to the artist, to the common individual, and finally right down to us, whoever we are. This kind of change leads inexorably to another important change in the sheer diversity of heroisms: female heroes, native heroes, exotic heroes, fantasy heroes, extraterrestrial heroes, almost any kind of heroes one could imagine. Our increasing willingness over thousands of years to experience and sympathize with heroisms beyond our immediate communal experience, to imaginatively join with an alien, with a troll, or even with someone of another gender, is a substantial change.

Second, these changes in turn are tied to the changing audiences of quest narrative. The communal audience of an oral story shares an immediacy and concreteness that is fundamentally social and interactive; private reading, distanced from the author, has different virtues and encourages a deeper individualism that is more introspective and psychological rather than physical, social, and external. The focus shifts from maintaining the coherence of the community to maintaining the coherence of the self or of the self in relation to one significant other. With the advent of electronic interactivity, the ethical focus may be undergoing yet another shift, even as the audience is vastly multiplied, as the printed text reaches thousands or even millions of readers, and the electronic narrative reaches even further.

And third, the physical challenges of an external quest are exchanged over this span of centuries for the arduous social and psychological challenges of an interior quest, sometimes even involving the reader. The gripping physical conflicts of Beowulf and the dragon give way to largely internal struggles, to what William Blake called the ongoing "mental fight" of the poet, the hero, or the reader. Rather than fleeing the mere physical hazards of Scylla and Charybdis, heroes attempt to escape the pressure of society's "mind-forg'd manacles," or even, with Joyce's Stephen Dedalus, to "fly by those nets" of nationality, language, and religion (Joyce 220).[9] Computer-mediated "virtual worlds," of course, create a narrative space where terms like *internal* and *external* seem to apply with less and less force.

But it is important to remember that the worlds of the narrative quest have no strict borders; simplistic, cookie cut-out heroes continue to exist in close proximity with sophisticated, difficult ones; Hollywood narratives straight off the monomyth assembly line coexist with many shambling or self-aware myths and stories that will not fit that formula. This chapter has attempted to outline matters of emphasis implicit in changing historical circumstances of production; so these are general tendencies and gradual changes, not hard and fast rules.

In the last part of this chapter, a distinction has been suggested between those narratives that simply reaffirm us in our comfort and those that coerce us outside our comfort zones—those that say, with Rilke's statue of Apollo, "Change your life." There is a great deal of value in exploring both kinds of quest narrative and perhaps especially in pursuing a balance between the affirming reward and the disturbing frustration. As with an ancient audience listening to *Beowulf* or the *Odyssey*, so with us rereading the *Lord of the Rings* or playing *World of Warcraft* may reaffirm our sense of our own skills and our sense of the world and may encourage us to encounter more serious narrative challenges. Even more important, it may encourage us, in our own worlds, to confront our own dragons.

Notes

1. While the aim is for simplicity and broad application in this definition, more elaborate definitions of the quest are readily available. The best known is Joseph Campbell's popular notion of the "monomyth" of the hero's journey and its three stages and many substages. (Among some audiences, Campbell's theory is particularly well known for its influence on the developing script of George Lucas's blockbuster, *Star Wars*.) Campbell's "monomyth" can be a useful conceptual tool, but it is limited by its tendency to reduce the differences between complex narratives into a bland soup of imagined universality. And unfortunately, even Campbell's simplest formulation of the quest is laden with misguided and unnecessary mysticism: "A hero ventures forth from the world of common day into a region of supernatural wonder: fabulous forces are there encountered and

a decisive victory is won: the hero comes back from this mysterious adventure with the power to bestow boons on his fellow man" (31). More practically, exploring the historical and material changes to elaborate schemes—whether those of Campbell, of Otto Rank or Lord Raglan or Vladimir Propp, or even that of Maureen Murdock—is beyond the scope of this short essay.

2. My use of the term *hero*, too, requires some definition. In contrast to idealist and ahistorical concepts of the "heroic," I use the term primarily to identify the chief protagonist of a narrative (roughly the way it is used in the small narrative segments of *The Iliad* and *The Odyssey* where the term appears). Thus the bookish, uncertain Dante is just as much a hero as the brutal, man-killing Achilles, even if students insist that neither is particularly "heroic" in the unexamined, idealized sense.

3. I do not mean to imply that narrative and other arts are not also built on the most mundane of objects and activities; rather, the perception and framing—of a found poem like Aram Saroyan's "oxygen," of Joyce's record of a single day in June, of Picasso's 1942 *Head of a Bull*—can allow us to perceive the mundane in entirely new and highly significant ways. That being said, historically most artists—and most quest narratives—have capitalized on certain kinds of built-in cultural significance in their choice of material.

4. The scholarship on oral cultures has grown substantially in the past thirty years. John Miles Foley provides a useful introduction; Albert Lord, Jan Vansina, Jack Goody, and Walter Ong remain classics in the field. I should also qualify my use of *Gilgamesh* in the context of orality. Though the ancient narratives of Mesopotamia were in the main orally performed and understood, we fortunately have access to substantial fragments of written material, laboriously incised on damp clay tablets. Scholars are still at work decoding and piecing together these materials.

5. It is difficult to exaggerate the impact of writing on human thought and culture. In company with the many oral theorists, Eric Havelock's *The Muse Learns to Write* and Goody's *The Logic of Writing* make strong introductions to this increasingly nuanced field of study.

6. A quick Internet search today shows Johannes Gutenberg in first place on almost everyone's list of who's important in the last millennium. There are many studies of the impact of print technology, but Elizabeth Eisenstein's *Printing Press as an Agent of Change* and Marshall McLuhan's famous *The Gutenberg Galaxy* form a crucial starting point.

7. The court culture of medieval Japan provided a strikingly different set of circumstances for women, of course, resulting in Murasaki Shikibu's great *Tale of Genji*, Sei Shonagon's *The Pillow Book*, and much more. Throughout history, too, there have always been women who succeeded—even against great odds—in making their voices heard.

8. In a special sense, of course, we have never *not* been the heroes of quest narratives. Any psychological approach to quest narrative will indicate how deeply we identify with the heroic figures through our narrative experience, whether

oral, written, or cinematic. But the participatory difference allowed in virtual worlds, where we invest ourselves much more fully in the narrative construction of heroic action, forces us to recognize this as a major shift in the nature of the quest narrative.

9. William Blake's well-known phrases come from the poems "Jerusalem" and "London."

Works Cited

Beowulf: A New Verse Translation. Trans. Seamus Heaney. Biling. ed. New York: Norton, 2000.

Blake, William. *Blake's Poetry and Designs.* Ed. John Grant and Mary Johnson. New York: Norton, 2007.

Campbell, Joseph. *The Hero with a Thousand Faces.* 1949. Princeton, NJ: Princeton UP, 1968.

Curtis, Gregory. *The Cave Painters: Probing the Mysteries of the World's First Artists.* New York: Knopf, 2006.

"The Descent of Inanna." *Inanna, Queen of Heaven and Earth: Her Stories and Hymns from Sumer.* Trans. Diane Wolkstein and Samuel Noah Kramer. New York: Harper, 1983. 51–90.

Eisenstein, Elizabeth L. *The Printing Press as an Agent of Change: Communications and Cultural Transformations in Early Modern Europe.* Cambridge: Cambridge UP, 1980.

Eliot, T. S. *The Complete Poems and Major Plays, 1909–1950.* New York: Harcourt, 1980.

The Epic of Gilgamesh. Trans. Maureen Gallery Kovacs. Stanford, CA: Stanford UP, 1989.

Foley, John Miles. *The Theory of Oral Composition: History and Methodology.* Bloomington: Indiana UP, 1988.

Goody, Jack. *The Domestication of the Savage Mind.* Cambridge: Cambridge UP, 1977.

_____. *The Logic of Writing and the Organization of Society.* Cambridge: Cambridge UP, 1987.

Havelock, Eric A. *The Muse Learns to Write: Reflections on Orality and Literacy from Antiquity to the Present.* New Haven, CT: Yale UP, 1988.

The Homeric Hymn to Demeter*: Translation, Commentary, and Interpretive Essays.* Trans. Helene P. Foley. Princeton, NJ: Princeton UP, 1993.

Joyce, James. *A Portrait of the Artist as a Young Man.* New York: Penguin, 1993.

Kane, Sean. *Wisdom of the Mythtellers.* Peterborough, ON, Can.: Broadview, 1994.

Lord, Albert B. *The Singer of Tales.* Cambridge, MA: Harvard UP, 1960.

McLuhan, Marshall. *The Gutenberg Galaxy: The Making of Typographic Man.* Toronto: U of Toronto P, 1962.

Miles, Rosalind. *The Female Form: Women Writers and the Conquest of the Novel.* New York: Routledge, 1987.

Milton, John. "Paradise Lost." *The Riverside Milton.* Ed. Roy Flannagan. Boston: Houghton,1998.

Murdock, Maureen. *The Heroine's Journey.* Boston: Shambhala, 1990.

Nungarrayi, Ngarlinjiya Mary Robertson. "Witikirli: The Travels with the Witi Poles." *Warlpiri Dreamings and Histories: Newly Recorded Stories from the Aboriginal Elders of Central Australia.* Trans. Peggy Rockman Napaljarri and Lee Cataldi. New York: HarperCollins, 1994.

Ong, Walter J. *Orality and Literacy.* 2nd ed. New York: Routledge, 2002.

Parry, Adam. "The Two Voices of Virgil's *Aeneid.*" *Arion* 2:4 (Winter 1963): 66 80.

Propp, Vladimir. *Morphology of the Folktale.* 2nd ed. Trans. Laurence Scott. Austin, TX: U of Texas P, 1968.

Raglan, Fitzroy R. *The Hero: A Study in Tradition, Myth, and Drama.* Westport, CT: Greenwood, 1975.

Rank, Otto. *The Myth of the Birth of the Hero: A Psychological Exploration of Myth.* Trans Gregory C. Richter and E. James Lieberman. Baltimore: Johns Hopkins UP, 2004.

Rappenglück, Michael. "The Pleiades in the 'Salle des Taureaux,' Grotte de Lascaux: Does a Rock Picture in the Cave of Lascaux Show the Open Star Cluster of the Pleiades at the Magdalenian Era, ca. 15,300 BC?" Trans. Jan Burgermeister. In *Actas del IV Congreso de la SEAC, Proceedings of the IVth SEAC Meeting, "Astronomy and Culture."* Eds. C. Jaschek and F. Atrio Barandela. Salamanca, Sp.: Universidad de Salamanca, 1997. 217–25. *Institute for Interdisciplinary Science.*

Rilke, R. M. "Torso of an Archaic Apollo." *Selected Poems.* Trans. C. F. MacIntyre. Berkeley: U of California P, 1940.

Vansina, Jan. *Oral Tradition as History.* Madison: U of Wisconsin P, 1985.

Modernist Quests: *Heart of Darkness* and *The Man Who Died*

Michael Bell

If informed readers were asked to nominate a single poem and novel as the most significant expressions of modernism in English, it is likely that T. S. Eliot's *The Waste Land* and James Joyce's *Ulysses* would be frequent choices. And it is surely not coincidental that both are fractured, displaced, ironic forms of quest: Eliot invokes the myth of the Fisher King and the medieval romance of the Holy Grail while Joyce chooses the more domestic of Homer's epic tales, the homeward journey of Odysseus.

Indeed the word *return* is a resonant one for the theme of the modern quest since an important aspect of the early twentieth-century literature we have come to know as modernist is its conscious return to fundamentals and to origins. The novel form, for example, had emerged partly out of ancient epic and medieval romance, in both of which the quest remained a prominent narrative structure. Of course, the novel as it developed over the eighteenth and nineteenth centuries was a reflection of modern society and was a very different form from the ancient epic. Yet, as other essays in this volume indicate, the quest motif continued to lurk within it, and early twentieth-century works of fiction, such as Lawrence's *The Rainbow* or Thomas Mann's *Joseph and His Brothers* as well as Joyce's *Ulysses*, return quite deliberately to the womb of epic and of myth. At the same time, the self-consciously modern nature of this return gives these elements a quite different value from their archaic forms.[1] Eliot, for example, remarked of poetry that it is at once the most primitive and the most sophisticated form (Eliot, "Tarr" 106). In all these works, archaic modes of thought and feeling are invoked within a new, modern mode of self-consciousness. So, too, the quest motif, as it survives into modernity, has the same complexity: at once archaic and contemporary, ionized yet indestructible. Perhaps the key feature of the works mentioned, however, is that the objective, communal form of the epic is internalized into the subjectivity of an individual mind and the quest is a way of focusing this inward turn.

In retrospect, it is evident that Eliot's overall poetic *oeuvre* represents a personal spiritual quest in which *The Waste Land* constitutes an early phase. Later works such as *Ash Wednesday* and *Four Quartets* are tentative re-creations, or rediscoveries, of lost religious meanings, but in *The Waste Land* a once meaningful language seems to have been hollowed out to be echoing emptily in the speaker's mind. Eliot structured the poem on the motif of the grail quest, yet it would take an exceptionally alert and cultured reader to recognize this just from an unguided reading. Most readers have been alerted by Eliot's notes and by a long tradition of pedagogical commentary to give a trained reading, but the true status of the quest motif remains equivocal. Is it really part of the public meaning of the poem, or is it the poet's private way of assembling the enigmatic fragments which, as the poetic speaker says, "I have shored against my ruin" (Eliot 50)? The resultant effect is that rather than the poem giving us an evident quest, which may or may not be successful in its outcome, the very notion of a quest seems to struggle for articulation. Eliot would have been aware of the great Victorian predecessor poem, Tennyson's *Idylls of the King*, in which the grail legend was already a story of failure and degeneration but in which the original model of the quest as a focus of moral meanings was still powerfully instantiated. In Eliot's case, by contrast, it is as if the poem's own moral compass had already lost its bearings because, even as the poem's speaker pursues his quest, its value seems to be denied by the world represented in the poem. Yet paradoxically, the underlying energy of the poem derives from the persistence of the quest.

It has become more evident in retrospect that *The Waste Land* arose from a deeply private condition of near breakdown in Eliot himself, yet generations of readers have responded to something representative in the way the poem's speaker turns over the cultural detritus of the postwar world to find some ground of meaning. And this suggests something significant about the nature of quest in general. If the quest is a moral and spiritual ordeal, something on which the protagonist stakes a whole existence, then it is likely to concern the most fundamental values of the culture, even if these are not recognized by the character or made explicit to the reader, and the modern quest of *The Waste Land* reflects a radical perplexity about belief and value. Such perplexity may not characterize every modern quest: Joyce's *Ulysses*, for example, is a comedic affirmation of humane values that cheerfully embrace the relative and arbitrary nature of all human forms of knowledge. It is hostile to all dogmas: political, moral, or religious. Two other quest stories, however, Joseph Conrad's *Heart of Darkness* (1899) and D. H. Lawrence's *The Man Who Died* (1931) record a similar perplexity to that of Eliot's speaker as they not only engage, but radically overturn, fundamental values of their culture.

Both of these latter works question deeply held traditional forms of idealism. Conrad's story is an early analysis of the evils of colonialism and racism beneath the high ideals of empire—evils that were to require the cultural work of the whole twentieth century for their proper recognition—his tale heralded one of the most important changes in human self-understanding in modernity. Lawrence's story challenges the traditional Christian culture of his time with a radical critique informed by modern anthropological, psychological, and philosophical understanding.

Heart of Darkness, set on a yacht moored in the River Thames, is narrated by one of a group of high-ranking men of affairs who listen to the story of a sea captain, Charles Marlow, who, as a young man, had been sent up the Congo River, then a Belgian possession, to find Kurtz, an ivory company's senior agent. Kurtz is a charismatic figure who went to Africa with a missionary zeal to spread the benefits of European civilization but has become a brutal exploiter of the native people and undergone what seems a deliberate collapse into barbarism. Marlow arrives in time to hear Kurtz's last words, "The horror! The horror!" (Conrad 117), and to be given the manuscript of his report for the International Society for the Suppression of Savage Customs, which Kurtz still hoped to have published. Marlow is intrigued by the perverse heroism that has lead Kurtz to explore and acknowledge the potential for selfish brutality underlying his idealism. Although committed to truth, Marlow visits Kurtz's fiancée and allows her to believe that Kurtz died with his ideals intact but, as his tale finishes, his auditors may feel a new implication in the darkness of the Thames at the heart of a commercial empire.

In Lawrence's tale an unnamed man awakes in a cave from near death after some terrible punishment. The slow return of life to his body attunes him to the vivid life in his natural surroundings. It seems that his former life as a spiritual leader had obscured the wonder of physical being to which he now responds. The physical world has a new intensity of active life such as one might imagine from a painting by Van Gogh. The man encounters several people, including a woman called Madeleine whom he forbids to touch him. He then comes to a site sacred to the ancient nature goddess, Isis, where a priestess is seeking the seasonal male god, Osiris. The man stays a while and makes love to the priestess before setting off in a small boat following the current with no apparent destination.

Before engaging these works more closely, it is worth noting a formal point about their genre. Both stories are in the form of the novella rather than either the novel or the short story. These categories can be somewhat arbitrary, but the distinction seems significant here. Whereas the longer form of the novel tends to favor a more inward account of character within a more solidly realized world, the central characters of these works, Conrad's Kurtz and Lawrence's unnamed man, are discursive constructs upon which meaning can be inscribed. Kurtz is removed from omniscient authorial understanding while the man in Lawrence's tale is constantly unaware of, and unprepared for, the bodily instincts on which he now acts. In Lawrence's case, the story is overtly closer to fable than to novelistic realism, while Conrad's story, despite its often painful detail and apparent realism, assumes in the mind of the principal narrator, Charles Marlow, a myth-like quality.

This makes the underlying motif of the quest more salient than it might be in the more fully fleshed-out world of a realist novel. The allegorical import of each tale is foregrounded. At the same time, both these works seem to be different from the typical short story, which is itself a creation of the modernist generation. The short story tends to encapsulate, with poetic concentration, a particular insight, what Joyce called an "epiphany," a single moment of recognition. By contrast, Lawrence's fable and Marlow's reminiscences carry a wide summative import that extends beyond their narrative frame. The quest structure points to the range and depth of ambition in these works.

Heart of Darkness is now a modern classic to be read alongside the greatest works of literature, yet when it first appeared in a magazine publication it would not have been so obviously distinguished from other popular patriotic British stories set in the colonies. Marlow tells how seeing the "blank space" on the map of Africa when he was a "little chap" inspired him to wish to explore it (Conrad 48). In this way, his quest is immediately placed within what Raymond Williams has called a "structure of feeling"[2] (Williams x). That is to say, within a given culture, certain objects or activities are imbued, as if naturally and inevitably, with a particular set of feelings. Indeed, contemporary geographical exploration, despite its political and scientific motives, embodied a structure of feeling ultimately descended from, and emotionally powered by, the models of ancient epic and romance. The quest is an emotional form created by a long history and is still active in the present. The younger Marlow had inherited these feelings even while his personal experience was still blank.

A world-view charged with feeling is hard to change, and *Heart of Darkness* records the confusion of this experience when what seems initially to be an exploration of the world becomes an exploration of the self. In other words, rather than responding emotionally to the given world, we have been emotionally sustaining a particular view of the world. Conrad's blend of realist narrative and nightmarish memory allows him to explore this ambiguity. Some quest narratives, such as the Elizabethan poet, Edmund Spenser's, *The Faery Queen* are overtly allegorical, dealing with the inner moral and psychic domain, and Spenser's exquisitely poetic world is appropriate to this internal focus. But in *Heart of Darkness*, a prose narrative with a harshly realist texture and historical specificity, the focus is more elusive as Marlow, and the reader, only gradually come to see that his is an essentially inner voyage. Whereas the great epic quests of antiquity often included a "Nekya," an episode in which the hero is required to brave the underworld, the region of the dead, Conrad's modern equivalent is rather an exploration of the subconscious.

Indeed, to appreciate the self-reinforcing nature of the emotionally charged colonial world-view of Conrad's time, it is worth noting its continuity with Sigmund Freud's contemporary understanding of the relation between the civilized and what was then thought of as the "primitive." In an inverted parallel with modern geographical and colonial exploration, and along with many modern writers, Freud explored the inner realm of the unconscious and the instincts. Most importantly, a similar model applied in both the outer and the inner domains. Freud saw the ego, the conscious moral self of the individual, as constantly negotiating between the pre-moral instinctual unconscious, which he called the id, or the "it," and the superego, a developed capacity for moral idealism and self-control. In Freud's tragic model of civilization, therefore, the realm of instinctual desire is intrinsically destructive and must be either repressed or sublimated; that is to say, it must be transmuted into a higher form.[3] So, for example, brute sexual rapacity has been converted into love, but the underlying power of precivilized instinct always lurks as a potential threat to the civilized self. Moreover, it was widely assumed under the influence of Victorian anthropology that all human cultures follow a single developmental process so that tribal peoples around the world were simply at an early, or primitive, stage of human evolution. Some modern thinkers reversed this evaluation. Lucien Lévy-Bruhl, in *How Natives Think* (1910), argued, like D. H. Lawrence, that "primitive" peoples enjoyed a different mode of life that was in emotional and psychological respects richer and more sustaining than modern rationality but even he, again like Lawrence, assumed that there was a generic world-view shared by archaic and tribal peoples, a world view that would inevitably give way to modernity. Freud likewise assumed that the study of such peoples gave insight into the workings of the instinctual and unconscious dimensions of the civilized. He had an extensive collection of "primitive" artifacts; and anthropological terms such as *totem* and *taboo* became key to his understanding of the psyche. But his scientific rationalism left little room for primitivist nostalgia and his thought seemed to support a self-evident parallel between the dutiful moral life of civilized man and the duty of the colonizer to protect, educate, and restrain native peoples.

Conrad and Marlow share this "Freudian" understanding of Africa not because they got it from Freud but because they shared the same mutually reinforcing assumptions. At the same time, Freud saw that moral ideals, while necessary to civilized existence, can also be self-deceptive rationalizations of darker desires and motives. He taught us not necessarily to reject but always to question moral ideals, especially when they are invested with higher orders of authority such as religion or patriotism. Conrad's novella records the shock of this recognition. Kurtz went, with apparent sincerity, to bring civilization to the African natives but suffered an internal collapse or degeneration. The reader has no direct access to the inner process here. The high-flown rhetoric of the civilizing mission in the manuscript of Kurtz's report is followed by the brief post-script: "Exterminate all the brutes" (Conrad 95). We do not know whether this represents a moral plunge from civilization to barbarism or whether it is, more subtly, a summative recognition of the true meaning of the civilizing project itself whose effect was indeed to exterminate indigenous cultures. Hence, in Marlow's quest for Kurtz, he does not just discover the great contemporary scandal of the cruel exploitation of the Belgian Congo under Leopold I, but he is driven to question the internal processes by which European peoples can perpetrate such evil.

Questions put to the hero are a traditional motif of the quest, but Marlow's quest dissolves into unanswered questions. Oedipus's answer to the riddling question of the Sphinx, "What goes on four legs, then two, then three?" was man. The philosopher Martin Heidegger said that anthropology is the essentially modern discipline because it treats man himself as a question (133). After many decades of studying native peoples around the world, anthropology came of age when it began to recognize that European man is not necessarily the human norm. In Marlow's and Conrad's story, precisely because it is set within the older world-view, we can see the beginning of this shocked recognition.

This chapter has emphasized that Conrad and Marlow still inhabit the older world-view. As Marlow remarks, the colonial venture is justified only by a certain moral idea and he clearly believes in that idea, however fragile and dishonored it may be, although he adds in an ominous image that the idea is itself "something you can set up, and bow down to, and offer a sacrifice to" (Conrad 47). His underlying commitment to the ideal is consistent with the Freudian understanding of civilization as a matter of duty and restraint, which is crucial to our understanding of the historical place of *Heart of Darkness* and explains in turn why the work has to be understood as an essentially inner quest.

In 1975, the Nigerian novelist Chinua Achebe wrote a blistering attack on *Heart of Darkness* as a racist work because it concerned only the moral lives of the European characters. It gave no native point of view. Achebe's essay is an important document of the post-colonial era but not well-judged as literary criticism. It is true that Conrad's novella does not tell the story as an African might do. It fell to a much later generation of African writers to do this, including most notably, of course, Achebe himself. But in his historical time and place Conrad performed a different function of European introspection.

Human cultures, particularly when they are under pressure from perceived threat or motivated by self-interest, tend to demonize and dehumanize particular "others," whether they be foreigners or internal subgroups. This is an evil that might be overcome by closer acquaintance through social interaction. Yet there is abundant historical evidence that close, even neighborly relations over many generations do not remove this xenophobic tendency because the humanity of the other is always in the eye of the beholder. Dehumanization is not a function of the other but of the perceiving self. This truth is, in both senses, blindingly obvious: It is banally true when recognized but invisible until the eyes are opened to it. *Heart of Darkness* is one of the great modern texts that began the slow process of this recognition in the world-historical context of colonization. Genuine decolonization only occurs in the mind and the heart. That is why, even as *Heart of Darkness* appears to concern a geographical journey to the heart of Africa, and indeed has to include that realistic encounter with the historical nature of colonialism, it has above all to be an essentially inner quest into the heart of European man by which the initial outer quest, the search for Kurtz, is subverted and superseded.

The shimmering interplay of inner and outer trajectories in the story explains why Marlow, as he looks on the African tribesmen dancing on the shore, is both appalled and fascinated. He is appalled at what, to him, is their incomprehensible otherness. Yet he is also fascinated because he recognizes his inner affinity with them: In his evolutionary thinking, they represent the ancestral past of European man, and the "past" is an ambiguous location. It may be seen as having been left behind in the process of evolution, and therefore as no longer relevant, or it may be seen, on the Freudian model, as a deeply buried layer still potentially active beneath the modern civilized psyche. Hence Marlow poses the ironic question to the surrogate readers, his audience within the tale: "You wonder I didn't go ashore for a howl and a dance?" (Conrad 80). For Freud, it is important to acknowledge, without succumbing to, the realm of primary instinct since repression was for him the principal source of neurotic symptoms. So, too, in keeping with what this chapter has called the Freudian spirit, Marlow balances identification and distance just as he does in his largely imaginative relation with Kurtz. He ruminates on the inner meaning of the spectacle but does not go ashore to join it as Kurtz effectively did.

D. H. Lawrence, by contrast, might be tempted to do just that: to affirm the manifestations of instinctual life but without fearing a collapse into barbarism. Lawrence represents an opposite wing of modern literature and thought, which, rather than fearing and repressing, seeks to honor the instinctual and the "primitive." The major philosophical proponent of this viewpoint was Friedrich Nietzsche (1844–1900) whose essential works were well known to Lawrence. In contrast to Freud's tragic view of civilization as dependent on the repression and sublimation of primordial instincts, Nietzsche and Lawrence emphasized how the instincts become dangerous through their repression. Marlow expresses puzzled admiration at the "restraint" of the hungry African crew in not killing and eating the Europeans (Conrad 85–86). While he contrasts this positively with Kurtz's lack of restraint, his observation is in keeping with the Freudian view that sees the irrational power of taboo as an early stage in the development of moral consciousness. These Africans are more civilized in their generation than the degenerate Europeans on the boat. But Lawrence would not have seen it in terms of restraint at all. His ideal of civilization, like Nietzsche's, was of an educated cultivation of instinctual impulse expressed in spontaneity and fullness of being. For both of them, the history of human civilization was one of increasing loss of connection with the sources of life, an increasing alienation from the world and from the self. Nietzsche expressed this in his first major work *The Birth of Tragedy* (1872), while Lawrence sought alternative cultural formations in Native American rituals or the art of the ancient Etruscan tombs. For both of them the privileging of "restraint" as the basis of moral order would be the symptom of a repressive culture.

Nietzsche and Lawrence thought that human culture had taken a wrong path at a very early stage and that their own European culture suffered from a widespread tendency to idealism. The word *idealism* has different meanings. In the first instance it is philosophical. Both men criticized the influence of the ancient Greek philosopher Plato, who posited a realm of ideal forms of which the phenomenal world was just an imperfect and shadowy reflection. His philosophical dualism, proposing a lower and a higher order of reality in which the everyday world of sensory perception was relatively devalued, had emotional and psychological consequences. Man comes to value the ideal world above that of the senses. For Nietzsche and Lawrence, Christianity was preeminently the form in which this psychological structure was embedded in European culture. Christianity is a dualistic religion whose God is above and beyond nature, as opposed to earlier religious forms in which divinity is mythically immanent in the natural world. Once again, what is at stake in the Nietzschean/Lawrencean critique is a structure of feeling too deep and naturalized even to be recognized by conventional inhabitants of the culture, let alone made into a possible object of critique.

No doubt that is why both writers, along with their subtle and powerful thought, also resorted to hyperbolic and challenging rhetoric. Lawrence's late work *The Man Who Died* (originally entitled *The Escaped Cock*) is a fable conceived in such a spirit of challenge. Lawrence's major novels, such as *The Rainbow* and *Women in Love*, are complex examinations of European culture, and his diagnostic thought is further elaborated in other writings such as *Studies in Classic American Literature*, but the present story does not rehearse these complex analyses. It simply encapsulates their significance in a condensed reimagining of Christ's resurrection.

Despite their radical critique of Christianity, both Nietzsche and Lawrence admired, and to some extent identified with, Christ himself whom, in common with many scholars and thinkers from the nineteenth century onwards, they thought of as a remarkable human being rather than as God. This was not just the familiar stance of admiring Christ while blaming the church for traducing his teachings. They thought Christ's mission was essentially mistaken and that disastrous consequences followed from his charismatic influence and moral insight. Crucially, therefore, Lawrence imagines a human rather than a divine meaning for Christ's resurrection, but not an irreligious one. Lawrence himself had been a pious Christian up to his young manhood and always thought of himself afterwards as a "passionately religious man" (Lawrence, *Letters* 165). For when he shed his Christian belief it was not to become secular or atheistical, but it was to rediscover a relation to the world for which archaic and "primitive" religions provided closer models.[4] Indeed, as with T. S. Eliot, albeit in a quite different sense, his whole life and work can be understood as a religious quest.

At the level of the public allegory, then, the unnamed "man" of Lawrence's fable is an alternative image of Christ, but he is also, more privately and intimately, an image of Lawrence himself, for whom the prophetic motive of his art often threatened to disrupt its artistic integrity. He was peculiarly aware of the temptations of prophecy. Moreover, he was not only terminally ill of consumption at the time of writing but had chronically poor health and always knew he would not live long. As with John Keats, this seemed to give him an extraordinary sensitivity to the sheer sensory quality of existence, which, also like Keats, he was able to put into language. Where he differed from Keats, however, was that Keats appreciated the richness of language for its own sake and sought to honor the richness of life by transposing its transience into the beauty and permanence of poetic art. Lawrence, by contrast, explicitly turned away from the "treasured gem-like lyrics of Shelley and Keats" for a poetry of "the immediate present" (Lawrence, *Phoenix* 218). The phrase "poetry of the present" may be applied to all of Lawrence's writing for what makes him uniquely valuable, despite the follies and failures arising from his prophetic ambitions, is his capacity to render living experience in such a way that the language, while richly metaphorical and active as a medium, seems never to intrude as a self-conscious "style." It seems just to render the object itself in its living quality. This is because Lawrence does not, strictly speaking, describe the object so much as he describes the experience of perceiving it or, better still, of responding to it. His writing is a continual exemplary lesson in response. All this compels the protagonist of Lawrence's story to undergo a peculiar inversion of the quest.

If Christ was seen as human, that did not stop him from being an archetype of the questing hero. Indeed, it heightened his stature in that regard. So the unnamed man's previous mission had features of the traditional quest. It had involved a preparatory ordeal in the desert as well as the Nekya, his final passage through the realm of the dead. But now, in the forced passivity of his weakened body, he attends to the natural and human world for its own sake. His former self has indeed died. Where Christ had taught that you must die to the old life in order to enter a new and more abundant one, the man discovers this to be true in a reversed sense. It is the abundance of sensory being to which he now gradually awakens, led by an instinct of the body rather than by his intellectual, cognitive self. The incipiently religious dimension here is that the man does not respond just to particular beings around him, such as the rooster, but to a wave-like or flame-like power of life in which any individual being is only the tip. He now sees the world as Van Gogh painted it: "a vast resoluteness everywhere flinging itself up in stormy or subtle wave-crests, foam-tips emerging out of the blue invisible, a black and orange cock or the green flame-tongues out of the extremes of the fig tree" (Lawrence, *Virgin* 129). His new sense of the sacred as immanent in the sensory world around him is a special vision not shared by the peasants, the slaves, or the mother of the priestess. Only in the priestess does he find a kindred spirit. She has been awaiting Osiris whom contemporary anthropologists, such as George Frazer in *The Golden Bough*, had recognized as an earlier type of Christ and who was clearly a nature god destroyed and reborn every spring. Sex for Lawrence always had something sacred about it as a contact with the larger life. That is why, at what one is tempted to call the climax of the *The Man Who Died*, the man offers his erection to the priestess with the words "I am risen." This is not a blasphemous reversal of Christ's meaning but an affirmation of the sacredness in sexuality. Yet along with this acknowledgment of sexuality runs an equally strong, apparently opposite motif focused by an internal inversion of the quest motif in the tale.

A peculiarly resonant and touching moment in the Gospels is Christ's turning from Mary Magdalene after his resurrection with the sentence *Noli me tangere* ("Do not touch me"). Lawrence's protagonist says, "Do not touch me" to Madeleine while he is still confusedly following his new instincts and later, just before he encounters the priestess, he begins to recognize the "irrevocable *noli me tangere* which separates the re-born from the vulgar" (Lawrence, *Virgin* 131, 148). *Vulgar* is not, of course, a socially snobbish term here: The priestess's high-ranking mother is vulgar in Lawrence's sense as she cannot see what her daughter sees. The priestess has above all held herself separate and has nurtured her own individuality. A major theme of Lawrence's writing is how the love relationship may be a threat to the integrity of the self. In thinking the relationship between man and woman was of central importance in human life, he was especially alive to its dangers. One danger is that love may be a cover for possessiveness. Madeleine's selfless and idealistic love is a possible example of this. A related danger lies in the romantic ideal of merging identities, of becoming one. In contrast, Lawrence thought that the love relationship must enhance the individual: If necessary, individuality must be jealously maintained within a relationship.

The man's need within his newly found sensory relatedness with the world to keep himself separate gives a peculiar, apparently undirected, character to his new life. Following the seismic shift in his relation to the world, and to his own being, he now allows himself to drift. In that respect, the very notion of the quest seems to be abandoned as an error. Yet by the same token, while responding so fully to the surrounding world as to yield himself passively to it, he maintains a strong sense of his own individuality. In that sense, he still has a quest: the quest to create or preserve an integral self, which is a task that Lawrence thought was a rare achievement and the most important responsibility of all human beings. A mission to save others may be a way of evading that task, yet neither does the man undertake an inner quest like Marlow's. Indeed, Lawrence thought some forms of moral introspection, such as he found in Dostoevsky, to be another unhealthy aspect of Christian culture. The man's present need is rather to free himself from an overly idealistic self-consciousness through an outwardly directed receptiveness to the life around him. For this purpose, he keeps on the move and with no specific goal located in the outer world.

In sum, although it would be unprofitable to generalize too far about modern uses of the quest motif, these two tales by Conrad and Lawrence suggest something of its enduring and protean potential under modern conditions. The tales concern difficult transformations of fundamental values in their culture, in the course of which the very notion, or viability, of a quest seems to be thrown into question. Yet in both cases an outwardly directed, public quest gives way to a more internal and personal one, which suggests that whatever irony may envelope it, the quest motive as such retains a persistent power. Even as the values invested in the original quest are found wanting, they are transmuted into the enduring human motive and the perennial literary form of the quest.

Notes

1. For an expanded discussion on this topic, see Bell.
2. Raymond Williams first used the phrase in *A Preface to Film* and then throughout his work including *The Long Revolution* (1961) and *Marxism and Literature* (1977).
3. This view is summarily expressed in Freud's *Civilization and Its Discontents*.
4. For a discussion of Lawrence's primitivism see the chapters on *The Rainbow, Women in Love* and *The Plumed Serpent in Bell.*

Works Cited

Achebe, Chinua. "An Image of Africa: Racism in Conrad's *Heart of Darkness*." *Hopes and Impediments: Selected Essays 1965–1987*. London: Heinemann, 1988. 1–13.

Bell, Michael. *D. H. Lawrence: Language and Being*. Cambridge, Cambridge UP, 2008.

Conrad, Joseph. *Youth, Heart of Darkness: The End of the Tether*. Ed. Owen Knowles. Cambridge: Cambridge UP, 2010.

Eliot, T. S. "Tarr." *The Egoist* 5.8 (Sept. 1918): 106.

_____. *The Waste Land. The Complete Poems and Plays 1909–1950*. San Diego: Harcourt, 1971. 37–55.

Freud, Sigmund. *Civilization and Its Discontents*. Trans. James Strachey. New York: Norton, 2010.

Heidegger, Martin. "The Age of the World Picture." *The Question Concerning Technology and Other Essays*. Trans. William Lovitt. New York: Harper, 1977. 115–55.

Lawrence, D. H. "The American Edition of *New Poems*." *Phoenix: The Posthumous Papers of D. H. Lawrence*. Ed. Edward D. McDonald. London: Heinemann, 1961. 218–22.

_____. *The Letters of D. H. Lawrence*. Vol. 2. Eds. George J. Zytaruk and James T. Boulton. Cambridge: Cambridge UP, 1981.

_____. *The Virgin and the Gipsy and Other Stories*. Ed. Michael Herbert, Bethan Jones, and Lindeth Vasey. Cambridge: Cambridge UP, 2005. 123–63.

Williams, Raymond, and Michael Orrom. *Preface to Film*. London: Film Drama, 1954.

CRITICAL READINGS

Quests for Immortality and Identity: *The Epic of Gilgamesh* and *The Odyssey*_____

Katherine C. King

An ancient epic hero goes in quest of something hugely important to himself or his social group. Normally he succeeds, but even if he fails, he brings back the story of his great adventure. The hero's name will be preserved in epic song, which is itself a major goal of epic heroes. The story of the quest allows the hero to transcend his human mortality and to live in memory as long as there are storytellers to repeat the tale. Apart from achieving poetic immortality, the goals of most ancient epic quests are related to kingship, either directly or indirectly. *The Odyssey*, composed around 700 BCE, recounts the adventures of the ancient Greek hero Odysseus as he travels homeward from Troy to Ithaka to reclaim his family and kingship. Using a combination of intellect, endurance, and physical strength, Odysseus succeeds both in regaining his throne and in establishing patrilineal monarchy as Ithaka's permanent system of government. Half a millennium earlier, around 1200 BCE, the Mesopotamian *Epic of Gilgamesh* celebrated Gilgamesh, a great hero but an irresponsible king, who abandons his responsibilities in Uruk to seek the secret of immortality. Although he fails to win immortality, Gilgamesh succeeds in learning a heretofore secret story and, chastised, returns home with it to be a wiser and better king to his people. For Western culture, these two epics define the idea of quest and give us models that shape how we think about subsequent literary adventures.

The Epic of Gilgamesh, which tells of deeds attributed to Gilgamesh, king of Uruk in Mespotamia in 2700 BCE,[1] contains two quests that set the pattern. In the first quest (tablets II–IV), Gilgamesh and his companion Enkidu go on a dangerous mission to conquer the "monster" guardian of a virgin forest and bring precious cedar wood back to his city. Gilgamesh is willing to enter the dangerous wilds because he believes that the glory of success will compensate for his finite human lifespan. He and Enkidu complete a seven-month journey in fifteen days, mercilessly kill Humbaba, clear-cut the forest, and float the timber down the Euphrates to Uruk. Gilgamesh has conquered the wilderness, domesticated it for the city, and glorified his name. This first quest is undoubtedly successful.

The audience that responds happily to Gilgamesh's success, however, soon discovers that the poet of *Gilgamesh* follows a tragic muse. Gilgamesh's arrogance in this and a subsequent adventure, in which he insults the goddess of fertility and conquers drought not by prayer but by violence, provokes angry gods to exact a price—the death of Enkidu—to teach respect for the forces of nature. The anguished death and rotting corpse of his beloved companion, whose immense strength paired with his own had brought them "through every danger" (X.57),[2] bring home to Gilgamesh the true horror of human mortality. "My friend Enkidu, whom I loved, has turned to clay," he laments several times. "Shall I not be like him, and also lie down, / never to rise again, through all eternity?" (X.69–71 *inter alia*). No longer satisfied with cultural immortality, Gilgamesh performs a second quest to seek physical immortality (IX–XI).

In this quest, Gilgamesh must go beyond the ends of the known earth to consult the only two human beings whom the gods have ever granted immortality, i.e., Utnapishtim and his wife. He leaves the city both physically and culturally, wandering in the wilderness and exchanging his kingly clothing for a lion's skin. Driven by his fear of death, he performs the superhuman feat of passing underground through the twin mountains that guard the Sun's rising and setting, a terrifying twelve-day journey through utter darkness. On the other side, in an immortal garden of glittering jewels, he finds a goddess who warns him that the Waters of Death lie between him and his goal. His haggard face and lament persuade her, as they did the Scorpion Guardians of the mountains, to help. She directs him to a boatman, who is ultimately also persuaded to help, despite Gilgamesh's initial violent destruction of the magic stones that had normally propelled the boat (X.92–106).

The boatman's help consists of technical expertise; as a substitute for the magic stones, Gilgamesh himself must provide the superhuman muscle to make 300 eighty-foot poles and then use them to propel the boat across the Waters of Death without being touched by a single fatal drop. Sunburned and frostbitten, with filthy skin and matted hair, clad in animal skins, and continually lamenting, Gilgamesh at last presents himself to Utnapishtim and his wife. He has accomplished a seemingly impossible journey. But will he accomplish his quest?

Gilgamesh's laments prove less persuasive with Utnapishtim than they did with his previous helpers. Utnapishtim chides him for his endless sorrow and for behaving like a lowly fool instead of a responsible king (X.270–95)[3], preaches a lesson about the coming and going of life and then gives him only part of what he asks for. He tells him the story of how he and his wife were granted immortality—the story of the great Flood from which he had saved the seeds of all life on earth—but he concludes, disappointingly, that the gods' gift was a unique event. "Who," he asks contemptuously, will "convene for you the gods' assembly, / so you can find the life you search for?" (XI.207–8). To prove his point that Gilgamesh is and always will be human and mortal, Utnapishtim asks him to stay awake for a week.

Despite his previous superhuman accomplishments, Gilgamesh cannot do this but instead sleeps for a week. As proof of Gilgamesh's mortality, Utnapishtim shows Gilgamesh seven loaves of bread baked as he was sleeping, the first one all dried up, the last one hot on the coals, and the others in various stages of declining freshness. Bread, the archetypal human food, perishes just as humans do; Gilgamesh understands the implications and cries, "[W]hat should I do? . . . wherever I turn, there too will be Death" (XI.243–46).

Utnapishtim, unsympathetic, dispatches Gilgamesh back to Uruk. First, however, Utnapishtim orders the boatman, whom he has banished for having brought a human being across the Waters of Death, to bathe and dress Gilgamesh in royal clothing that will magically stay clean until he enters Uruk. In other words, Utnapishtim insists on restoring

Gilgamesh from savage to civilized humanity. Despite the despair in his heart, Gilgamesh will return home as the dignified king the gods made him to be, with Urshanabi as requisite servant-companion. Second, at the instigation of his compassionate wife, Utnapishtim grants Gilgamesh a reward for his arduous journey: information about a restorative plant growing at the bottom of the ocean. Once Gilgamesh performs an additional amazing feat to acquire it, he possesses the means to an extended, always youthful life.

The promise of extended youth evaporates, however, when Gilgamesh leaves the plant unattended while he refreshes himself in a pool during the journey home. A snake eats it, sloughs its old skin, and slithers off, leaving Gilgamesh to age and die like all human beings.

Periodically throughout the epic, the poet stresses that Gilgamesh has superhuman power because of his divine mother. The reader has been told that "two-thirds of him is god and one third human" (I.48; X.51), or, in other words, that his divinity is twice as important as his humanity. As the epic comes to its conclusion, however, the poet focuses on the "one third human."

Gilgamesh's second quest is a failed one precisely because he is human. We cannot characterize him as a failed hero because *human* heroes, by definition, *cannot* achieve physical immortality. Instead, Gilgamesh is a tragic hero. Tragedy is about human limits, and Gilgamesh sadly learns his limits. As a tragic hero, Gilgamesh is often seen as a model for the hero of *The Iliad* rather than of *The Odyssey*.

And yet, unlike Achilles but like Odysseus, Gilgamesh's career is intimately associated with the well-being of a city-state. Like Odysseus, Gilgamesh achieves the most a man can do, and his culture benefits greatly by his deeds (note the long list of achievements—walls, temples, roads, wells, agriculture, religious ritual, story—that the poet lists at the beginning of the epic). The last verses of the epic bring Gilgamesh back to his city with words of pride. In a repetition of the poem's opening lines, in which the poet took his readers on a tour of the city, Gilgamesh urges his companion to "climb Uruk's wall. . . . Survey its foundations, examine the brickwork! . . . three square miles and a half is Uruk's expanse" (XI.323–29 and I.18–24). His evident pride indicates that, as the poet promised at the beginning (I.9), Gilgamesh has "found peace" despite his failed quest.

What makes *The Epic of Gilgamesh* a model for *The Odyssey* is its intertwining of quest and kingship and its emphasis on learning from experience. Its introductory lines indicate that Gilgamesh "was wise in all matters" and that his journey had taught him "the sum of wisdom" (I.2, 4, 6). They also indicate that upon returning to Uruk, Gilgamesh "set all his labours on a tablet of stone" (I.10). In other words, like Odysseus, Gilgamesh is capable of telling his own culturally significant story. Gilgamesh comes back from the second quest a sadder man but, we can assume, a better king because of the grief he has experienced and the humility and wisdom acquired by going beyond the end of the known world. Something similar happens with Odysseus.

The word *odyssey* has come to denote a story of adventurous wandering. It signifies wandering that may seem purposeless but that in fact leads somewhere, often to inner knowledge and a recognition of one's professional or personal identity. Most quests, like that in *The Epic of Gilgamesh*, lead away from home; some, like that of the Argonauts, focus nearly equally on the going and the return; but *The Odyssey* focuses entirely on the return home. Home itself—and everything home signifies—is the goal of the quest. Achieving home in *The Odyssey* has three complementary significations: on the social plane it means restoring or re-creating personal relationships and demonstrating that Odysseus's unique character and skills make him superior to all others who contend for the kingship; politically, it signifies stabilizing the community, which has been in political limbo for nineteen years; and symbolically it signifies a return from obliteration in nature to full individuated humanity.

To give his story the deepest possible resonance, Homer employs symbols and figures that either represent or pose threats to human and cosmic order. Cosmic time, for example, is evoked by the 360 male pigs in Odysseus's herds (which represent the solar year), the 350 immortal cattle of the Sun (which represent a lunar year), and the conjunction of the new lunar and new solar years (which happens roughly only once every nineteen years) on the day Odysseus "remarries" his wife.[4] Threats to order are most prevalent in the Great Wanderings of Books 9–12: Divine Circe confuses the categories of human and animal; giant one-eyed Polyphemus performs the "civilized" human tasks of herding, milking, and making cheese, but he also eats raw human flesh like a beast and acknowledges no law; the flesh of the wrongfully butchered cattle of the Sun is cooked and yet moves and bellows, thus confusing the living and the dead and symbolically turning the companions into raw-meat-eating beasts (12.395–96); cave-dwelling Kalypso, or "Concealer," hides Odysseus on an island termed the "navel of the sea"(Allen 1.50),[5] offering an immortality that is paradoxically death (or, as the word *navel* suggests, pre-life). Figurative elements like these have inspired some scholars such as Joseph Campbell to regard the epic as a personal spiritual journey to enlightenment (Campbell *Hero* 39, 58; *Masks* 162–73).

Other elements, however, give Odysseus's journey a more political and ethical cast. One of these is the "woeful homecoming" (1.326–27) of the other Greek kings who fought at Troy. Greek storytellers did not end the saga of the Trojan War with the destruction of that great city. When the heroes headed for home, only a few made it there quickly and safely. Many suffered greatly, and a few died either on the way or upon reaching their homeland shores. Ajax, son of Oileus, for example, was wrecked at sea and drowned as punishment for hubris against both Athena and Poseidon, two gods that also figure prominently in *The Odyssey*. Agamemnon reached home quickly but died at the hands of his queen and her lover. His brother, Menelaus, meanwhile, took more than seven years to get home after having been blown off course to Egypt with his reclaimed adulterous wife Helen. The poems that told of these returns were called *Nostoi* or *Homecomings*; none of them survives in epic form except *The Odyssey*, but we know of them from fragments and references in other works, not least in *The Odyssey* itself. In this longest and greatest of the *Nostoi*, Homer uses the other returns, with their issues of vengeful gods, treacherous wives, and wanderings off course, as a foil to set off the extraordinary characteristics of his own hero and his faithful Penelope.

The character of Odysseus and the ethical program of *The Odyssey* are presented in the opening lines of the epic: Odysseus is introduced as "that versatile man . . . who wandered far and long after sacking Troy's holy city," who "saw many men's cities and learned their ways of thought," and who "suffered much woe on the sea, blows to his spirit, / while striving for his own life and the homecoming of his companions" (1.1–5). Versatility, the ability to change and devise new strategies as occasion demands, is key to his success as is his associated ability to learn the "ways of thought" of those he meets. But also key is his ability to endure "woe" and "blows to his spirit" without losing self-control, an ability his companions lack. The companions, the poet continues, "perished because of their very own recklessness"; yielding to hunger, "they devoured the cattle of Helios . . . / and he took away from them their day of homecoming" (1.7–10). Odysseus's supreme self-control despite extreme provocation and his steadfast refusal to forget his goal of reuniting with his wife in Ithaka despite extreme temptation is what turns a journey home into a truly heroic quest.

The Odyssey begins with Odysseus alone and "longing for homecoming and his wife," trapped on Kalypso's island after he has already lost all his shipmates (1.13). Odysseus is in an idyllic location, and a goddess, who has promised him immortality in order to have him for husband, is exuding charm to make him forget Ithaka (1.48–57). He should be happy—is this not immortality, after all, exactly what Gilgamesh was seeking? But instead, Odysseus is weeping and longing to die (1.57–58). He does not really want to die, of course. What he wants is to escape the goddess's immortal world and rejoin the world of mortals, to change his generic male status (his only activity appears to be sex, eating, and sleeping) for the singular identity of the individual named Odysseus, to exchange the effortless existence in which every biological and sensual need is met for one that requires painful struggle against and with other human beings. It is not difficult to make an analogy between Kalypso and the womb and see Odysseus's yearning as for birth, or, rather, rebirth into his previous fully human status.

When Odysseus's ceaseless laments impel his patron Olympian goddess Athena to intercede with Zeus to release him from Kalypso's hold, Kalypso benevolently supplies Odysseus with the means to effect and survive his exit from the "navel of the sea." These include food, drink, sailing instructions, and—instead of a ready-made boat— an axe and adze with which Odysseus exercises his unforgotten human skill of building. In other words, it is without magic but only with human tools and human skills that Odysseus sets off across the "unspeakable" span of water that separates Kalypso's island from "cities of men" (5.100–1).

Odysseus's use of technology (tools and the science of steering by the stars) marks his reentry into the normal human world and symbolically makes his crossing of the waters a self-propelled rebirth.

Poseidon, who hates Odysseus because he blinded his Cyclops son, makes Odysseus's crossing a painful parturition, ripping away every vestige of technology and leaving Odysseus with nothing except his naked body. He raises a ferocious storm that bit by bit tears away pieces of the raft, tossing it about like thistledown (5.328–30) and finally scattering its timbers like a pile of husks (5.368–70). These two similes of seed-bearing and seed-dropping plants contribute to the imagery of rebirth, with Odysseus as the seed that survives.

It is now that Odysseus's heroic greatness—physical strength combined with his famous power of endurance—comes into play. Homer subjects his hero to intense fear but also makes clear that despite his fear, Odysseus keeps his extraordinary intellect and strength intact. When a minor sea goddess, Leukothea, advises him to abandon the battered raft and begin to swim toward land, giving him an immortal scarf to use as a life preserver (5.343–47), Odysseus accepts the scarf, but in a characteristic moment of careful deliberation and mistrust, decides to stay put until the raft splits apart completely (5.354–64). Immortal scarf or no, Odysseus must still struggle through two days of difficult swimming, then be driven against a huge rock that tears the skin from his hands, and then swim far along the coast before he finally finds a quiet place to come ashore.

Having survived the angry sea, Odysseus deliberates about where best to sleep and restore his exhausted body. Choosing a spot beneath two conjoined low-growing trees, he covers (*kalupsato*) himself in leaves for warmth (5.491). A simile compares him to a man covering a burning log in dark embers to keep alive the seed of fire (5.388–91). The man who had been passively concealed by Kalypso at the navel of the sea now actively conceals himself in order to conserve his own seed of life. Odysseus, reborn into the world of mortality, has taken charge of preserving his precarious human existence.

The trees that shelter Odysseus at this crucial moment are olive, a tree integral to ancient Greek life and an important symbol of civilization in *The Odyssey*. Odysseus will sleep twice more in the shelter of the olive: next on the coast of Ithaka, where the Phaiakians deposit him caught in a magical coma (13.122), and finally in his palace bedchamber, where one of the bedposts is an olive tree still fixed in the ground (23.190–224). With each appearance of the olive, Odysseus moves a stage closer to his goal of integration into his own human, Ithakan community. Here on the Phaiakians' island, the double olive is significant: The cultivated olive conjoined with a wild one is a fitting symbol of the duality of Scheria, whose utopian community contains both real and mythic aspects (Vidal-Naquet 47–51; Segal 27–32). It is also a fitting symbol of Odysseus's liminal position on the verge of civilization before he has discovered what kind of people he has come to, before he has proved his worth to them and they to him, and before he has identified himself and thereby shifted himself fully into the realm of cultural existence with its own promise of immortality in *kleos*, or epic song.

Like a newborn baby, Odysseus awakens naked and in need of everything: food, drink, clothing. Once again he is helped by a female, the charming teenage daughter of the king of the Phaiakians who, inspired by Athena, has come to the shore to wash clothes in the river that empties there. Showing great bravery as well as the commitment to hospitality for which the Phaiakians have become famous, Nausikaa provides means for him to bathe, olive oil for his skin, and freshly washed royal clothing. Like Gilgamesh with Utnapishtim, the bathed, groomed, and dressed Odysseus emerges a new man, his looks reflecting his true status as hero and king.

Odysseus's noble appearance now provokes a new danger to his homecoming: Nausikaa indicates clearly that if the stranger were so inclined, she would look favorably on his asking to wed her (6.244–45). Her father later explicitly makes marriage with his daughter a true alternative to Odysseus's returning to Ithaka (7.311–15). It is an appealing alternative, for the Phaiakians are a highly cultured people with a beautiful city and royal palace, games, dances, and even a bard who knows stories of Odysseus's heroic role in the Trojan War. But utopia does not appeal to Odysseus, whose sights remain fixed on Ithaka with its hot and cold seasons, its rocky landscape, its quarrels, its tears, and most importantly, Penelope.

The utopian Phaiakians are a way station between Kalypso's mythic island and the real world of Ithaka, where actions always have consequences. While he is with them, Odysseus, whose very name means "painful," tells the Phaiakians a story of painful loss whose adventures are almost all lessons about actions and consequences. Most teach "the value of restraint and caution, of refusing the easy way, especially when it comes to eating" (King 95). The necessity to eat sets human beings apart from gods, and the way one eats sets human beings apart from beasts. Beasts eat their food raw, in whatever condition they find it; humans cook food or otherwise alter it, which means they must wait while it is prepared. Rituals of sacrifice and libation to the gods accompany its preparation and consumption, as do rituals of hospitality between human beings. All these things require a person to restrain the urgent demands of what Odysseus calls the "loathsome" stomach (7.216) until the proper time.

The Great Wanderings contain many instances of wrong eating. In the raid on the Kikones, their first adventure after leaving Troy, Odysseus's companions eat at the wrong time, falling on the spoils immediately rather than waiting until they have escaped as Odysseus has advised (9.43–46). Six men in each ship die as a result. Bestial Polyphemus and the Laistrygones invert the rites of hospitality by eating their guests raw (9.289–93, 311, 344; 10.116). Six men and eleven ships are lost to these bad eaters. Odysseus's companions three times eat the wrong thing when it is offered: lotus near the beginning of the adventures (9.91–97), Circe's porridge in the middle (10.233–40), and, finally, the cattle of the Sun in Book 12. Odysseus rescues them from their first two mistakes, but the last is irremediable. The companions, who know they must not eat the sacred cattle, hope that the god can be appeased with gifts; if he cannot, they feel that anything is better than dying of slow starvation. Not fully understanding the necessity for restraint or not having the inner strength to exercise it, they symbolically eat up the days of their lives and die. Odysseus, who can endure the pain of extreme hunger and knows there can be no redemption from sacrilege, alone survives.

The behavior and fate of Odysseus's companions prepare the reader for what happens to Penelope's 108 suitors when Odysseus returns. Unrestrained eaters of Odysseus's household (16.389–90 *inter alia*), bad guests and worse hosts, self-indulgent, arrogant, and disorderly, Homer casts them as both bestial, like Polyphemus, and foolish, like the companions who eat the cattle of the sun. During their final feast on Odysseus's livestock, they begin laughing uncontrollably, and the cooked meat they are eating begins to bleed as if it were raw (20.345–49), a sign of wrongful eating and imminent punishment similar to the twitching, bellowing cooked beef that the companions ate on the Sun's island (12.395–96). Once Odysseus reveals himself, the suitors, like the companions, vainly hope that offering recompense will save their lives. Later after Odysseus attacks and Athena magnifies Odysseus's power by lifting her terrifying aegis, the suitors stampede like cattle and end up piled in heaps like fish (22.299, 384–88) as befits their sub-human behavior.

Merely arriving in Ithaka does not win Odysseus his former status as husband and king. He does not march in and announce himself to the suitors, whom he learned about from Teiresias in Hades and from Athena on the shore of Ithaka. In stark contrast to the incautious Agamemnon, he returns slowly in four stages, each shift of position marked by his revealing his identity to a select one or two on a need-to-know basis. Going in disguise to the faithful swineherd Eumaios on the outskirts of the estate, he scopes out how things are going in the palace and makes himself known first to his nineteen-year-old son, Telemakhos. Reunion with his son achieves two things: It establishes Odysseus's status as father and furnishes him a partner with whom to strategize.

In the second stage, Odysseus kills the suitors and establishes his right to be Penelope's husband. Infiltrating the palace disguised as an old beggar, he tests and unsettles the suitors, makes allies of three servants, and exploits Penelope's plan to set up a contest to shoot an arrow cleanly through twelve lined-up axe sockets with Odysseus's great bow. This hunting bow, safely kept in the storeroom while Odysseus went to Troy to wield man-killing spears and swords, is a symbol of the prewar husband Penelope wants back. The suitors' failure even to string it certifies their inferiority and impudence in aspiring to the queen's bed and king's palace. Odysseus's subsequent use of the bow as a weapon to murder all 108 suitors may make the audience, as well as Penelope, wonder whether the resulting "lion-like" hero (22.401–02) is, in fact, that same husband. The immediate effect of Odysseus's successful archery is to validate in the minds of the audience his claim to be master of this household. The third stage of return begins when Odysseus reveals his identity to his wife. Given his sexual desirability, as established previously through Kalypso and Circe, the audience, like Telemakhos, may expect Penelope to fall into her husband's arms. Not so. She does not—or does not want to—recognize this blood- and gore-splattered man as her husband. First making him wash off the blood of the murdered suitors, she tests him, provoking him to reveal their most intimate shared secret, which is that Odysseus built their marriage bed around the trunk of an olive tree (23.188–204) Clean of battle filth and emotionally disarmed, occupying this bed marks Odysseus's full return from Troy to Ithaka, from warrior to husband. Penelope and Odysseus consummate their remarriage not just physically but also spiritually: They have sex and share stories of their suffering. This husband and wife, contrary to Klytemnestra and Agamemnon or Helen and Menelaus, exemplify that ideal marriage extolled by Odysseus to Nausikaa, "a household maintained by a man and woman who think alike, a source of pain to their enemies, delight to their friends" (6.182–85).

Many people think that *The Odyssey* should end when Odysseus and Penelope finally fall asleep in each other's arms. Since Odysseus is once again father of his son, master of his household, and husband of his wife, his quest for home and identity ought now to be complete. However, a fourth, political stage still remains: reclaiming the kingship of Ithaka. Kingship has been associated previously in *The Odyssey* with being husband of Penelope and master of Odysseus's extensive property, but this association is not absolute. As Telemakhos says in Book One, there are many aristocrats in Ithaka who could be king (1.394–96), and now after the slaughter of several among the suitors, the community is truly divided about who merits being king. In order to win the kingship for himself and for his son to follow, Odysseus must leave the "female" domestic space that contains Penelope, and he must journey to the masculine source of his political power, his father Laertes.

Elderly Laertes, previous king of Ithaka, has retired to a farm far from town and has become decrepit through grief over Odysseus's nineteen-year absence. When, after some testing on both their parts,

Laertes accepts Odysseus as indeed his son, he comes back to life. Then, joined by Telemakhos and some faithful retainers, grandfather, father, and son arm themselves to face the onslaught of the suitors' furious fathers. Fittingly, Laertes, father of Odysseus, kills Eupeithes, father of Antinoos, worst of the suitors. This is the only bloodshed, for Zeus stops the civil war proclaiming that Odysseus will "always be king" and that the relatives of the justly slain suitors will "forget" that Odysseus murdered them (24.482–85) Zeus's fiat taken together with the masculine trio of Odysseus flanked by his rejuvenated father and his grown-up son implies that Odysseus's household will rule Ithaka from now on, the kingship passing from father to son in an unchallenged patrilineal hereditary monarchy.[6]

Odysseus's identity is therefore complete not only in the moment but for the future. Despite the fact that he will have to leave home again soon to offer compensation to Poseidon, another father whose son was justly harmed, his quest is complete. He has gone from generic male humanity on Kalypso's island to a fully individuated social and familial identity at home.

Odysseus's successful quest has also established the dominance of one of two competing social ideologies presented in *The Odyssey*. One ideology views group survival or loss as entirely dependent on the virtues or mistakes of the leader and regards murder, regardless of motive, as necessitating vengeance. This group is represented in *The Odyssey* by Poseidon and by the Ithakan fathers who lost sons at Troy, on the voyage home, or in the slaughter in the palace. They are the majority in Ithaka, according to the vote taken after the slaughter is discovered (24.463–64). The other point of view recognizes justifiable homicide and gives priority to the individual over group responsibility. This minority point of view is represented by Mentor and Halitherses, who focus on the destructiveness of the suitors (24.455–60) just as Homer focuses on the companions' "very own recklessness" at the beginning of the poem (1.7). Zeus's fiat validates the minority view and thereby certifies that the specific talents of Odysseus—the intellectual agility, self-control, and physical strength that he shares to a large degree with both his father and his son—merit his rank at the top of Ithaka's hierarchy.

Gilgamesh leaves the civilized world for the wilderness and then crosses into the supernatural realm where he hopes to find humans who have escaped mortal limitations. Driven by fear, he seeks the humanly impossible and fails. Although returning to his city and kingship appears to give him peace, they are nonetheless a consolation prize. Odysseus, however, encounters in the supernatural world challenges similar to the real-world ones he confronts on Ithaka. He seeks and finds what every man in the world of *The Odyssey* is expected to seek: a rightful position in a community of men who govern themselves with civilized laws. Both heroes learn painfully that physical immortality and humanity are incompatible categories, but Odysseus chooses humanity willingly, while Gilgamesh is forced into tragic acceptance. Eternal life is, however, the ultimate reward for what they achieve in their quests: Their stories will endure as the cultural immortality proper to humankind.

Notes

1. The first integrated version of the epic was composed in Babylonia circa 1700 BCE; the mini-epic plays from which it took its substance were composed in ancient Sumer (later subsumed into Babylonia) between 2200 and 1800 BCE. See George xvi–xxvii.
2. The translation is Andrew George's minus the brackets that indicate restorations. The Roman numerals designate the particular Tablet; the numbers following the period refer to the line numbers in George's text.
3. Like many scholars, George (xliii) interprets this fragmentary passage as a criticism of Gilgamesh.
4. See Murray 211–12 for a thorough exposition of mythic elements. Meton constructed an official nineteen-year calendar for Athens in 433 BCE.
5. Translations are my own from volumes 3 and 4 of T. W. Allen (ed.), *Homeri Opera*. For my complete translation of the poem (1.1–10), see *Ancient Epic*, 81.
6. See Thalmann for a thorough discussion of tensions between aristocracy and monarchy, inherited rank and achieved rank, in *The Odyssey* and in the eighth century BCE.

Works Cited

Allen, T. W., ed. *Homeri Opera*. 2nd ed. Vols. 3 and 4. Oxford: Oxford UP, 1917, 1919.

Burkert, Walter. *Structure and History in Greek Mythology and Ritual*. Berkeley: U of California P, 1979.

Campbell, Joseph. *The Hero with a Thousand Faces*. 2nd ed. Princeton, NJ: Princeton UP, 1968.

_____. *The Masks of God: Occidental Mythology*. New York: Viking, 1964.

Foster, Benjamin R. *The Epic of Gilgamesh*. New York: Norton, 2001.

George, Andrew R. *The Epic of Gilgamesh*. London: Penguin, 2003.

King, Katherine C. *Ancient Epic*. London: Wiley, 2009.

Murray, Gilbert. *The Rise of the Greek Epic*. 2nd ed. Oxford: Clarendon, 1911.

Segal, Charles. "The Phaeacians and the Symbolism of Odysseus' Return." *Arion* 1.4 (1962): 17–64.

Thalmann, William G. *The Swineherd and the Bow: Representations of Class in the "Odyssey."* Ithica, NY: Cornell UP, 1998.

Vidal-Naquet, Pierre. "Land and Sacrifice in the *Odyssey*: A Study of Religious and Mythical Meanings." *Reading the Odyssey: Selected Interpretive Essays*. Ed. Seth L. Schein. Princeton, NJ: Princeton UP, 1996.

Virgil's *The Aeneid* and the Ambivalence of Aeneas's Heroic Quest _____

Eric Sandberg

Virgil's great epic *The Aeneid*, the story of one man's heroic quest to realize Rome's imperial destiny, has been enormously influential, serving as a literary model, a textbook, and even a tool of prophecy. It is, however, very much a product of its particular historical moment of upheaval and transition.

Virgil was born in 70 BCE and died, with *The Aeneid* still unfinished, in 19 BCE. This means that in his relatively short life he lived through the Catiline conspiracy to overthrow the Republic; the civil war between Julius Caesar and Pompey the Great; the assassination of Caesar and the civil war that followed it; as well as a third civil war between Octavian, Caesar's heir, and Mark Antony. These were violent times characterized by an atmosphere of apprehension: The 500-year-old Republic was dangerously unstable, lurching from one crisis to the next, and there seemed every prospect of its ultimate collapse. The emergence of the stable political structure of the Principate under a bloodstained Octavian, now transformed into a benevolent Augustus, offered Rome a stability it had not had for generations. On the other hand, it meant an end in all but name to the traditions of the Republic. Virgil's epic is on one level a celebration of this new political dispensation, and it was quickly recognized as such by contemporary readers and commentators: Virgil praises Augustus by associating him with his illustrious mythological ancestor Aeneas (Bell 12–13). Until relatively recently, this view of *The Aeneid* as supportive of Augustan imperial policy was widely accepted (Kennedy 39). There is, however, another case that can be made, arguing that the epic simultaneously casts doubt on Augustus's achievement, or at least looks as much to its costs as its benefits (Thomas xiii). Augustan stability and peace had been preceded by a bloody political reckoning, and it was not guaranteed to last. Indeed, when Virgil wrote *The Aeneid*, the Principate was only a handful of years old, and Augustus's health was poor: He was certainly not expected to live to seventy-five as he did (Griffin 60). The Augustan system was in fact at this point as much plan and hope as reality (Bell 20).

Thus, while *The Aeneid* undoubtedly celebrates the rise of the Roman Empire under Augustus, it simultaneously looks backward in sadness to the bloodshed that preceded it and forward in trepidation to an uncertain future, holding these seemingly irreconcilable perspectives in "a powerful and continuing tension of opposites" (Tarrant 180). It accomplishes this by narrating the heroic quest of Aeneas, who is a particularly suitable figure for Virgil's purposes: Augustus's adoptive family, the Julii, claimed descent from this legendary Trojan, and he thus provides a direct link between contemporary imperial reality and the heroic mythology of Homer's *The Iliad* and *The Odyssey*. He allows Virgil to offer up to his patron Augustus a laudatory epic that intertwines his personal achievements with Rome's mythological and historical past. Aeneas's story is also, however, that of a reluctant hero who unwillingly sets out on a quest shaped by powers beyond his control and of the price he and those around him are forced to pay to reach what may be an uncertain goal.

The story of this quest is quickly told. Aeneas, son of Anchises and the goddess Venus, survives the sack of Troy by the Greeks. Fleeing the city with his father and a group of followers, he is tasked by the gods with establishing a new city and kingdom. During his search for its destined location, he encounters a number of perils. The enraged goddess Juno drives Aeneas's ships off course, and while sheltering from the storm he falls in love with Dido, Queen of Carthage. Reminded by the gods of his destiny, however, he abandons her and journeys to the underworld to visit the shade of his father who has died during the journey and foretells Rome's majesty. Finally, Aeneas arrives on the banks of the Tiber in Italy, the destined home of the exiled Trojans. This part of the story is related in the first six Books of *The Aeneid* and is closely modeled on the *Odyssey*. The second half of the epic is modeled on *The Iliad*, and after Aeneas's peaceful settlement with the local Latins is disturbed by Juno, war breaks out. Terrible bloodshed ensues before Aeneas is able to fulfill his destiny by marrying the Latin princess Lavinia and establishing the line that will culminate in Rome's imperial destiny as embodied by Augustus. In outline this all seems clear and even predictable: The hero sets out on a journey, overcomes temptation and danger, arrives at his destination, fights to accomplish his goal, and ultimately triumphs. This conforms broadly to the structure of the heroic quest as outlined by Joseph Campbell, a process of "separation from the world, a penetration to some source of power, and a life-enhancing return" (35). But elements of Aeneas's quest are more ambivalent than might at first be apparent.

One such element is Aeneas's extreme reluctance to assume his heroic role. As soldiers slip out of the Trojan horse and open the doomed city's gates, he is visited in a dream by the ghost of Hector, the prince of Troy slain by Achilles, who warns Aeneas of the impending danger and gives him explicit instructions:

> 'Ai! Give up and go, child of the goddess,
> Save yourself, out of these flames. [. . .]
> [. . .] Her holy things, her gods
> Of hearth and household Troy commends to you.
> Accept them as companions of your days;
> Go find for them the great walls that one day
> You'll dedicate, when you have roamed the sea.
> (Virgil 2.387–97)

Having received this otherworldly command, Aeneas's course is clear: He must obey Hector, who speaks with the knowledge peculiar to the dead and with the authority of his position as the prince and hero of Troy. Aeneas's duty is to the future of Rome, not the past of Troy, and the outlines of his quest, if not the details, are clear. This is his moment to embrace his heroic destiny.

Yet Aeneas is reluctant to obey. Of course, this does not disqualify him from heroic stature; Campbell has pointed out that "the dull case of the call unanswered" can be a feature of the hero's quest (59). But something strange is going on here. Campbell argues that the refusal of the call to heroism is a refusal to give up one's own misguided perception of self-interest (60). Yet Aeneas is refusing his destiny not to protect himself, but to die in battle in direct contravention of Hector's commands and his heroic destiny. In part, Aeneas's insistence on fighting is a way to justify his eventual flight, which is not a transparently heroic action; his eagerness to fight in the face of certain death confers upon him the heroic stature that his actions might otherwise belie (Griffin 83). Yet his struggle against the attacking Greeks is only ambivalently heroic (Parry 44). He and his band of soldiers dress themselves as Greeks in order to surprise the enemy, a tactic that is explicitly acknowledged as being less than heroic—"Trickery, bravery: who asks, in war?"—and that in any case succeeds only in bringing them under attack by their fellow Trojans (Virgil 2.517). Aeneas then impotently witnesses the slaughter of the Trojan King Priam and his family, and he is only prevented from murdering the unprotected Helen "in fury past control" by the intervention of Venus (2.781–82). Even if one accepts as natural Aeneas's reluctance to fulfill his destiny through flight, assuming a disguise in battle only to end up fighting your own side is not particularly heroic nor is watching your king be slain or attempting to murder an unprotected woman.

Eventually, Aeneas leaves Troy, although only after repeated divine interventions: First Hector's ghost and then Venus urge him to flee, followed by the appearance of "a tongue of flame that touched but did not burn" above his son Iulus's head, a sign reaffirmed by a star "trailing flame" as it falls "through depths of night" (Virgil 2.893, 2.904). Campbell has argued that heroes who initially refuse their quest may be guided towards the right course by supernatural guardians, and this is precisely what happens to Aeneas (73–74). However, his reluctance is unusually pronounced; four separate supernatural signs are required to set him on his path, and his unwillingness does not end when he has fled Troy. When he takes refuge in Carthage and finds love in Queen Dido's arms, he is content to stay and revel "all winter long" until the gods remind him of his duty, rebuking him as a "tame husband" who has forgotten his duty (Virgil 4.264). Attempting to explain himself to Dido, Aeneas admits that his first wish is not to go onward to Italy, nor even to stay in Carthage with her, but to "look after Troy and the loved relics / Left me of my people [. . .]" (4.472–73). "I sail for Italy," Aeneas admits, "not of my own free will" (4.499). Although some critics see in the second half of *The Aeneid* a hero who has finally embraced his destiny, even after arriving in Italy Aeneas continues to exhibit an unheroic reluctance to pursue his inevitable course (Franke 80). War breaks out with the Latins, and Aeneas, "heartsick at the woe of war," is compared to "weary living things / of bird and beast kind" (Virgil 8.38, 8.36–37). This is hardly an image of heroic acceptance of destined greatness: Aeneas is a hero in spite of himself.

The ultimate manifestation of Aeneas's reluctance is his persistent death-wish. Of course, heroes are not afraid of death, and it may be understandable that for a warrior like Aeneas "death was beautiful in arms" (Virgil 2.426). However, Aeneas expresses with disturbing frequency not just a willingness, but a desire to die. In fact, his first words in the poem, spoken in the midst of a storm at sea, are a paean to death: "Triply lucky, all you men / To whom death came before your fathers' eyes / Below the walls of Troy! [. . .]" (1.134–36). The dead are paradoxically the lucky ones, while those who have survived to participate in the heroic quest, and particularly Aeneas himself, are to be pitied. This death-wish is a Homeric echo, as Odysseus too, when caught in a storm, claims that he would rather have died in battle at Troy than drown at sea. But it also distinguishes the heroism of Aeneas, who wishes to sacrifice himself for his father and city, from that of Odysseus, who longs for individual glory (King 152). In another Homeric allusion, Aeneas later travels to the underworld to visit his father's shade, just as Odysseus does in the *Odyssey*. However, it is instructive to note the difference between their attitudes. When Odysseus meets the shades of the dead, he must master "blanching terror" both at the beginning and end of the encounter (Homer, *Odyssey* 11.48, 11.725). Aeneas, on the other hand, plunges "boldly" into the cavern that leads to the underworld (Virgil 6.362). This demonstrates heroic bravery but also an unusual enthusiasm for death. Once in the underworld, Aeneas sees the souls of the unburied who are thus unable to cross the river Acheron aboard Charon's boat. The poem's description of this scene is astonishing:

> [. . .] as many souls
> As leaves that yield their hold on boughs and fall
> Through forests in the early frost of autumn,
> Or as migrating birds from the open sea
> That darken heaven when the cold season comes
> And drives them overseas to sunlit lands.
> There all stood begging to be first across
> And reached out longing hands to the far shore.
> (6.418–25)

Virgil offers images of both a resigned acceptance of early mortality and of a positive longing to cross the barrier between the chill of life and the warmth of death. As Harold Bloom points out, it is a tragic affair to stretch one's hands out and beg for what is, after all, merely death (7). All of this has lead Virgil to be frequently identified as a "poet of refined melancholy" (Tarrant 179). Thus while fearlessness in the face of death is a traditionally heroic virtue, Aeneas goes beyond mere absence of fear in ways that suggest a reluctance not just to undertake his quest, but to live. He is certainly not what Campbell describes as "the life-eager hero" (359). In the world of *The Aeneid*, death may be more attractive than life.

In a real sense, neither Aeneas's reluctance nor his death-wish matter: He possesses so little agency—the ability to decide and act on his own—that they can have no real impact on the outcome of his quest.

As we have seen, Aeneas flees Troy only after several divine messengers have told him what he must do. In fact, even then it is Aeneas's father who ultimately makes the decision to escape, and until his death, Anchises leads the Trojans. Having escaped the wrath of the Greeks, they build a fleet, and it is Anchises, not Aeneas, who gives "word / To hoist sail to the winds of destiny," and it is Anchises who misinterprets the prophecy of Apollo to indicate that they should settle on Crete (Virgil 3.12–13). To this point, Aeneas simply accompanies his father. On one level this demonstrates Aeneas's *pietas*, which many view as his defining trait (Condon 177). *Pietas* was a complex and highly-valued virtue in Roman culture, indicating an emotionally charged sense of duty that is directed towards both family—most specifically from sons to fathers—and country (Griffin 64; Garrison 11). While his father lives, Aeneas is duty-bound to respect, love, and obey him. But it is also an indication of Aeneas's lack of self-directed agency and his tendency to drift at the mercy of people and forces more powerful than himself.

The gods are the most important of these forces. The epic opens by explicitly attributing Aeneas's tribulations to the divine anger of Juno, who "galled / In her divine pride" and "sore at heart / From her old wound[,]" forces Aeneas "[t]o undergo so many perilous days / And enter on so many trials" (Virgil 1.13–18). Juno has not forgiven the Trojans for Paris's decision in favor of Venus in a divine beauty competition and thus drives Aeneas through the series of misadventures that make up his quest. She conspires with Aeolus, king of the winds, to drive Aeneas off course, arranges the storm that drives Aeneas and Dido into the cave that sees their dubious nuptials, and unleashes the fury Allecto, "grief's dear mistress with her lust for war" upon the Latins and the Trojans (7.445). This last and cruelest act of divine opposition is not even intended to stop Aeneas from fulfilling his destiny, for by this point Juno has recognized that she will not be able to "keep the man from rule in Italy" (7.428). Instead, with preternatural malignancy she simply wishes to "drag it out, to pile delay / Upon delay" while she destroys both Trojan and Latin (7.430–31). This is the act of a divine personification of the cosmic irrationality that largely shapes Aeneas's quest (Quint 291). His task is simply to suffer the anger of Juno, for as a mortal he cannot actively oppose it.

Juno's malignancy is counterbalanced by the favor of Venus, who champions Aeneas's cause. For instance, she covers her son in a "grey mist, a cloak / Of dense cloud [. . .] so that no one / Had the power to see or accost" him as he enters Carthage and Dido's palace, and then sends Desire to infatuate the Carthaginian queen, "inflaming her with lust to the marrow of her bones" (Virgil 1.564–66; 1.900–01). As Jasper Griffin has pointed out, however, Venus's aid is both coldly impersonal and ultimately ineffective (82). Aeneas's plaintive cry to his divine mother to "join hands and speak and hear / The simple truth" is ignored; instead, he is dragged into the fearful emotional quandary of his relationship with Dido, which ultimately leads him to the grotesque betrayal of denying his marriage, however plausibly, after attempting to sneak ignominiously away (Virgil 1.560–61). When he meets Dido's shade in the underworld, his tearful plea for forgiveness is rejected: she has become and will always remain "his enemy," and there is no avoiding the terrible Punic wars between Rome and Carthage, the "fire and sword" that are the legacy of Venus's divine succor (6.635; 4.870). When read in this way, it is difficult to see in Venus the "benevolent, protective female figure" some critics associate with her (Quartarone 179). She is less malignant than Juno, certainly, but not less dangerous or unpleasant, and certainly not less prone to directing Aeneas's course.

Ultimately the arbiter of Aeneas's fate is Jupiter, father of the gods and the source of authority in the Virgilian world. This is revealed early in the epic when Jupiter explains what will happen to both Aeneas and his descendants, an act of prophecy that reveals a future that is simultaneously the Roman past (Franke 76). *The Aeneid* displays the Trojan future as Roman history, from its foundation after the "massive war" chronicled in the second half of the poem, through centuries of warfare culminating in the Augustan age when "the Gates of War" will be finally shut (1.355; 1.394). Jupiter knows—and tells us—how Aeneas's quest will end even before it has properly begun. This prophecy is refined and elaborated on throughout Aeneas's journey. In fact, when he is not being stage-managed by the gods, Aeneas relies on oracles and soothsayers for indications of divine will to make what cannot really be called his decisions. This leaves little room, of course, for Juno or Venus to genuinely affect the outcome of Aeneas's quest, and if these mighty goddesses cannot hinder or help him, what chance does Aeneas himself have to affect his destiny? Thus his passive acceptance of his fate, his stoic resignation to the divinely mandated course of events, is perhaps understandable. As Susanna Morton Braund has pointed out, the autocratic universe of *The Aeneid* offers no room for free will, as humans are merely subjects of divine power (211). Aeneas's heroism takes the particular form of submission to his fate: he does not will his quest, accepts it only with great reluctance, and is guided through it as a passive object of divine will.

Aeneas requires all of his fortitude to face the horrors that lie at the end of his quest, horrors foreshadowed by the fates of two of his companions, Palinurus and Caieta. Aeneas's steersman Palinurus is overcome by sleep and plunges into the ocean. As Aeneas learns from his shade in the underworld, he does not drown but struggles to shore after three nights adrift. This is in fact a miniature version of Aeneas's own journey. His reception in Italy is also similar to the disaster that awaits Aeneas:

> By turns I swam and rested, swam again
> And got my footing on the beach, but savages
> Attacked me as I clutched at a cliff-top,
> Weighted down by my wet clothes. Poor fools,
> They took me for a prize and ran me through.
> (Virgil 6.483–87)

Palinurus reaches Italy only to be murdered as the result of a delusion: he is no rich prize, but an exhausted refugee whose death can benefit no one. The only compensation offered Palinurus for his hard fate is a form of cartographical memorial: his tomb will be built "on a cape forever named for Palinurus" (6.512). Some critics view this as a substantial and effective recompense (Henry 136). However, others have pointed out that it is only temporary: "The pain / Was for a while dispelled from his sad heart," but the poem leaves us in no doubt that the pain will return in spite of this reward (Feldherr 119; *The Aeneid* 6.513–14). "Caieta's port," named after Aeneas's nurse, is another potentially ineffective memorial (Virgil 6.1221).

> [. . .] in death you too
> Conferred your fame through ages on our coast,
> Still honored in your last bed, as you are,
> And if this glory matters in the end
> Your name tells of your grave in great Hesperia.
> (7.1–5)

At first, all may seem well here: this is a demonstration of *pietas* on Aeneas's part, and an indication of the consolations of posterity. But the narrator of the poem asks a question that is as pointed as it is telling. Palinurus's consolation is only temporary, but it is at least real, whereas here the very meaning of memorialization is questioned: its value is conditional upon an *if*. Thus seeds of doubt as to the efficacy of the future in remedying the ills of the present lie at the center of *The Aeneid*.

This doubt cannot help but color our reading of Aeneas's arrival in Italy, where he is greeted with the same misguided savagery as Palinurus. Latinus, King of Latium, welcomes Aeneas, but Juno's unleashing of the Fury Allecto derails the peaceful union between Trojan and Latin: first Latinus's wife is "enflamed / By prodigies of hell" into deranged opposition to the prophesied marriage of Aeneas and her daughter Lavinia, and then Turnus, king of the Rutulians, is "driven wild" with lust for war (Virgil 7.518–19; 7.633). The second half of *The Aeneid* narrates the ensuing conflict but displays a clear and pronounced aversion to war (Tarrant 179). At its cleanest, Aeneas's war is a series of bloody battles, ambushes, murders, and betrayals; at its worst it is the lovers Nisus and Euryalus, whose night sortie to recall Aeneas to the besieged Trojan camp turns into a grotesque slaughter of sleeping drunkards who "Belched out [. . .] crimson life, wine mixed with blood" (Virgil 9.495). This is certainly not heroic warfare. Nor is it even strategic: Euryalus and Nisus should not be killing sleeping men, but instead they should be summoning help. Ultimately, Euryalus is captured and killed by the Latins, and Nisus, refusing to abandon him, is also killed. Their story moves from the erotic to the heroic to the brutally violent and ultimately to the pointlessly futile (Ross 37). They kill and are killed gratuitously. This becomes particularly clear if we compare this episode with its Homeric model, the night sortie of Odysseus and Diomedes in *The Iliad*. While equally bloody, if less grotesquely so, the Homeric attack is at least based on "cunning tactics" as the Greek warriors attempt to gain information about their sleeping foes, kill while the killing is good, and then return safely laden with spoils and information to their camp (10.51). This is quite different to the sort of activity that characterizes Aeneas's war: meaningless bouts of intense violence linked to no rational plan that kills off young men like the Arcadian Pallas and the Etruscan Lausus, who though enemies are equally admirable, "Not much disparate in age, and both / Splendid in height and build [. . .]" (Virgil 10.599–600). Aeneas too suffers in the war. He is particularly horrified to have killed Lausus, but his "profound pity" cannot bring the young man back to life (10.1151). War is of course always terrible, and *The Aeneid*'s Homeric models certainly did not shy away from representing its horrors, but Virgil's focus on its irrational, grotesque, and senseless elements is striking. Aeneas's heroism lies here not in his victory, but in his mute endurance of the unavoidable catastrophes connected with it.

The culmination of this violence, and of *The Aeneid*, is the killing of Turnus. Significantly, this is the only important action Aeneas takes on his own authority. During single combat with Aeneas, Turnus is dismayed by one of the Dirae, terrible monsters controlled by Jupiter. "Unstrung by numbness, faint and strange," Turnus can offer but little resistance (Virgil 12.1174). Turnus's defeat is thus a clear product of divine will, and Aeneas has no more control over the outcome of this fight than he does over any of the other challenges he has faced during his quest. The problem here lies not in Aeneas's victory, although it should be recognized that there is nothing especially heroic in defeating an enemy who is already dazed and disoriented, but in what he does with it. As the wounded Turnus pleads for mercy, Aeneas notices that he is wearing Pallas's swordbelt as a trophy. Enraged by this reminder of his young companion's death, Aeneas "sank his blade in fury in Turnus's chest" (12.1295). Critics have noted that Turnus's death results from his own impious decision to wear the spoils he has stripped from the dead Pallas (Martino 432–33). Turnus, it is also pointed out, is far from being an admirable character, and his fate would have elicited no sympathy from a pagan Roman reader (Galinsky 324). It could also be argued that this is the moment when Aeneas's personal will coincides perfectly with the will of the gods; Aeneas achieves his heroic maturity by becoming what fate demands he be. Yet as many recent critics have argued, and indeed as was noted in antique Christian sources, there remains something terrible in Aeneas's furious execution of a man literally on his knees begging for his life (Galinsky 322). This is arguably slaughter, not battle, reminiscent of Aeneas's earlier vengeful desire to murder Helen of Troy. On that occasion, divine intervention saved him from his "fury / Past control" that would have held Helen responsible for the "harsh will of the gods" (Virgil 2.781–82, 2.792). Now, no divine hand interposes, and Aeneas commits an all-too-human murder in spite of the fact that Turnus is no more responsible for his actions than Helen was.

Aeneas's rule is thus established in Latium, albeit in a troubling fashion, and the path is clear for the realization of Rome's destiny. *The Aeneid* may end with Turnus's death, but we know that Aeneas's story will continue. However, this is where the prophetic fates of Palinurus and Caieta again become relevant. Aeneas himself, Jupiter has already proclaimed, will only live for three more years; his son Iulus will rule for thirty, his Trojan descendants for three hundred, and the Romans will rule "empire without end" (1.375). Aeneas himself, having killed Turnus in a fit of rage, bereft of his wife and father, his homeland, and his love Dido, anguished by the bloodshed he has caused, and married to a woman whose mother has strangled herself "in hideous death" rather than see her daughter wed him, will soon die (12.822). The longevity of his race, the eternal empire of Rome will, however, be his reward: for uncounted generations his people will remain a living monument. But we are already prepared by the fates of Palinurus and Caieta to doubt the significance of this memorial. Will Aeneas's relief be more than temporary, and does the glory of his people ultimately even matter? Will the result of his heroic quest be worth the price that it has demanded?

In fact, an even more radical doubt than the stories of Palinurus and Caieta might suggest is cast on Aeneas's accomplishment, as his memorial is taken from him at the moment of his victory. Juno, having done everything she can to hurt the Trojans, finally begs Jupiter for a last concession: "Never command the land's own Latin folk / To change their old name" (Virgil 12.1116–17). Jupiter lightly grants the request, thereby at a stroke extinguishing the Trojan people who will "mingle and be submerged, incorporated" into the polity and culture of the Latins (12.1134). Aeneas's monument on Italian soil, his Cape Palinurus or Port Caieta, will simply not exist: Rome is Romulus's city, not his. What Aeneas gets instead is the history of the Roman people. His quest is no more than a partial fulfillment of the Roman destiny revealed throughout the epic: the long story of Roman mythology and history from Aeneas's day to Augustus's is unfolded for the reader who knows exactly what is going to happen. For instance, the shield forged for Aeneas by the god Vulcan depicts in exhaustive detail "[. . .] the future story of Italy, / The triumphs of the Romans [. . .]," a clear parallel to the shield Vulcan forges for Achilles in *The Iliad* (Virgil 8.850–51). But Aeneas's shield, unlike Achilles's, does not depict a total cosmos: It represents nothing but war and violence (Griffin 93). Roman history as represented in *The Aeneid* springs from mythological war, develops through the wars of the Republic, and culminates in Augustus's victorious civil war to found the empire. Aeneas, "knowing nothing of the events themselves" is able to take "joy in the pictures," but this is a naive and childish pleasure (Virgil 8.989–90). The Roman future arguably holds no genuine reward for the horrors of Aeneas's quest, only further horrors for his descendants.

There is a further twist in this ambivalent epic that has seen Aeneas give up so much, unwillingly journey so far, and unintentionally commit so many crimes for so little reward. After the bloodshed depicted so vividly on Aeneas's shield, Roman history culminates in the triumph of Augustus and the end of the long years of violent chaos and civil war that accompanied the decline of the Republic. Jupiter prophecies that with his ascension "the Gates of War / Will then be shut [. . .]" (Virgil 1.394–95). Peace will be granted. In an epic that has consistently downplayed Aeneas's "personal glory" in favor of the "hero's fulfillment of his public destiny" this is the ultimate reward, and the genuine and valid conclusion to the hero's quest (Bell 14). But Virgil's epic hints at another possible ending: When Anchises shows Aeneas the souls of future Roman heroes, the display culminates with Marcellus, Augustus's son-in-law and intended successor, who will die tragically young. On a poetic level, Marcellus represents youthful promise; on a more prosaic level he represents the hope of a swift and stable succession after Augustus's death. For Aeneas, his death interrupts the line of prophetic succession, and the future becomes once more unknowable. For Virgil and his Roman readers, Marcellus's death in 23 BCE was a recent and shocking reminder of the potential instability of the new political dispensation. Thus the very certainty and stability with which Aeneas's heroism is to be rewarded, albeit only in the future, is questioned even as it is promised.

Aeneas is undoubtedly a hero, but he is very different from his Homeric predecessors, and perhaps also from some modern versions of the hero. He is reluctant to embark on and to continue his quest, and while this does not place him outside what is commonly defined as heroic, it is striking, and certainly inflects our understanding of his quest. At its most extreme, Aeneas's reluctance becomes a sort of death wish, a desire for an end to the suffering that is life. His heroism consists not in overcoming the fear of death, but in resisting its allure. Aeneas is also strangely inactive, guided and instructed throughout his quest by his father, seers and oracles, and the gods. He rarely makes a decision on his own, waiting instead for more of the "perpetual guidance" so "repugnant to romantic notions" upon which he depends (Syme 462). This is a key point in understanding Aeneas's heroism, for it is the heroism of "an instrument of heaven, a slave to duty" rather than the heroism of an active agent (Syme 462). His heroism, somewhat counterintuitively, lies in doing what he is told.

That this is compatible with genuine heroism is demonstrated by the price Aeneas is forced to pay so that Rome's imperial destiny, manifested in the figure of Augustus, can be realized. This is the second aspect of his heroism: his ability to suffer. Aeneas's quest is one of renunciation of personal desire—and some would even argue of personality—in the interests of something larger. He is a "sort of moral Hercules" whose labors are a series of suffered renunciations, of home, of family, of love (Quinn 81). Aeneas as an individual, with independent desires and longings and needs, is subsumed in a destiny that is not even really his, but the destiny of Augustan Rome (Parry 44). He is, in the words of one critic, "a man without hope, living from a sense of duty" (Dudley 59). Much of our interpretation of the poem as a whole, then, must rest on our interpretation of that to which Aeneas owes this duty and that for which he suffers "the pressures and cruelties" placed upon a man who embodies the nation and Rome's imperial destiny (Feeney 219).

Thus, on one level *The Aeneid* is a clear and explicit celebration of the Roman and Augustan achievement, a hymn to past republican glory and to future imperial greatness, a paean to peace and stability after long years of war and strife, an allegory of the establishment of a "new golden age" in Roman history by Augustus (King 133). But exactly this point is a key area of critical disagreement in the reception of Virgil's epic: Whether it is a conservative or subversive text is, in the words of John Martino, a "classic matter of personal interpretation" (436). What is clear is that Aeneas's heroic quest culminates in an achievement that is both indisputable—for who can deny the greatness of Rome?—and tendentious, for who can deny the loss of personal freedom, the cost in blood and sorrow of an empire? Aeneas pays a huge price to fulfill Rome's destiny, and this constitutes his heroism. The remaining question is whether the destiny is itself worth the price that has been paid. It may be going too far to argue, as some critics do, that "Aeneas's tragedy is that he cannot be a hero" (Parry 53). On the contrary, his heroism is his tragedy. It is reasonable, however, to ask if this heroism is directed towards a worthwhile end. The fates of Palinurus and Caieta cast some doubt on the validity of Rome's destiny as a compensation for Aeneas's suffering, and the death of Marcellus undercuts the certainty of the stability and peace that lie at the end of the Roman quest. These elements introduce a level of ambiguity that allows *The Aeneid* to be read as an ambivalent epic, and it is perhaps this simultaneous questioning and embracing of the heroic that makes the tale of Aeneas's heroism so fascinating and relevant more than two thousand years after Virgil's death.

Works Cited

Bell, Kimberly K. "*Translatio* and the Constructs of a Roman Nation in Virgil's *Aeneid.*" *Rocky Mountain Review* 62.1 (2008): 11–24.

Bloom, Harold. Introduction. *Modern Critical Views: Virgil.* Ed. Harold Bloom. New York: Chelsea House, 1986. 1–7.

Braund, Susanna Morton. "Virgil and the Cosmos: Religious and Philosophical Ideas." *The Cambridge Companion to Virgil.* Ed. Charles Martindale. Cambridge: Cambridge UP, 1997. 204–21.

Campbell, Joseph. *The Hero with a Thousand Faces.* Princeton, NJ: Princeton UP, 1968.

Condon, James P. "Notes on T. S. Eliot's 'What Is a Classic?': The Classical Norm and Social Existence." *The Classical Journal* 73.2 (1977): 176–78.

Dudley, D. R. "A Plea for Aeneas." *Greece & Rome* 8.1 (1961): 52–60.

Feeney, D. "The Taciturnity of Aeneas." *The Classical Quarterly* 33.1 (1983): 204–19.

Franke, William. "Virgil, History, and Prophecy." *Philosophy and Literature* 29.1 (2005): 73–88.

Galinsky, Karl. "The Anger of Aeneas." *The American Journal of Philology* 109.3 (1988): 321–48.

Garrison, James D. *Pietas from Vergil to Dryden.* University Park: Pennsylvania State UP, 1992.

Griffin, Jasper. *Virgil.* Oxford: Oxford UP, 1986.

Henry, Elisabeth. *The Vigour of Prophecy: A Study of Virgil's* Aeneid. Carbondale: Southern Illinois UP, 1989.

Homer. *The Iliad.* Trans. Robert Fagles. New York: Penguin, 1990.

———. *The Odyssey.* Trans. Robert Fagles. New York: Penguin, 1996.

Kennedy, Duncan F. "Modern Receptions and Their Interpretative Implications." *The Cambridge Companion to Virgil.* Cambridge: Cambridge UP, 1997. 38–55.

King, Katherine C. *Ancient Epic.* London: Blackwell. 2009.

Martino, John. "Single Combat and the *Aeneid.*" *Arethusa* 41.3 (2008): 411–44.

Parry, Adam. "The Two Voices of Virgil's *The Aeneid.*" *Modern Critical Views: Virgil.* Ed. Harold Bloom. New York. Chelsea House, 1986. 41–53.

Quartarone, Lorina. "Teaching Vergil's *Aeneid* through Ecofeminism." *The Classical World* 99.2 (2006): 177–82.

Quinn, Kenneth. "Did Virgil Fail?" *Modern Critical Views: Virgil.* Ed. Harold Bloom. New York: Chelsea House, 1986. 73–83.

Quint, David. "Virgil's Double Cross: Chiasmus and the *Aeneid.*" *American Journal of Philology* 132.2 (2011): 273–300.

Ross, David O. *Virgil's The Aeneid: A Reader's Guide.* Malden, MA: Blackwell, 2007.

Syme, Ronald. *The Roman Revolution.* Oxford: Oxford UP, 2002.

Tarrant, R. J. "Poetry and Power: Virgil's Poetry in Contemporary Context." *The Cambridge Companion to Virgil.* Cambridge: Cambridge UP, 1997. 169–87.

Thomas, Richard F. *Virgil and the Augustan Reception.* Cambridge: Cambridge UP, 2001.

Virgil. *The Aeneid.* Trans. Robert Fitzgerald. London: Everyman's Library, 1992.

The Hero's Quest in *Beowulf*_____

James B. Kelley

Beowulf presents itself as a rewarding but not particularly easy text for the modern reader, who usually encounters it in a present-day English translation rather than in Old English. Part of the challenge for the modern reader comes from the work's having been written over a thousand years ago in an early, very different form of English. Reading the poem as a manifestation of a timeless and universal hero's quest may make the poem more accessible to many of us, but we should take care at the same time to appreciate the specific elements of the poem that make it both a unique literary work and a representative of early medieval literature in English.

Beowulf follows Old English poetic conventions that often seem strange to us at first. For one, it is written in alliterative verse. Each line of the poem has four stressed syllables, two in the first half of the line (the a-verse) and two in the second half (the b-verse), and a twice-used consonant in the a-verse usually repeats once in the b-verse of the same line. The poem is also full of kennings, compound nouns that describe the subject metaphorically rather than literally. When first introduced to the title character in the 1910 translation by Francis B. Gummere, for example, we read about how after learning of the predations of a human-eating monster named Grendel in the nearby kingdom of Hrothgar, Beowulf immediately resolves to travel there from Hygelac's kingdom by boat and to provide assistance:

> This heard in his home Hygelac's thane,
> great among Geats, of Grendel's doings.
> . . .
> stalwart and stately. A stout wave-walker
> he bade make ready. . . .
> (lines 194–95, 198–99)

These lines marking the hero's entrance in the story show both the poem's alliterative structure (in the repeated "h" sound in *heard, home, Hygelac's* and the repeated "g" sound in *great, Geats,* and *Grendel's*) and the poem's use of kennings. Beowulf is not introduced by name here. In fact, he is not named until line 343 when he presents himself to Wulfgar in order to seek audience with the troubled King Hrothgar. Rather, in the reader's first glimpse of the hero, he is identified only as "Hygelac's thane" (one of King Hygelac's respected underlings or warriors), as "great among Geats," and as "stalwart and stately." Similarly, the boat that he has prepared for the trip is not simply called a "boat" or "ship" or "vessel" but rather is described poetically as a "stout wave-walker."

A related difficulty of the poem is that, from its opening lines, *Beowulf* often assumes that we, as its audience, possess knowledge of a number of important social ranks and practices, such as the meaning of terms like *thane* or *man-price* (*wergild*, which is the monetary compensation that is paid to atone for a wrongful death in order to avoid a lasting blood feud), as well as familiarity with allusions to long past events, groups, and individuals (whether historical or fictional). Information of this sort is often presented in the poem's so-called "digressions," in which the poem's speaker seems to stray far from the topic of Beowulf's heroic battles with various monsters. Many modern editions of the poem—including the one by Gummere—make extensive use of footnotes to define the poem's more challenging terms and to explain, in various ways, the possible relevance of some or all of the digressions to the main storyline.

Critics who have studied the poem in depth do not always agree on what to call it. *Beowulf* is most commonly labeled an epic poem (due to the highly formal or lofty style and the depiction of the cultural values of the ruling class of an ancient Germanic culture) or a historical poem (due to the incorporation of many real-world events into the narrative). However, in his highly influential essay "*Beowulf*: The Monster and the Critics" (1936), J. R. R. Tolkien argues that the work should be called an elegy:

> *Beowulf* is not an "epic," not even a magnified "lay." No terms borrowed from Greek or other literatures exactly fit: there is no reason why they should. Though if we must have a term, we should choose rather "elegy." It is an heroic-elegiac poem; and in a sense all of its first 3,136 lines are the prelude to a dirge: *him Þa gegiredan Geata leoda ad ofer eorðan un-waclicne* ["then fashioned for him the folk of Geats / firm on the earth a funeral-pile"]: one of the most moving ever written. (34)

More recently, Stanley B. Greenfield reads *Beowulf* as epic tragedy in his book *Hero and Exile*, and Natalia Breizmann argues that it can be read as a quest romance:

> If epic can be described as a narrative of society, then romance is a narrative of the individual. The plot of *Beowulf* presents a fictive history of a nation and is in this sense "epic." However, the plot also resembles an archetypal quest story, of the sort that reaches its apogee [i.e., its highest point or peak] in the courtly literature of the High Middle Ages—a story with elements of fantasy. The motif of adventure in which the protagonist fights monsters as well as human opponents and performs other deeds of valor is widespread in medieval romance. (1022–23)

Beowulf can thus be read and appreciated in any number of ways, and reading it as a retelling of the hero's quest can help make the story more understandable to the modern reader.

The story of *Beowulf* certainly follows the archetype of the hero's quest in a number of ways. This archetype has perhaps been most famously articulated in Joseph Campbell's highly influential work, *The Hero with a Thousand Faces*, which argues that myths and other fantastic tales from around the word tell a single story over and over, a story that follows a hero through the three stages of departure, initiation,

---

and return. In a statement summarizing what he calls the "monomyth," Campbell writes: "A hero ventures forth from the world of common day into a region of supernatural wonder: fabulous forces are there encountered and a decisive victory won: the hero comes back from this mysterious adventure with the power to bestow boons on his fellow man" (23). Although the title character is the one who most clearly undertakes the hero's quest in *Beowulf*, the search for self-transformation is not an exclusively male endeavor even in the male-dominated world of this ancient story. Citing the work of a number of influential scholars who have examined the roles of women in *Beowulf* and other works in Anglo-Saxon literature (including critics such as Jane Chance, Shari Horner, Stacy Klein, and Gillian Overing, for example), Semira Taheri has recently traced the various quests for individuality that are undertaken by four easily overlooked female characters in the story: Thryth (or Modthryth), Hygd, Wealhtheow, and Grendel's unnamed mother.

Viewed in terms of the hero's quest, Beowulf himself undertakes a literal journey: He sails from the kingdom of Hygelac and the Geats in present-day Sweden to the friendly kingdom of Hrothgar and the Danes (or Scyldings) in present-day Denmark, and he returns home once he has saved that neighboring kingdom from ruin. Similarly, Beowulf encounters Campbell's "fabulous forces" and exhibits his heroism three times in the course of the main story: he stays overnight in the grand mead hall of Heorot and mortally wounds Grendel in unarmed combat; he then ventures into an underwater lair to confront and defeat Grendel's mother, who has killed a Dane to avenge the death of her son; and finally, some fifty years later, he tracks down and kills a dragon that has been attacking his own kingdom. Beowulf also pursues one or more objects or objectives of great importance. Grendel's severed body parts (an arm and the head) and the dragon's hoard may be seen as the literal objects that he seeks, but the greater objective is more abstract: the restoration of peace first in Hrothgar's kingdom and then the restoration of peace in his own kingdom.

Indeed, Beowulf may be said to pursue one, two, or three quests in this one work, depending on how one divides up the story. In an early and influential essay, W. P. Ker identifies what he sees as a flaw in the structure of *Beowulf*: "A third of the whole poem is detached, a separate adventure. The first two-thirds taken by themselves form a complete poem, with a single action" (28). Ker uses the term *sequel* twice to distinguish the final third of the poem, which details Beowulf's battle with the dragon, from the first two-thirds of the poem, which Ker finds to be structurally superior (27, 28). Another important early critic, Friedrich Klaeber, similarly sees a flaw in the work's inclusion of the final section on an aged Beowulf-as-king and the battle with the dragon: "The poem of *Beowulf* consists of two distinct parts joined in a very loose manner and held together only by the person of the hero." The third section, Klaeber writes, "only serves as a supplement to the preceding major plot" (l ii).

As Jane Chance has more recently noted, the opposing view of *Beowulf* as a unified work that presents three interrelated trials of the title character—the battle with Grendel, the battle with Grendel's mother, and the battle with the dragon—has become "increasingly popular" among critics of the poem (258). Chance establishes a number of significant connections among the three sections of *Beowulf*. For example, she observes that all three monsters—Grendel, Grendel's mother, and the dragon—are described in terms at once human and monstrous and that they are humanized in part through their connection to treasures and to that central human dwelling and symbol of early Germanic civilization, the great hall (249). A review of Gummere's translation certainly supports this claim: Grendel terrorizes the gilded hall of Heorot for twelve years; Grendel's mother lives in "some hall" furnished with ancient treasures below the waters of the "mere," or swamp (line 1518); and the dragon's lair and hoard of gold in the third section are described through a series of kennings built around the word "hall," including "cavern-hall," "that hall in earth," "the ring-board hall," "earth-hall," "treasure-hall," and "that hall within" (lines 2419, 2728, 2849, 3056, 3063, and 3069).

Important developments in the poem, as well as the overall structure of the hero's quest in *Beowulf*, can be brought into focus through the application of archetypal criticism, whether the specific approach is grounded in the work of Campbell or in the theories of C. G. Jung, on which Campbell's ideas are partly based. Campbell makes no direct references to *Beowulf* in two of his immensely popular works presenting what he calls the monomyth, for example, but the multiple stages of the hero's journey that he has outlined can often be discerned for each of the three quests in the poem. The poem contains clear examples of the initial stage of the Call to Adventure. For example, troubadours' "sorrowful songs" bring news of Hrothgar's suffering to the court of Hygelac and the ears of Beowulf in the first section (line 151), Hrothgar tells Beowulf that he must seek out and kill Grendel's mother in the second section ("Now is help once more / with thee alone!" lines 1380–81), and the dragon announces itself as a threat to Beowulf in the third section by burning down the king's buildings:

> To Beowulf then the bale [i.e., evil] was told
> quickly and truly: the king's own home,
> of buildings the best, in brand-waves melted,
> that gift-throne of Geats. . . .
> (lines 2333–36)

Similarly, there are several clear instances of Crossing of the First Threshold, a stage signaling the hero's initial movement from the safe, everyday world into a realm of unknown dangers and new possibilities. In the first section, when he first arrives in Hrothgar's kingdom, Beowulf must answer the questions of the guard watching the coast, just as he must restate the purpose of his arrival again to gain entrance to Heorot. Similarly, in the third section, Beowulf's safe, everyday world is disrupted by the enraged dragon, and with his band of eleven men, he is led by a slave to the monster's den. The most compelling instance of Crossing of the First Threshold in *Beowulf* is the hero's dive and slow descent into the waters of the mere in the second section, and this section also contains the most compelling instance of the stage of the Belly of the Whale. In *The Hero with a Thousand Faces*, Campbell defines this stage as being marked by an apparent or symbolic death: "The hero, instead of conquering or conciliating the power of the threshold, is swallowed into the unknown, and would appear to have died" (74). Indeed, when the Danes and Geats who accompanied Beowulf to the mere and await his return see the waters turn red and boil with the blood of Grendel's mother, they believe that he, not his foe, has died in the battle.

Other stages of Campbell's journey of the hero are not so clearly present in the poem. Beowulf experiences neither the Refusal of the Call nor the Refusal of the Return, and he does not receive external aid in two of the three battles. In fighting Grendel and Grendel's mother, there seems to be no Rescue from Without; only in the third battle does Beowulf need and receive assistance from the brave young warrior Wiglaf, and even with that assistance, although the dragon is killed, Beowulf is mortally wounded in the battle.

Campbell's model of the monomyth has received criticism for reputedly failing to respect local differences and culturally determined meaning in specific literary works and pieces of oral traditions. Regardless of when and where the stories originate, everything is read the same way by Campbell, these critics argue. In *Theorizing about Myth*, for example, Robert A. Segal offers an extended, enumerated critique of Campbell's widely popular approach to myth. "Campbell is lopsidedly universalistic . . . in his search for similarities Campbell brazenly ignores lingering differences. Though he continually professes interest in differences as well as similarities, he finally dismisses all differences as trivial" (140). Segal goes on to contrast Campbell's "universalism" to Jung's approach to mythology:

To interpret a myth, Campbell simply identifies the archetypes in it. . . . Jung, by contrast, considers the identification of archetypes merely the first step in the interpretation of a myth. One must also determine the meaning of those archetypes in the specific myth in which they appear and the meaning of that myth in the life of the specific person who is stirred by it. One must analyze the person, not just the myth. (140)

Readings that explore Jungian archetypes in *Beowulf* often explore the idea that Grendel is Beowulf's "shadow self," the dark and destructive side of the title character's heroism. Such a reading can help explain, for example, the characterization of Scyld the Scefing in the poem's Prelude, who is held up as a "good king" by the speaker even as he resembles Grendel in his wanton destruction of mead halls in his enemies' kingdoms. Similarly, the poem's frequent references to blood-feuds and kin-slaying make clear that the poem may be read as being as much about internal dangers (whether within a social group or within the psyche of an individual person) as it is about external threats (represented by hostile neighboring kingdoms and by the three monsters that lash out at civilization from their remote lairs).

One of the most sustained Jungian analyses of *Beowulf* is presented in Judy Anne White's book *Hero-ego in Search of Self: A Jungian Reading of* Beowulf. This analysis is useful both for its commentary on specific details in the poem and for its interpretation of the work as a whole. For example, White sees the mere as symbolizing the unconscious in both its depths and its terrifying unknowability, and she notes that Beowulf must face his second foe not "in the familiar environment of the hall," with his men present, but rather on his own and in the deep waters of the mere (55). White sees the full set of conflicts between the hero and monsters in *Beowulf* as illustrating the Jungian concept of individuation, the process of individual psychological development. The conflict is a mental one within the hero and the unconscious; it is merely symbolized by an outer, physical conflict. In particular, White reads the victory over Grendel's mother as a transformative moment in this process of individuation:

> [Beowulf] now seems to have a new sense of purpose and a new ordering of priorities. He seems to be comfortable in his relationship with Hrothgar and the comitatus itself; he no longer seems to be fighting for himself, with thoughts of the Danes lurking somewhere in the back of his mind. This is the Beowulf who will become a wise and trusted king. (72)

Strictly, a Jungian approach would make this transformation inward rather than outward, though the transformation would be symbolically expressed outwardly.

What White sees as the significance of the second section is supported by scholars who are not specifically Jungian in their approach to the poem. For example, in *Beowulf: The Poem and Its Tradition*, Niles similarly identifies Beowulf's battle with Grendel's mother as the "structural center of the epic" and notes that at this point in the poem "the young hero has his closest brush with death" (159). From a Jungian point of view, the battle would be between ordinary ego consciousness and the archetype of the Great Mother, which really stands for the unconscious as a whole.

Whether or not Beowulf fully experiences all three stages of the hero's quest—in particular, whether he returns to his normal world after having experienced an all-important self-transformation and from that time onward lives as a more complete and integrated person than before—is a complicated and necessary question. *Beowulf* is marked by extreme detail to physical objects, including weapons, armor, jewelry, and drinking vessels. George Clark has presented a rich discussion of the meaning of the various treasures in *Beowulf*, and John D. Niles similarly observes in the "Afterword" to the 2008 illustrated edition of Seamus Heaney's verse translation that the poem "revels in hard, shining objects" ("Afterword" 244). At the same time, however, the work may not always provide enough detail about the inner world of

Beowulf or of the other characters to allow the reader to determine easily whether or not the title character experiences a meaningful and lasting transformation and, upon returning to his everyday world, is able (in Campbell's words) to "bestow boons on his fellow man."

Readers who believe that Beowulf is indeed transformed, whether internally or externally, are likely to focus on the middle section of the story: the battle with Grendel's mother. As a young man, the title character comes to Hrothgar's aid perhaps more out of a personal desire for fame and reward than out of need to fulfill an inherited obligation to a neighboring king. He boasts to everyone gathered in Heorot of his past accomplishments; he uses one of these accomplishments (the swimming contest with Breca) to mock Unferth and perhaps even overstates all of his past accomplishments much as he distorts the truth about how the announcement of his plan to confront Grendel was received in Hygelac's kingdom. Beowulf asserts in Hrothgar's hall that his own people, fully confident in his ability to overcome all obstacles, encouraged him without reservation to make the journey and to confront the monster:

> So my vassals advised me well,
> brave and wise, the best of men,
> O sovran Hrothgar, to seek thee here,
> for my nerve and my might they knew full well.
> Themselves had seen me from slaughter come
> blood-flecked from foes, . . . (lines 416–21)

However, once Beowulf has returned home to Geatland, we learn from Hygelac firsthand that the king had serious reservations about allowing Beowulf to make the journey in the first place. Hygelac says to Beowulf:

> . . . With waves of care
> my sad heart seethed; I sore mistrusted
> my loved one's venture: long I begged thee

---

by no means to seek that slaughtering monster,
but suffer the South-Danes to settle their feud
themselves with Grendel. . . . (lines 2001–06)

The returned Beowulf seems very different, too. In recounting his experiences to Hygelac, for example, he does not begin by boasting of his heroic battles with Grendel and Grendel's mother but rather talks first about court politics, as might a politician rather than an adventure-seeking youth. Gummere explains in a footnote: "Beowulf gives his uncle the king not mere gossip of his journey, but a statesmanlike forecast of the outcome of certain policies at the Danish court" (xxviii, n1).

The key to this transformation may be the exchange between Beowulf and Hrothgar in the middle section of the poem. When Beowulf returns to Hrothgar's court after defeating Grendel's mother alone in her underwater hall, he listens to Hrothgar's speech (or "sermon," as it is often called by critics of the poem). Hrothgar explains that after fifty years of rule, he had grown so confident in his own authority and power that he had come to believe no one could challenge him, a belief that made Grendel's unstoppable attacks all the more distressing:

. . . till it seemed for me
no foe could be found under fold of the sky.
Lo, sudden the shift! To me seated secure
came grief for joy when Grendel began
to harry my home, the hellish foe
(lines 1,780–84)

Hrothgar recounts the painful lessons of his own overconfidence, warns Beowulf that a warrior's physical strength does not last forever, and urges him to reflect on how he might change his life for the better: "temper thy pride" (line 1,768).

Beowulf's seemingly newfound ability to temper his potentially dangerous character trait of *oferhygd* (arrogance, pride, or reckless self-indulgence) may be seen in his changed treatment of Unferth. Newly arrived in Heorot, Beowulf had mocked Unferth as a drunkard and kin-slayer, but after hearing the words of wisdom from Hrothgar, Beowulf treats Unferth with great respect. Here he shows gratitude to Unferth for having lent him the sword Hrunting, and he does not mention how the sword proved useless in the fight with Grendel's mother. In offering thanks rather than throwing insults, Beowulf earns a positive comment from the speaker of the poem:

> Bade then the hardy-one [Beowulf] Hrunting be brought
> to the son of Ecglaf [Unferth], the sword bade him take,
> excellent iron, and uttered his thanks for it,
> quoth that he counted it keen in battle,
> "war-friend" winsome: with words he slandered not
> edge of the blade: 'twas a big-hearted man!
> (lines 1,816–21)

With this maturation, Beowulf now seems prepared to govern his own kingdom well. He acts to defend his charges and, ultimately, as an aging king, he willingly sacrifices his own life for the good of his kingdom.

By contrast, readers who believe that Beowulf fails to experience a meaningful and lasting self-transformation (from being driven by narcissism to being guided by altruism) are likely to focus on the battle with the dragon in the final third of the poem. Such readers may view this battle with the dragon as a sign of Beowulf's failure to mature in his understanding of his changing position in the world and his changing responsibilities to his people; at this point in the poem he is no longer a young warrior seeking fame and reward for himself but rather a old king who has ruled for fifty years, a period of rule lasting just as long as that of Hrothgar when Grendel's attacks began.

In this third section, the speaker in the poem reports Beowulf's views on the impending battle with the dragon. Beowulf believes that it would be less than honorable behavior on his part—it would be a "shame" (line 2,354)—for him to send an army rather than for him to go alone to hunt down the dragon, and as he prepares for the battle he reflects on many of the same heroic achievements of his youth about which he had boasted when, as a much younger man, he first entered Hrothgar's hall. Before the battle with the dragon in this third section, he vows to "once again . . . do doughty [i.e., fearless, valiant] deeds" (lines 2,521; 2,523) and even wishes that he could fight the dragon in unarmed combat, as he had defeated Grendel many years ago (lines 2,527–33). In this section of the poem, Beowulf is called twice the "folk-defender" (lines 2,522; 2,653), and the dragon is his opposite, the "folk-destroyer" (line 2,698), but the distinction between defender and destroyer becomes blurred as the king puts himself unnecessarily in mortal danger. With no heir in place to inherit the throne, Beowulf's death leaves the kingdom vulnerable to attack by several powerful and hostile neighbors.

John Leyerle's essay "Beowulf the Hero and the King" stands out as an early, important work supporting this view of Beowulf's failed or incomplete self-transformation. Beowulf is found by Leyerle and others to be guilty of *oferhygd*, but the fault may lie not with Beowulf himself but rather with the larger cultural expectations of how a king should behave. Leyerle identifies what he sees as "a fatal contradiction at the core of heroic society": the heroic king must expose himself to danger in order to demonstrate his worthiness to rule even as he must be cautious in order to protect his people and himself from harm (89).

Retellings of *Beowulf* in popular culture sometimes move away from the story of the hero's outward quest and possible inner transformation toward a collapsing of conventional distinctions between the heroic and the monstrous. These retellings often present versions more sympathetic to Grendel. In at least two recent film adaptations, for example, Hrothgar emerges as the instigator of Grendel's predations. In

Beowulf & Grendel (2005), it is Hrothgar who kills Grendel's father and thus begins the feud; in *Beowulf* (Zemeckis, 2007), Hrothgar is himself Grendel's father. William F. Hodapp examines the question of Grendel's paternity in recent film adaptations, and María José Gómez-Calderón examines the transformations of the Beowulf story in other new media.

"Critics have disagreed . . . about Beowulf's 'perfection,'" Greenfield writes in his concise summary of this lack of consensus among critics as to whether or not Beowulf has experienced a meaningful and lasting self-transformation:

> A few have seen the young warrior as brash, maturing only after he has killed Grendel's mother. Many more have seen Beowulf as 'flawed' in his eagerness for treasure, overreliance on his own strength, and impudence in fighting the dragon; they see him thus exemplifying the degeneration and sinful pride which Hrothgar had warned him against in his sermon after his conquest of Grendel's mother. (Greenfield, Calder 140)

Natalia Breizmann makes the insightful argument that Beowulf's decision to battle the dragon singlehandedly contains both motivations, the selfless and the selfish: "The fundamental discrepancy between Beowulf's loyalty to his people and the demands of his ambition is finalized in the very last line of the poem, which describes him as both most kind and most eager for fame." The final line to which she refers, in the Gummere translation, ends the poem by praising Beowulf above all others and by using two superlatives, "kindest" and "keenest": Beowulf was "to his kin the kindest, keenest for praise" (line 3,192). This complex or conflicted characterization of Beowulf, Breizmann explains, places the burden of interpretation on the reader of the poem. The final line of *Beowulf* "juxtaposes the mortal sin—vainglory—and the highest virtue—charity—and leaves the task of resolving this dilemma to the audience. With the end of Beowulf's adventure the quest of the reader begins—the quest for reading and understanding the poem's ideological message" (1,033).

A second challenge facing the reader may be to appreciate *Beowulf* both for its overarching, often already somewhat familiar hero's quest structure and for its strangeness and complexity. In his essay, "Myth and History," John D. Niles argues that "[a]ny approach to *Beowulf* that reduces a long, involuted narrative action into a single pattern of initiation . . . is missing too much." Niles believes that a full approach to the poem must take into account the large number of lines devoted to subjects such as blood feuds and *wergild,* gift-giving and leader-thane loyalty, or to the alliance-building practices of exogamy and fosterage (224). If *Beowulf* is read solely as a straightforward quest narrative and is not appreciated also for its depictions of the cultural values and practices of an ancient Germanic people at a time when those practices were about to vanish or had already vanished, the Old English poem risks becoming nearly indistinguishable from contemporary blockbuster films such as *Star Wars* and *The Matrix* or enduring fairy tales such as "Little Red Riding Hood" and "Hansel and Gretel." These stories, and many others, indeed have much in common, but they can be appreciated—by a reader who rises to the challenge—for both their commonalities and their distinctive elements.

Works Cited

Beowulf. Dir. Robert Zemeckis. Perf. Robin Wright, Anthony Hopkins, and Angelina Jolie. Paramount, 2007. Film.

Beowulf. Trans. Francis B. Gummere. New York: Collier, 1910. "Harvard Classics." *Medieval Sourcebook: Beowulf, 8th Century.* Web. 15 Dec. 2011.

Beowulf & Grendel. Dir. Sturla Gunnarsson. Perf. Gerard Butler, Ingvar Eggert Sigurðsson, and Stellan Skarsgård. Movision, 2005. Film.

Breizmann, Natalia. " 'Beowulf' as Romance: Literary Interpretation as Quest." *MLN: Modern Language Notes* 113.5 (Dec. 1998): 1022–35.

Campbell, Joseph. *The Hero with a Thousand Faces.* Novato, California: New World Library, 2008.

Campbell, Joseph, with Bill Moyers. Ed. Betty Sue Flowers. *The Power of Myth.* New York: Anchor, 1991.

Chance, Jane. "The Structural Unity in Beowulf: The Problem of Grendel's Mother." *New Readings on Women in Old English Literature*. Ed. Helen Damico and Alexandra Hennessey Olsen. Bloomington: Indiana UP, 1990. 248–61.

Clark, George. "Beowulf's Armor." *English Literary History* 32.4 (Dec. 1965): 409–41.

Gómez-Calderón, María José. " 'My Name Is Beowulf': An Anglo-Saxon Hero on the Internet." *Journal of Popular Culture* 43.5 (Oct. 2010): 988–1003.

Greenfield, Stanley B. *Hero and Exile: The Art of Old English Poetry*. Ed. George H. Brown. London: Hambledon, 1989.

Greenfield, Stanley B., and Daniel Gillmore Calder with Michael Lapidge. *A New Critical History of Old English Literature*. New York: New York University Press, 1986.

Hodapp, William F. " 'no hie fæder cunnon': But Twenty-First Century Film Makers Do." *Essays in Medieval Studies* 26 (2010): 101–08.

Ker, W. P. "Beowulf." *Bloom's Literary Themes: The Hero's Journey*. Ed. Harold Bloom and Blake Hobby. New York: Infobase, 2009. 25–38.

Klaeber, Friedrich. *Beowulf and the Fight at Finnsburg*. Boston: Heath, 1922.

Leyerle, John. "Beowulf the Hero and the King." *Medium Ævum* 34 (1965): 89–102.

Niles, John D. "Afterword: Visualizing Beowulf." *Beowulf: An Illustrated Edition*. Trans. Seamus Heaney. New York: Norton, 2008.

_____. *Beowulf: The Poem and Its Tradition*. Cambridge: Harvard UP, 1983.

_____. "Myth and History." *A Beowulf Handbook*. Ed. Robert E. Bjork and John D. Niles. Lincoln: U of Nebraska P, 1997. 213–32.

Segal, Robert A. "The Romantic Appeal of Joseph Campbell." *Theorizing about Myth*. Amherst: U of Massachusetts P, 1999. 135–41.

Taheri, Semira. "Feminine Quest for Individuality in *Beowulf* and Kate Chopin's *The Awakening*." *Journal of South Texas English Studies* 2.2 (Spring 2011). 10 May, 2011. Web. 15 Dec. 2011.

Tolkien, J. R. R. "*Beowulf*: The Monster and the Critics (1936)." *Interpretations of Beowulf: A Critical Anthology*. Ed. R. D. Fulk. Bloomington: Indiana UP, 1991. 14–44.

White, Judy Anne. *Hero-ego in Search of Self: A Jungian Reading of Beowulf*. New York: Peter Lang, 2004.

The Chivalric Quest: *Sir Gawain and the Green Knight*

Anthony Adams

The chivalric quest is arguably the literary genre best associated with medieval literature, containing elements of feudal society, knightly combat, courtly love, noble sacrifice, and religious introspection. The word *chivalry* entered Middle English in the fourteenth century as a borrowing of the Old French word *chevalerie*, which referred to knighthood or cavalry, and literally meant soldiers who rode on the back of a horse (Fr. *cheval*). The tales and songs that were told about brave cavaliers and their deeds became popular first in France, and these tales in time made their way to England. It is somewhat ironic that many of the characters and settings most associated with French chivalric literature were British in origin. Although romances were written concerning early French heroes such as Charlemagne and Roland and heroes of antiquity such as Alexander the Great, the most popular and lasting form proved to be those associated with the "Matter of Britain," or the world of King Arthur and the Round Table. These Arthurian romances came in the Middle Ages, and in endless variations down to the present day, to be the tales most closely associated with the world of knightly heroism, and Arthur, Lancelot, Guinevere, Camelot, and the Holy Grail have become forever linked with the chivalric quest. Although the genre came late to England, it quickly became as popular there as on the continent, spurring numerous imitations of French precursors as well as some truly original works. *Sir Gawain and the Green Knight,* while neither the first nor the last Arthurian romance of medieval England, is undoubtedly its most polished, accomplished, and courtly emanation. The poem, comprising (in modern editions) four distinct parts (or "fitts") in 2,531 lines, contains all of the expected elements of the chivalric quest narrative—the grave challenge and intrepid response, the journey into the unknown and toward self-discovery, the pleasure of amorous pursuits, the combination of martial prowess and religious faith—while also calling into question many conventions and ideals of the romance tradition. It is also an unsurpassed glimpse of attitudes toward late-fourteenth-century English court culture as well as being a literary reflection of it.

The appeal of the chivalric hero rose from the fusion of earlier traditions with newer ones that blended the virtues of a simpler age with the best of the contemporary world and evinced significant nostalgia for a time when the world was young and pure. The earliest traditions included, on the one hand, the distinctly martial or heroic element that could be found in Anglo-Saxon poetry such as *Beowulf* and *The Wanderer*, and in Celtic literature such as the Old Irish *Táin Bó Cúailnge*, as well as in Old Norse poetry and saga; and, on the other hand, they included a powerful Christian ethos that invoked virtues such as self-sacrifice, chastity, and pity, all in some way diametrically opposed to the heroic code. The third strand was also the newest, and it celebrated the secular virtues of ennobling love, such as that between a knight and the beautiful lady to whom he has dedicated himself and his service, the yearning at the heart of the courtly love tradition. It was the commingling of these three powerful strands of human feeling that gave rise to the medieval romance (Keen 116). It was this last strand that provides chivalric romance with its peculiarly passive quality compared to earlier heroic material, such as the French *chansons de geste* ("songs of action"), which are roughly contemporaneous with Chrétien's romances, but which have an entirely different and more warlike flavor. Despite the apparent masculine appeal of tales of knightly combat and daring, the appeal of medieval romance had as much to do with the central role they gave to women, both as amorous objects of worship and as actors (and villains) themselves. The notion of *amour courtois* or "courtly love" that arose among the troubadours and trouvères in twelfth-century France was manipulated and enhanced by the later romance tradition, first by French writers such as Chrétien de Troyes, the acknowledged early master of chivalric romance, by German poets such as Wolfram von Eschenbach and Gottfried von Strassburg, and finally in England, in a tradition that in the Middle Ages would reach its terminus with Sir Thomas Malory, but which would continue, in England as in all the western world, to be revived and revisited down to the present day.

The hero of the chivalric quest has a great deal in common with the protagonist in a type of fairy tale known as the "exile and return" narrative. In this tale-type, a young man or male child is driven or sent away from his home and community, whether by enemies or unpleasant circumstance. Following his departure he must make his way in the world by means of his wits and his physical skills, oftentimes finding surrogate fathers or families to aid him. Eventually, after overcoming a series of obstacles, he succeeds in winning his proper inheritance or in establishing a new one for himself. His identity and position within the community restored, the hero begins his new life with gained maturity and reputation. In contrast to the fairy tale hero, the chivalric hero is more likely to choose his quest consciously, possibly in response to some perceived danger to his own community; in other cases, the choice is thrust upon him, perhaps by an emissary from another world. Once bound to seeing the quest through, the hero can expect to travel through strange places and harsh climates, often alone or with a small company, and his progress along the journey will be interrupted periodically by obstacles such as monsters or unusual barriers. The chivalric hero is expected to make his values visible to the often hostile world outside the court, values that are both sacred and profane, including the love of a woman (or, in the case of knights protected by the Virgin Mary, two women). He will traverse liminal and transitional spaces, seeking external and visible objects but also seeking greater self-knowledge and awareness; and he will prove the equal of any task or trouble, whether these are physical, ethical, or psychological in origin. It is well to keep in mind that the chivalric quest romance offers its readers a blend of the predominant Christian themes of humility, passivity, spirituality, and mercy, and of the heroic and epic themes of triumph, physical superiority, and vengeance. The Christian story stressed worldly defeat as necessarily a precursor to spiritual victory; the heroic epic celebrated martial prowess in this world as the best way to ensure a lasting reputation. Arthurian romances, as the preeminent examples of chivalric literature, offered then an often attractive commingling of these two disparate ethical realms.

Sir Gawain and the Green Knight, despite being one of the best known of the Arthurian romances, remains for several reasons a deeply distinctive work. First, the poem is unusually detailed in its descriptions of the physical world of the court and courtiers. From the bangles on the clothing and the gleam of the jewelry, to the heft and shine of the weapons and armor, to the dressage upon the horses and the sweetmeats upon the tables, Gawain is placed undeniably within a world of real things. This attention to realistic detail does not preclude the irruptions of the marvelous that are expected in romance—the eerie appearance of the Green Knight, the efficacy of Morgan's magic—yet it does provide an unexpected vantage point from which to view it. More than most romances, *Sir Gawain and the Green Knight* presents a world of wonder, one in which people do not merely accept the marvelous without comment but gaze upon it, gossip about it, and perceive the uncanny in their presence (Putter, *Introduction* 38–45). Second, the poem can be read as offering a series of commentaries upon the very nature of the chivalric quest. It is a poem that is very aware of itself as being of a type of literature or genre, one in which the characters are supposed to act in certain ways that the audience is aware of. The poem's tremendous sense of suspense plays on the audience's and the characters' own expectations of what will happen, only to surprise us in the end, for the quest that Gawain undertakes ostensibly for one purpose turns out to be for another. The assumed goal of the quest, the final terrible encounter with the Green Knight at the Green Chapel, turns out to have been an elaborate stratagem to test the hero in an entirely different way, and the many signs and symbols of the world turn out to be more cryptic and slippery than the hero, or the audience, suspect (Putter, *Introduction* 77–8).

The setting for the adventure is situated in a courtly milieu that is set against the backdrop of time long past. The poet lets us know that Arthur's court is of a distant era, yet one with certain known boundaries—those of the Trojan War and the mythical settlement of Britain by Brutus, descendent of Aeneas (Borroff and Howes ll. 1–19). Against that historical past is then set another romantic past, one less remote than antiquity, but at a far enough distance to allow for chivalric nostalgia (Bloomfield 18). The poet declares that he will tell an "adventure" of Arthur's court that has never been heard before (l. 29). Against a background of similar romance conventions he composes his own, raising expectations and supplanting or tormenting them during the progression of his narrative. The very word *adventure* highlights one of the crucial aspects of all such chivalric romances in that the hero must undertake some unexpected, dangerous, and arduous journey or undergo some trial or often both. While readers are familiar with knights seeking a longstanding goal, such as the Grail, it is more common to have the adventure insert itself rather abruptly into the life of the hero, coming as it does from an unexpected visitor to court or a chance encounter in a forest or other space equally wild and uncivilized. The word, coming into Middle English from the Old French *auenture,* "a thing that comes about by chance," hints at the usually unexpected nature of the event. Such a chance event comes about with the arrival of the Green Knight. When the emerald-hued horse and rider cross the threshold of Arthur's court, the assembled knights and ladies are amazed by his marvelous appearance, and unlike many unusual opponents in romances, he is described in immense detail. The portrait of the knight is the head-to-toe description (Lat. *descriptio*) adapted from the classical tradition and most commonly associated with the appearance of a beautiful woman (Pearsall); in fact, the *Gawain*-poet will return to this device in Castle Hautdesert when he describes the two ladies (ll. 947–69). Moreover, the Green Knight bears not one but two visages, the initial terrifying and grotesque in its aspect, the second noble and handsome. As we read the lines devoted to his appearance, he changes in our mind's eye from one sort of figure to another, providing an ambiguous and alternating perspective on romance ideals as he shimmers and alters between two opposing points of view (Benson 61). He is called an *aghlich mayster* (l. 136), a "fearsome lord," an epithet that in itself combines the terrible and the courtly. The poet describes him as *half etayn* (l. 140), "half a giant," but he was also "the seemliest in his stature to see, as he rides" (l. 142). The particular color of green mentioned, *enker grene* ("intense green" l. 150), indicates a thriving, flourishing color, not a sickly hue (Saunders 34). The potential associations of this eerie visitor with the natural and vegetative world underscore the impossible quality of the color on a man. The significance and interpretation of his arrival has remained debatable. Whether the Green Knight is a personified echo of the seasons of Christmas and the pagan solstice, symbolizing life over death in his color and his actions, is unclear. The Christmas celebrations were well-established in medieval festival culture at the time *Sir Gawain and the Green Knight* was written, and many motifs found in the poem would have been associated with the season, including superstitions over New Year and the "crossing of the threshold," the colors green and red, the holly bush, and the sense that the Other World and its spirits were nearest to this one when December came around (Kirk 104–5). Moreover, the season of Christmas then, as now, was one of heightened sensory contrasts in northern Europe, between the icy world outdoors and the brightness and security within (Kirk 108).

As an apparent denizen of that other world, the Green Knight presents the court with a challenge in the form of a "Christmas game" (l. 283), one aimed not immediately at the hero Gawain but at the entire court of Camelot; although Gawain provides the heroic focus, it is the court itself, and its way of life, that is being tested (Stevens 69–70). Often referred to as the "Beheading Game," the form of combat requested by the Green Knight has a clear analogue in an earlier French tale, the *First Continuation* of Chrétien's *Perceval*. In that version, as the older challenger turns out to be the younger man's father, and the contest proves a suspenseful means by which to reveal a previously hidden family truth. In *Sir Gawain and the Green Knight*, the contest serves to outline the inexorable nature of *trawþe* ("honor, loyalty, integrity, righteousness") and the slippery world of sign and play that the hero finds himself within (Putter, *Introduction* 64). The "exchange of blows" offers an indirect parallel with the "exchange of winnings" agreed upon later in Bertilak's castle, and the cautious way that Gawain approaches the former game underscores his own carelessness, or disloyalty, towards his *trawþe* later in the poem. The outlandish "Christmas game" proposed by the Green Knight seems straightforward enough: One of the assembled knights must accept the giant axe and strike a blow. That man must then journey one year hence to the Green Knight's own court, whereupon he will receive an answering blow. The challenge is initially accepted by Arthur himself; Gawain inserts himself into the action, and proceeds to display his noted gift for fine language, first by establishing his own fitness for the game (he is not as important as Arthur, thus his loss will not be as grievous to the court), and then through clearly establishing his own understanding of the terms that the Green Knight had laid out. The language here in the poem is that of legal contracts, and as the Green Knight asks his challenger to "recount we our contract" (l. 378), Gawain rises to the verbal challenge by rehearsing the exact nature of the rules of this game as if he were going through the fine print (Putter, *Introduction* 65). It is only after Gawain has brought the axe down upon the Green Knight's neck, and the visitor responds by picking up the decapitated head, which proceeds to speak to Gawain, that Gawain and the audience understand the horrifying nature of the contract entered into.

The inexorable nature of the contract is entwined with the cycle of the year as we move into Fitt Two and the time of Gawain's departure draws near. In this chivalric tale, the hero undertakes the onset of his journey with a heavy heart, and the onlookers grieve rather than rejoice. *Sir Gawain and the Green Knight* offers at this point a rather poignant reflection on the pointless nature of such heroic quests, for one of the greatest heroes in Christendom and Camelot is sending himself to certain death, not on a noble quest, but on a foolish errand: "Ill fortune it is / That you, man, must be marred, that are most worthy!" (ll. 674–75) Gawain's preparation for his departure for the Green Chapel comes on November 1 of the year following the encounter with the Green Knight, on the Feast of All Saint's Day, and begins with his literal and metaphorical arming for the grievous journey to come. The notion of the chivalric hero preparing for his dangerous journey in an uncertain world of temptation and sin is drawn from the sixth chapter of Paul's Letter to the Ephesians, a famous reference point for the image of the *miles Christi* ("soldier of Christ") defending himself against a profane world. The language of the arming of Gawain focuses on images of brightness and enclosure, emphasizing the interlocking nature of the armor and the man, who thus presents an inviolable presence to the sinful world. Moreover, this inviolability extends to the sense of integrity within. For its medieval audience, the splendor of the knight's external appearance would signify a parallel splendor within the man (Mann, "Courtly Aesthetics" 244–48). Much attention has been paid to the symbolic meaning of the image of the pentangle that emblazons his shield (Green). This is the symbol that emphasizes Gawain's *trawþe*, or "honor," arguably a knight's most essential chivalric characteristic. The pentangle is a public symbol that displays for onlookers the central virtues of the man who bears it, and one is meant to read and recognize its meaning (Howard 427–28). The symbol itself, not Christian in origin, was submitted to allegorical exegesis, which could claim to see within it memory of various "fives" of Christian worship, such as the Five Joys of Mary, or the Five Wounds of Christ. Crucially, the five points of the symbol also represent for Gawain the five knightly virtues of *franchise, fellowship, cleanness, courtesy,* and *pity.* The poet makes it clear that Gawain is suited to bear such an emblem, for in this land he is the finest hero, the paragon of chivalric values, and as such he is best fitting to carry out the quest (Green 135–36). Yet within this symmetrical and interlocking knot of meaning borne by the knight remains the vulnerable man who will have his right to bear the device tested by dangers within and without (Hollis 271–72; Mann, "Courtly Aesthetics" 248). Both Gawain and the audience expect this, for such is the chivalric hero's lot; moreover, the substance and quality of the Arthurian court, the chivalric community, will itself be tested as the Green Knight had made clear upon his entrance when he asks if "any in this house such hardihood claims, / Be so bold in his blood, his brain so wild, / As stoutly to strike one stroke for another" (ll. 285–87).

The quest has commenced, but readers looking forward to Gawain's solitary combat against evil men, ogres, dragons, and other creatures of the wild world outside will be disappointed, as these conventional battles of the chivalric romance are summed up in a single stanza (ll. 713–39). This surprises the attentive reader of romance who might expect more of such adventures to follow only to learn much later that these typical feats were a mere digression for the poet (Ganim 380–81). In contrast with many romances, *Sir Gawain and the Green Knight* offers a far more realistic topography for its hero to traverse. Gawain wanders through the outskirts of North Wales before passing through the borderlands of Wirral, but he is most harshly treated not by creaturely threats but by the bitter winter weather itself. In his exhaustion and in a spirit of religious supplication, he prays for a place that he might hear Mass, and in so doing he sees Castle Hautdesert appear out of the mists as if a "castle cut of paper for a king's feast" (l. 802). A magnificent and majestic species of the medieval fortress, it is also summoned out of the recesses of Gawain's expectations, for a central concern of our poet is the glory of courtly and civilized society in the dreary wilderness of the real world. The power and ritual of each court's hospitality is considered alongside the knight's need to keep up appearances and maintain his poise. Once inside, Gawain is greeted like royalty and is much impressed by the courtliness and hospitality found within. His own reputation for amorous dalliance is well-known, and the rumor quickly makes the rounds that Sir Gawain, "without a peer on earth / in martial rivalry" (ll. 874–75) shall also teach the assembled guests the art of "love's language" (l. 927). The true tests of Gawain, though he does not suspect it, will occur within these castle walls as he shall be tested not in martial arts but in the virtues of *trawþe* and *clannes*, or "purity," chivalric virtues that the hero must always manifest to the watching world and over which he must remain ever vigilant, lest his reputation fail (Mann, "Courtly Aesthetics" 253–4, 258).

With this in mind, the hunting and temptation sequences take on a new and heroic urgency. In the third fitt, the heroic and the courtly realms, the overtly masculine and subtly feminized worlds are knotted keenly as the poet juxtaposes the intricate action of the hunting scenes out of doors, in which Gawain does not take part, with the equally intricate verbal scenes of flirtation and temptation indoors, in which he is the object. The descriptions of the hunts repay close technical reading, for the poet was clearly experienced with both the action and the language of this activity. The modern reader can benefit much from examining this section of the poem alongside the medieval manuals of hunting. Books such as the Anglo-Norman *Les Livres du Roy Modus et de la Royne Ratio* (ca. 1375) and Edward of Norwich's *The Master of Game* (ca. 1410) make it clear that the audience of the poem saw hunting as a splendid metaphor for many aspects of life, including courtship, and the daily scenes with the three featured beasts of the hunt— the deer, the boar, and the fox—all run parallel to the scenes playing out within the knight's chambers (Burnley 3–6). *Sir Gawain and the Green Knight* is not the only medieval hunting poem to offer thinly veiled allegorical suggestions of the multiple meanings contained in the activities of the hunt, but it may well be the most sophisticated. Yet it is good to keep in mind that, although the language of these scenes is rich with the jargon and energy of the hunt that might well have pleased a knowledgeable reader, the world of the hunters is divided into nobles and the professional laborers of the hunt. The manuals mentioned above pay greater attention to the elaborate drama of the hunt and the requirements of the roles within it than they do to the practical matters of hunting, and they, like the courteous nobles of *Sir*

Gawain and the Green Knight, are most interested in these matters of rituals and reward.

The first day sets a comic tone, one that has reminded some readers of the fabliaux, when we observe Galwain lying awake under his covers as the Lady lifts the latch: a "corner of the curtain he caught back a little / And kept watch warily, to see what befell" (ll. 1185–86). The Lady laughs at him as she greets him, warning that " 'you are taken in a trice—a truce we must make, / Or I shall bind you in your bed, of that be assured' " (ll. 2210–11). Her language is replete with double entendres, expressions and words that are drawn from other contexts, such as the hunt, and become sexualized in the bedroom (Mills 613–15). The Lady's seeming offer of herself (" 'My body is here at hand, / Your each wish to fulfill; / Your servant to command / I am, and shall be still' " ll. 1236–40) surprised earlier readers with its seeming disregard for courtly norms (Benson 50); yet this speech, like all of the speech in this section of the poem, draws its electricity from the nature of verbal and physical ritual. Speech is part of the elaborate game of courtship and retreat, of vulnerability and defensiveness (Putter, *Sir Gawain* 244–47). The game escalates over time, and at the close of each day, Gawain and Bertilak each agree to exchange with the other their "winnings" from that day's adventures. The chivalric hero is caught up in an elaborate and courtly game of gift-giving, and the reader is led to compare the currency of one realm with that of the other (Mann, "Price and Value" 300–01).

The language of the second day changes from wordplay and sexual banter to the more elaborate chivalric rhetoric of the slighted beloved, as the Lady accuses Gawain of treating her poorly and in a manner ill-befitting a knight: "it seems a great wonder" that he "cannot act in company as courtesy bids" (ll. 1481, 1483). The seriousness of his situation is underscored by the poet, who informs us that "thus she tested his temper and tried many a time, / Whatever her true intent, to entice him to sin" (ll. 1549–50). The third day begins in darkness as Gawain awakens from "black dreams" (l. 1756) to the Lady's emotional appeal as she challenges him with coldness "toward a creature so close by your side, / Of all women in this world most wounded in heart" (ll. 1780–81). The poet tells us the knight is in "great peril" (l. 1768) and reminds us of the hero's quest and his essential virtues by referencing the Virgin Mary (and by extension his shield [Mills 627]). As the emotional heft and peril of the courtship sequences increase, so too do the hunting scenes change and escalate in power. The boar hunt of the second day is more dangerous to horse and rider than the previous day's deer drive, and it ends with Lord Bertilak himself submitting to single combat with his foe. The third day of hunting, with its slippery and stealthy fox, might well mirror the desperate state that the fearful Gawain finds himself in. Believing himself to be in mortal danger, Gawain accepts the green silken girdle from the Lady in order that he, unlike the fox, might "escape unscathed" (l. 1858) from the completion of the grim game awaiting him.

Revealing once more the *Gawain*-poet's love of structural patterns, the girdle functions in symmetrical opposition to the earlier symbol of the pentangle (Howard 430–32). Whereas the latter device of Gawain's was public and legible, the girdle is equally powerful but essentially private, meant to be kept concealed from view, and Gawain exacerbates its privacy by choosing to keep it a secret from Bertilak when he reports to him the winnings of that day. Moreover, its significance proves less "legible" than the pentangle, as first the Lady, unbeknownst to Gawain, misrepresents to him its powers, and the knight then mistakes its purpose on his quest (Hanna 145). What at first seems to be an exceedingly useful gift, one whose power justifiably will counteract the other-worldly magic of the Green Knight, is revealed by him to have been the central means to test Gawain. This simple, illegible, and ultimately ordinary garment is the powerful token that reveals the knight to have been less loyal to the virtues he bore upon his shield than either he himself or the world had realized. The poet also designs this sequence so as to downplay the girdle's significance to the greater story and to distract Gawain from its potential ethical import (Putter,

Introduction 90–96). Yet it will prove to be the act of interpretation itself that is in flux as the poem comes to its conclusion since the desire to understand the meaning of the girdle—and of the adventure as a whole—becomes pressing to many of the actors and most pressing to Gawain (Hanna 294–96).

The journey to the Green Chapel is also part of the elaborate system of patterns that the poet has constructed. The journey to the Castle is bookended by the journey from it to the Green Chapel, and each location involves an arming sequence and a description of the dwelling: magnificent and comforting at Hautdesert, "bleak" and "hideous" at this "Chapel of mischance" (ll. 2189–90; 2195), the approach to which is made worse by the ominous sound of the great axe being sharpened upon a grindstone. After his arrival at the place where the Green Knight is waiting for him, the two rehearse the arrangement once more, and Gawain readies himself to "stand still, / And you may lay on as you like till the last of my debt / is paid" (ll. 2252–54). As there were three temptations within the Castle, so at the Chapel will there be three strokes of the axe. At the first, Gawain's flinching causes the giant to accuse him of cowardice, which leads Gawain in turn to swear on his honor to be still. A second stroke proves but a feint, as "merrily does he mock him" (l. 2295); and the third only scratches the skin so that "a little blood lightly leapt to the earth" (l. 2314). His failure, he and the audience now learn, came earlier when he accepted and hid the girdle: "you lacked, sir, a little in loyalty there," but he is forgiven because the hero loved not cunning nor courtship, but his own life (ll. 2367–68). In response to Gawain's inquiry as to his real name, the Green Knight tells him that he is Bertilak of Hautdesert, the very man who had been his host for the past three nights. The elaborate ruse was the work of the notorious magician Morgan le Fay, Gawain's aunt and the sworn enemy of Guinevere; she resides at his castle, and Gawain saw her himself, for she was the old woman who accompanied the Lady in the procession the day of Gawain's arrival (ll. 947–69). It was Morgan's intention, we learn, to frighten Guinevere to death; it was her magic that enabled Bertilak to appear as the Green Knight, and it was at her behest that the Lady tempted Gawain for three days.

Mindful of the defeated Morgan le Fay, we should remember that medieval romance draws its power not from the masculine energy, but from the feminine; that although male figures are the actors, female figures remain the directors and producers of much of the events and narratives that invigorate romance. To read *Sir Gawain and the Green Knight* with appropriate attention to the importance of the female characters is to become momentarily and pleasantly disoriented; their presence, at the periphery and at the core, highlights many of the problems encountered by Gawain in his efforts to make certain and solid just what has happened to him, what is happening to him, and the significance of it all for his chivalric sensibility (Heng 502–04; 508). If *Sir Gawain and the Green Knight* offers a brilliant celebration and biting critique of chivalric custom and courtly ceremony, the poet provides ample opportunity to witness a hero striving both to revere and deracinate a mystery set in motion and imagined by women around a world of men.

Gawain's reaction to the truth about his *trawþe* ("honor") and *clannes* ("purity") is far less joyful than the reaction of either the Green Knight or Arthur and the rest of Camelot when he eventually returns home to tell them what has befallen him. He feels that he must first admit to, even embody, his great shame and his failure to live up to the virtues symbolized by the points upon his shield; he curses his "cowardly and covetous heart! / In you is villainy and vice, and virtue laid low!" (ll. 2374–75). With the circumstances of his failing having been revealed, Gawain goes on to make a short but famous speech in which he lays the blame for his failings, and those of other men, upon women: "if a dullard should dote, deem it no wonder, / And through the wiles of a woman be wooed into sorrow, / For so was Adam by one" (ll. 2414–16), and Solomon, and Samson, and David, and many more were the heroes brought low by the women they loved. The girdle, among the most difficult objects to interpret in the poem, becomes first an object of magic; then of scorn; then, the Green Knight suggests, a mere "token" of their meeting (ll. 2398–99). Gawain decides to make it the emblem of all his sins, his cowardice, and his covetousness (ll. 2374–5), and while refusing the offer of continued fellowship in the castle, he claims the girdle as his own; he takes it, in all of its brightness and beauty, so as to display it as "the badge of false faith that I was found in there, / And I must bear it on my body till I breathe my last" (ll. 2509–10). Yet here too our hero is defeated by the sense of game and fun that King Arthur insists upon, for when Gawain returns and tells the story of his failure as the "blood burns in his cheeks" (l. 2503), Arthur comforts him, and the court all together laughs; instead of betokening an individual knight's shame, it will become a token of the court's fellowship and continued joy (Hanna 297–98). The romance concludes with a reminder of the antiquity of the tale and the hope for eternal bliss shared by the poet and his audience. The quest has ended with much learned and much still misunderstood—and so, the poem suggests, is the lot of humankind, who along with Sir Gawain bear tokens of wonder that they do not understand and play a game whose rules remain forever in need of another reading.

Sir Gawain and the Green Knight presents readers with a flawed but keenly appealing hero on a quest that questions the value and composition of such heroism. At the start of the poem, Sir Gawain's reputation is at its zenith, his character and virtue emblematic of the best of Arthur's court. Yet the adventure on which he embarks demonstrates that neither he nor the chivalric code by which that court claims to live is as perfect in their virtue, or as prepared to be tested, as was thought before the Green Knight rode into Camelot. The model for the chivalric quest allows it to conclude either in gracious victory or noble defeat, and Gawain's adventure stays true to this in form. But the unusual power of the poem comes from the unexpected manner in which both victory and defeat are framed; Gawain is not allowed to set the terms of the various conflicts he takes part in, but he must accede to terms set by others, and the battles he fights turn out to have significances he is unaware of until they have been completed. He believes himself ready for the game, but he is not able to discern fight from folly or truth from fiction. Above all else, *Sir Gawain and the Green Knight* suggests that the true chivalric hero is one who must rejoice to falter, as it were, by marveling at his own mistakes along the way; and it reveals the hero's quest as a journey through a rough, wonderful, and very real landscape, but where the toughest trials take place within himself.

Works Cited

Andrew, Malcolm, and Ronald Waldron, ed. *The Poems of the Pearl Manuscript*. 3rd ed. Exeter: U of Exeter P, 1996.

Benson, Larry Dean. *Art and Tradition in Sir Gawain and the Green Knight*. New Brunswick, NJ: Rutgers UP, 1965.

Bloomfield. Morton W. "*Sir Gawain and the Green Knight*: An Appraisal." *Proceedings of the Modern Language Association* 76.1 (Mar. 1961): 7–19.

Borroff, Marie, trans., and Laura L. Howes, ed. *Sir Gawain and the Green Knight*. New York: Norton, 2010.

Burnley, J. D. "The Hunting Scenes in *Sir Gawain and the Green Knight*." *The Yearbook of English Studies* 3 (1973): 1–9.

Burrow, J. A. *A Reading of* Sir Gawain and the Green Knight. London: Routledge, 1965.

Ganim, John M. "Disorientation, Style, and Consciousness in *Sir Gawain and the Green Knight*." *PLMA* 91.3 (May 1976): 376–84.

Green, Richard Hamilton. "Gawain's Shield and the Quest for Perfection." *English Literary History* 29.2 (June 1962): 121–39.

Hanna, Ralph. "Unlocking What's Locked: Gawain's Green Girdle." *Viator* 14 (1983): 289–302.

Heng, Geraldine. "Feminine Knots and the Other *Sir Gawain and the Green Knight*." *PLMA* 106.3 (May 1991): 500–14.

Hollis, Stephanie J. "The Pentangle Knight: *Sir Gawain and the Green Knight*." *The Chaucer Review* 15.3 (Winter 1981): 267–81.

Howard, Donald R. "Structure and Symmetry in *Sir Gawain*." *Speculum* 39.3 (July 1964): 425–33.

Keen, Maurice. *Chivalry*. New Haven: Yale UP, 1984.

Kirk, Elizabeth. "'Wel Bycommes Such Craft Upon Cristmasse': The Festive and the Hermeneutic in *Sir Gawain and the Green Knight*." *Arthuriana* 4.2 (Summer 1994): 93–137.

Mann, Jill. "Courtly Aesthetics and Courtly Ethics in *Sir Gawain and the Green Knight*." *Studies in the Age of Chaucer* 31 (2009): 231–65.

_____. "Price and Value in *Sir Gawain and the Green Knight*." *Essays in Criticism* 36.4 (1986): 294–318.

Mills, David. "An Analysis of the Temptation Scenes in *Sir Gawain and the Green Knight*." *The Journal of English and Germanic Philology* 67.4 (Oct. 1968): 612–30.

Pearsall, Derek A. "Rhetorical *Descriptio* in *Sir Gawain and the Green Knight*." *Modern Language Review* 50.2 (Apr. 1955): 129–34.

Putter, Ad. *An Introduction to the* Gawain-*Poet*. London: Longman, 1996.

_____. Sir Gawain and the Green Knight *and French Arthurian Romance*. Oxford: Clarendon, 1995.

Saunders, Corinne. "The *Gawain*-poet and Medieval Romance." *The Cambridge History of English Poetry*. Ed. Michael O'Neill. Cambridge: Cambridge UP, 2010. 26–42.

Stevens, Martin. "Laughter and Game in *Sir Gawain and the Green Knight*". *Speculum* 47.1 (Jan. 1972): 65–78.

Trigg, Stephanie. "The Romance of Exchange: *Sir Gawain and the Green Knight*." *Viator* 22 (1991): 251–66.

Dante's Quest and the Sublimation of Heroic Combat in *The Divine Comedy*_____

Matthew Bolton

Virgil presents his epic hero Aeneas as a man of many virtues: He is a good son and father, a pious worshipper, a self-sacrificing leader, and the progenitor of the Roman people and culture. Yet undergirding all of these noble qualities is a more primal qualification. To serve as the hero of Virgil's epic, Aeneas must be a warrior, a man ready to take up arms against any nemesis that stands in his way. Virgil announces this martial theme in his opening line, *"arma virumque cano"* ("I sing of arms and the man"), and he closes his epic with the image of Aeneas driving his sword through the fallen Turnus. When Dante casts himself as the hero of his own epic *Commedia*—and casts his "great master" Virgil as his guide—he places himself in a complex relationship with the heroes who have come before him. Dante is not a warrior, but a poet, and so he is strikingly different from men like Aeneas, Perseus, Theseus, or Achilles. Unlike the heroes of classical mythology and the classical epic, Dante makes his quest unarmed, and though he encounters any number of monsters and horrors, he has no sword or spear with which to prove his mettle. Instead, the heroic impulse toward combat is sublimated in a series of fascinating negotiations with the value system of the classical tradition. By reconfiguring the role of combat in the hero's quest in his *Inferno*, Dante presents the poet as the successor to the warrior and establishes a new kind of epic hero.

In the *Inferno*, Dante and Virgil make their way through a landscape that is an amalgam of classical and Christian elements and that is peopled not only by mythological and historical figures but by Dante's own contemporaries. Because sinners are sorted according to the crimes they committed while on earth, people from wildly different places and times rub shoulders. Dante may speak to a figure from mythology one moment and to a former Florentine neighbor the next. And while the tripartite division of Dante's cosmos (into Hell, Purgatory, and Heaven) reflects Christian theology, his *Inferno* owes much of its geography to the Greek and Roman underworld. The rivers that Dante and his guide must cross, the city of Dis that they must enter, the monstrous guards whom they must face down or flee—all are drawn from classical culture rather than from the Christian one that followed it. As a result, Dante and Virgil make their journey in the footsteps of various Greek and Roman heroes and encounter the very same monsters that Hercules, Theseus, Aeneas, and others bested. At the beginning of the third circle of Hell, for example, the poets face Cerberus, the three-headed dog whom the Ancient Greeks depicted as guarding the entrance to the underworld. Hercules's twelfth labor involved his picking the beast up and carrying him out of the underworld. Dante and Virgil cannot hope to compete with this kind of accomplishment. They do, however, engage in what one might term "heroic evasion." Faced with an imminent threat, the eminent poets take action:

> When the slimy Cerberus caught sight of us,
> he opened up his mouths and showed his fangs;
> his body was one mass of twitching muscles.
> My master stooped and, spreading wide his fingers,
> he grabbed up heaping fistfuls of the mud
> and flung it down into those greedy gullets.
> (VI. 22–27)

Having distracted the monster, Dante and Virgil are able to move past it and enter the third circle of Hell. While the two men never engage in combat with any of the monsters they encounter, they often must rely on physical actions rather than on their words. In diverting Cerberus, Virgil shows that he has some of the bravery and physicality of his epic protagonist, Aeneas. In the sixth book of the *Aeneid*, Virgil's hero journeyed to the underworld, and Dante found in Virgil's account of this journey "themes, characters, and topographical features that he could transform to meet the demands of his own poem" (Raffa 267). One of

Dante's demands was that the Christian Hell be a more violent, dangerous, and threatening place than the pagan underworld, and in many respects the two poets' quest therefore becomes a more treacherous one than that of Hercules or Aeneas.

Like Aeneas, the poets will face the Furies, whose hair is made of "horned snakes and little serpents" (IX. 41), and like Perseus they will shield their eyes from the approach of the gorgon Medusa, whose gaze turns men to stone. In the seventh circle, the poets again find themselves in the position of a classical hero when they face the minotaur. This is the area of Hell inhabited by sinners who acted in violence, and the raging minotaur—the man-bull who was kept in a labyrinth on Crete—is therefore a fitting guard for this realm. In mythology, Theseus, with the help of the monster's human half-sister, Ariadne, slays the minotaur. When the poets encounter this creature in Hell, they make no attempt at combat. Instead, Virgil uses the beast's anger against it, riling it up to the point where it is too enraged to effectively attack the poets. He taunts the minotaur by describing the way in which Theseus and Ariadne tricked and killed it. In a fitting attack for a poet, Virgil antagonizes the monster with his knowledge of classical mythology and through the cutting accuracy of his depiction. Like the bull he resembles, the minotaur "sees red" and gives the poets an opportunity to engage again in heroic evasion:

> The way a bull breaks loose the very moment
> he knows he has been dealt the mortal blow
> and cannot run but jumps and twists and turns,
> just so I saw the Minotaur perform,
> and my guide, alert, cried out: "Run to the pass!
> While he still writhes with rage, get started down."
> (XII. 22–27)

They may not slay the minotaur, but as Dante and Virgil run past the baffled monster and into the terrain he was guarding, it is clear who has won this engagement.

If a hero and the monster he defeats are somehow reflections and inversions of each other, then in defeating the minotaur Dante implicitly compares Virgil and himself to the heroic Theseus. After all, they have survived an encounter with the beast that is forever associated with the Athenian hero. Dante himself must therefore have some common qualities with the hero of Athens. The identification with Theseus is further reinforced by the fact that he, too, made a journey into the underworld. Theseus's attempt to rescue Persephone ends in defeat with the hero finding himself trapped in a chair that makes him forget his original intentions and perhaps his very self. Virgil and Dante, on the other hand, will successfully navigate Hell with all their faculties intact. Moreover, whereas the classical underworld is a place dominated by sadness and gloom, the Hell of the Christian Dante is marked by anger and violence. Nothing is forgotten or forgiven in this Hell. In many respects, then, Dante raises the stakes of his own journey, making it more dangerous than those undertaken by Theseus, Hercules, and Aeneas. The encounters with Cerberus and the minotaur add an element of physicality and risk to Dante's narrative, establishing that the personas of Dante and Virgil are susceptible to harm. Their quest does not involve merely a passive viewing of the sights of Hell but rather an active engagement with its inhabitants. Taken in this light, the encounters with mythological creatures put the fictionalized versions of Dante and Virgil on common ground with the heroes of antiquity.

Dante and Virgil's later encounter with a band of devils known as the *Malebrache* furthers this sense of Hell as a place in which the poets face bodily harm. Armed with their own teeth and claws (*malebrache* means "evil claws") and with sharp hooks for holding sinners under the lakes of burning pitch, these devils are ferocious. Though they are drawn from medieval folklore rather than from the classical tradition, the devils nevertheless cast Virgil and Dante in a role where they must be either victors or victims. Virgil shows a readiness to face them, despite their threats. He positions the frightened Dante behind an outcropping and says:

> Whatever insults they may hurl at me,
> you must not fear, I know how things are run here;
> I have been caught in as bad a fix before.
> (XXI. 61–63)

Susan Mitchell's translation of this assurance (*"ch' i'ho le cose conte / e altra volta fui a tal baratta"* in the original) gives Virgil the earthy line: "This isn't the first scuffle I've had" (Halpern 97). In fact, throughout the riotous happenings of Cantos XXI–XXIII, Virgil shows a swagger and a roughness that can be a bit jarring for both Dante and the reader. It is a bit like the scene in which Hamlet, who has seemed bookish and cerebral throughout much of the play, shows a sudden assurance of winning a fencing match. Horatio says, "You will lose, my lord," to which Hamlet replies, "I do not think so; since he went into France I have been in continual practice. I shall win at the odds" (V.ii. 209–12). Virgil, who has been a figure of reason and prudence throughout the *Inferno*, suddenly shows himself ready to wade into a pack of devils rather than skillfully evade them. This dramatic shift in Virgil's character befits the actions of this region of Hell, one in which the sins of fraud are punished. Their journey across this bolgia (or subcircle) is punctuated by burlesque, darkly comic confrontations between the Devils, the sinners, and the two poets. Devils and sinners alike engage in a series of deceptions and acts of violence and betrayal. Virgil's readiness to stand up to the *Malebrache*, and his admission that he has been in this kind of situation before, sets the tone for these rough-and-tumble passages.

Interestingly enough, Dante becomes increasingly cautious and skeptical as Virgil becomes increasingly headstrong and heedless. He urges his guide not to trust the devils, who have promised to accompany them safely to a bridge by which they may pass to the next bolgia. By the end of their passage across this terrain, Dante's caution is vindicated: Virgil has been deceived by the devils into taking a route that leads them into a trap. Again the poets take evasive action:

> . . . down that sloping border my guide slid
> bearing me with him, clasping me to his chest
> as though I were his child, not his companion.
> (XXIII. 49–51)

Virgil will return to his circumspect ways after this, and the implication may be that the reasonable individual finds less combative ways to overcome obstacles. Hercules might batter a foe into submission and Theseus might use strategy to get close enough for a killing stroke, but Virgil and Dante will continue to rely on their words and their wits—to say nothing of their feet—to evade danger.

At the very center of Hell, the logic and necessity behind Virgil and Dante's heroic evasions becomes clear. Frozen in the center of the lake of Cocyctus is the monstrous figure of Satan. With his giant body, three faces (with their three mouths busily devouring Brutus, Cassius, and Judas Iscariot), and three pairs of batlike wings, he is more fearsome than any of the monsters the poets have previously faced. Indeed, he is perhaps more fearsome than any of the monsters of the classical world. Satan's perversion of the human and the angelic form is an affront to the sensibilities of both the classical and Christian ethos, and his size and ferocity put him in a different class from monsters like the minotaur or the furies. But more daunting than his physical size or appearance is his moral resonance. A person may resist Satan, but only God and Christ can actually defeat him. The arch-fiend therefore operates on an entirely different moral and eschatological plane than do any of the monsters of antiquity. In the Greek and Roman traditions, evil was assailable. The minotaur brought suffering to the people of Athens, but Theseus was able to defeat him and so free his city from sacrificing youths to the monster's anger. Cerberus guards the underworld, but Hercules was able to bring him to heel as proof of his own heroic strength. But for a mortal to enter into combat with Satan—much less to defeat or kill him—is not only impossible but possibly heretical. To presume to "slay" Satan would be to take on God's and Christ's power for oneself. According to most Christian doctrine, it is Christ alone who can defeat Satan. The Gospel of John, for example, posits Christ as such a champion: "The Devil sinneth from the beginning. For this purpose the son of God appeared, that he might destroy the works of the Devil" (1 John 3:8). Greek monsters could be fought and defeated by mortal men, but Satan is a different order of foe. Dante and Virgil, of course, make no attempt to fight with Satan or to destroy his works. Rather, as they have with so many threatening creatures before, they find a way past him. Dante clings to Virgil, who makes one last heroic evasion:

> I held onto [Virgil's] neck, as he told me to,
> while he watched and waited for the time and place,
> and when the wings were stretched out just enough,
> he grabbed on to the shaggy sides of Satan;
> then downward, tuft by tuft, he made his way
> between the tangled hair and the frozen crust.
> (XXXIV. 70–75)

Halfway down the devil's body—at the very center of the earth—they turn themselves 180 degrees and then climb up his legs to emerge in the southern hemisphere. The strategy that the poets have relied on throughout their journey pays off, as they use Satan himself as their ladder for climbing back out of Hell. Dante here suggests that even a combatant as strong as Hercules or as wily as Odysseus could have fought his way past Satan. The two poets unquestioningly accept the doctrine that he is a foe who can be evaded but not destroyed, and their readiness to find a way around or past the obstacles that threaten them is vindicated here at the center of Hell. This points to a larger philosophical distinction by which Dante reevaluates the role of combat in defining heroism. The Hell that Dante describes in the *Inferno* is a violent, bloody place, and many of its inhabitants are damned to an eternity of combat and suffering. The devils and sinners of Cantos XI–XIII, for example, seem to act out an endless series of skirmishes and reversals. In the frozen lake of Cocytus at the center of Hell, sinners are locked together in combat:

> Wood to wood with iron was never clamped
> so firm! And the two of them like billy-goats
> were butting at each other, mad with anger.
> (XXXII. 29–51)

In that same circle of Hell, Count Ugolino famously gnaws on the head of Archbishop Ruggiero, the man who imprisoned and starved him and his sons. After telling his story, Ugolino renews his attack on his enemy:

> He spoke these words; then, glaring down in rage,
> attacked again the live skull with his teeth
> sharp as a dog's, and as fit for grinding bones.
> (XXXIII. 76–78)

Moreover, Dante will encounter any number of epic and mythological heroes who have been consigned to Hell. Ulysses (the Latin rendering of Odysseus) and Diomedes, for example, burn in a twin flame for their deception in inventing the Trojan horse. Virgil says that they "are suffering in anger with each other . . . And they lament inside one flame the ambush / of the horse" (XXVI. 56–58). The mythological hero Jason, who piloted the Argo and found the Golden Fleece, likewise suffers in Hell for deceiving Hypsipyle and Medea (XVIII. 86). Despite living in an age before Christ, characters like Ulysses, Diomedes, and Jason have been judged, anachronistically, according to a Christian moral framework; these and other heroes of antiquity now suffer for

---

the sins of fraud or violence, although in the heroic discourse of classical epic, these qualities would be considered as cunning, crafty, and strategic behavior. It is worth noting that Dante, through his literary source Virgil, sympathizes primarily with the Trojan forces and therefore sees the heroes of Homer's epics as betrayers. Yet even Trojan heroes like Hector and Aeneas are consigned to Limbo (IV. 122), for their noble characters and actions are not enough to compensate for the fact that they lived before Christ and consequently are damned. Dante views classical mythology and literature through the lens of a medieval Christian worldview, and he therefore sees in many classical heroes faults and sins that must be punished. In this context, the combat that was so valorized in the classical world becomes a potentially damning activity in the Christian one, demonstrating the social construct of both value systems.

The epic hero of Dante's poem therefore must be more than a warrior; he must first and foremost have a moral sense of whether a particular act would partake of virtue or vice. For while some acts of violence on earth are punished in Hell, some of the violence in Hell is praised as a sign of God's goodness and power. Dante describes the punishments of Hell as "God's justice in its dreadful operation" (XIV.6). In other words, violence undertaken in accordance with God's will can be just and virtuous —a logic that can have calamitous results as seen in both the crusades and the ethos of jihad. Even Dante himself can sometimes act violently without rebuke; for example, he sets upon one of the sinners frozen in the ice of Cocytus:

> At that I grabbed him by his hair in back
> and said: "You'd better tell me who you are
> or else I'll not leave one hair on your head."
> I had my fingers twisted in his hair
> and already I'd pulled out more than one fistful,
> while he yelped like a cur with eyes shut tight. . . .
> (97–99; 103- 05)

Dante is no pacifist, and his notion of Christianity does not preclude a judicious use of violence—as the tortures of his Hell clearly indicate. Violence and combat are not inherently good or bad in Dante's cosmology; instead, all such valuations must be subordinated to the question of whether they do or do not accord with the will of God. Yet the simple fact that so many of the damned are made to enact scenes of violent combat suggests that combat itself partakes of a fallen state, and that men like Dante and Virgil, who use reason to avoid combat, are operating at a higher intellectual and moral level than the warriors who struggle on earth or in Hell.

Yet Dante and Virgil's interactions with mythological monsters are only one of several devices by which Dante casts his persona paradoxically in the mode of the classical hero. Several times in the *Inferno*, Dante, overcome by the sights and experiences of his journey through Hell, swoons. On the banks of the River Styx, as Virgil argues with the boatman Charon, Dante succumbs to the fierceness of the terrain:

> Out of the tear-drenched land a wind arose
> which blasted forth into a reddish light,
> knocking my senses out of me completely,
> and I fell as one falls tired into sleep.
> (III.133–36)

Again in Canto V, after talking with the doomed Paolo and Francesca, he is overcome: "Pity / Blurred my senses; I swooned as though to die, / And fell to Hell's floor as a body, dead falls" (V. 140142). And, of course, the poem opens with Dante having awoken ("*mi ritrovai*") in the dark wood (I. 2)—which means that he had fallen asleep or fainted. Dante's swooning might be interpreted as another means by which he sublimates and redirects the classical tradition of heroic combat. The hero risks falling in battle, and Dante's falls seem calculated, in part, to make him one with these heroes. Fainting may be less valorous than, say, falling under the onslaught of a foe or collapsing from exhaustion.

Nevertheless, Dante's fainting speaks to the trials that he suffers in the underworld. The sights and sounds of Hell assault Dante and take their toll on him, and his response is a physical one. His fainting episodes therefore do not undercut, but rather establish, his heroic status. Dante pays a physical price for his journey through the underworld.

This points to a larger truth about Dante's narrative: It is the landscape itself, rather than any one of its inhabitants, that takes the greatest toll on Dante. Their journey across the infernal landscape makes these two poets into heroes, putting them on level footing with their epic and mythological forerunners. And Dante does not pass into Hell and back, but rather he passes all the way through to its center. Dante's endurance therefore becomes epic in scope. Like Homer's Odysseus, Dante is "long-suffering" (*Odyssey* I.2), and his ability to endure a journey becomes the truest mark of his heroism. If the Christian Hell he traverses is worse than the pagan underworld, then Dante's alter ego in some respects has accomplished more than any of the heroes who have come before him.

Yet Dante's true rivals are not so much the heroes of the classical world as they are the poets who wrote of those heroes. The most profound and pervasive way in which Dante sublimates the epic impulse toward combat is by entering into competition with Virgil and other classical writers. One of the running themes of the *Commedia* is Dante's own place with respect to other poets. In Limbo, where the virtuous pagans reside, Dante meets the greatest poets of antiquity. Homer, the "sovereign poet" (88) Horace, Ovid, Lucan, and, of course, Virgil all welcome Dante. Dante writes:

> And after they had talked awhile together,
> they turned and with a gesture welcomed me,
> and at that sign I saw my master smile.
> Greater honor still they deigned to grant me:
> they welcomed me as one of their own group,
> so that I numbered sixth among such minds.
> (IV. 97–102)

Dante is characteristically humble and understated in relating this event, as he is throughout so much of the *Commedia*. Yet at the same time, the poet has composed a scene in which the greatest poets of antiquity acknowledge him as one of their own. The humility of the character Dante within the poem belies the bold assurance and self-regard of the poet who composed it. Dante goes to great lengths to suggest to the reader that he himself is an equal to the great writers of antiquity.

It is not just the poets of antiquity who give deference to Dante, but also the writers of his own time. Brunetto Latini, a Florentine who wrote prose in French and whose books were important to Dante, is consigned to the circle where sodomites are punished. He speaks in praise of Dante, saying to him:

> . . . Follow your constellation
> and you cannot fail to reach your port of glory,
> not if I saw clearly in the happy life;
> and if I had not died just when I did,
> I would have cheered you on in all your work,
> seeing how favorable Heaven was to you.
> (XV. 55–60)

Again, Dante portrays his persona as the humble recipient of such praise and encouragement. Yet Dante has composed Latini's lines as well as his alter ego's response and composes for his famous contemporary a speech in praise of himself. Moreover, there are no extant references—outside Dante's text—to Brunetto Latini having committed sodomy. One might wonder at Dante's decision to broadcast Latini's vice, be it real or imagined, to his entire readership. Dante both damns his mentor to Hell and then has that mentor give Dante his blessing. One might see in Dante's conflicted representation of Latini a Freudian wrestling with a father-figure or the artistic struggle that Harold Bloom terms the anxiety of influence. Dante feels indebted to Latini, and he therefore feels toward the older writer an uneasy combination of affection and resentment.

Dante's relationship with Virgil—perhaps the most significant and profound relationship in the entire *Commedia*—writes large the extent to which this poem is about Dante creating for himself a place in Western literature. Virgil's *Aeneid* was profoundly important to Dante as a literary model and as a trove of classical lore and literary effects. Dante calls Virgil the "light and honor of the other poets" and speaks of "my long years of study, and that deep love / that made me search your verses" (I. 82–84). By electing Virgil as his guide, Dante makes clear his sense of indebtedness to the Roman author. Yet doing so also draws the two poets into a relationship in which comparisons will inevitably arise and in which some of those comparisons will be favorable to Dante. On one level, the *Inferno* is a massive expansion and reworking of Book VI of the *Aeneid*. In this section of Virgil's epic, Aeneas journeys into the underworld to consult with his dead father and with the shades of great heroes and leaders. Dante anatomizes this book and then redeploys its elements in a new, more expansive mode. To use a musical analogy, he takes a musical phrase from the *Aeneid* and makes it the starting point for a symphony. Dante writes of Virgil and himself crossing an infernal landscape that is conceived on a far grander scale than is the underworld of the *Aeneid*.

Dante sees himself as surpassing Virgil in another way: As a baptized Christian, Dante assumes that he can understand God's design in a manner that the pagan Virgil cannot. Time and again, Virgil is puzzled by references in Hell to the presence of Jesus Christ. His account of Christ's harrowing of Hell, in which Jesus used the three days between his death and resurrection to carry the virtuous biblical patriarchs to Heaven, centers around a great mystery: Virgil simply cannot conceive of who this powerful interloper was. Similarly, Virgil is puzzled by the sight of a traitor in the seventh bolgia who has been crucified. Dante says:

And I saw Virgil staring down amazed
at this body stretching out in crucifixion,
so vilely punished in the eternal exile.
(XXIII. 124–26)

The Roman poet knows that he is looking at something of profound significance, and yet he lacks the key to unlock its meaning. Medieval scholars believed that Virgil, in his Fourth Eclogue, had unwittingly predicted the birth of Christ. Dante, too, seems to ascribe some measure of prophetic vision to Virgil—and yet whatever vision Virgil possesses is not enough to allow him to see clearly the mystery of Christ's birth and resurrection. Throughout most of the *Inferno*, Virgil stands as a symbol of reason, intellect, and moral probity. Yet having lived before the birth and death of Jesus Christ, he is lacking the one virtue that would allow him to be saved: Virgil died without having been baptized into the Christian faith. For Dante, this is the essential element of salvation. It does not matter that Virgil had no exposure to Christianity—or, indeed, that such exposure was impossible given the time in which he lived. Dante sees Virgil's lack of faith and his subsequent damnation as a sad but necessary consequence of the pre-Christian age in which he lived. Such claims to religious and moral superiority rest entirely on the benefits of hindsight and are as ethnocentric as they are sectarian. Many of the damned pre-Christian figures have in fact disobeyed the dictates of their own gods or the ethical standards of their own times. Jason, for example, knew he was wrong to abandon Hypsipyle and Medea, and his punishment is appropriate in both a classical and a Christian moral framework. Yet Virgil commits no such offense; he is damned not for a moral lapse, but for a theological one. That Dante did not hesitate to employ the trick of hindsight to establish his superiority over Virgil would seem, by his own logic, as cunning and as shrewd as the tactic of introducing the Trojan horse that had earned Odysseus and Diomedes their dreadful punishment in the Hell of the Christian Dante. Dante may feel as conflicted about the great Virgil as he does about the minor poet Latini: He owes so much to Virgil, and yet that very sense of indebtedness fosters in Dante a sense of competition and resentment. Dante's own Christianity is his ultimate means of one-up-manship on a poet who died before Christ was born.

Though Virgil will guide Dante all the way through Hell, there comes a point in the *Commedia* where the disciple Dante must continue on without his master. After Virgil guides Dante up the mount of Purgatory, Dante will continue his journey without the Roman poet—ascending the rest of the Mount of Purgatory in order to describe the sights of Heaven, a realm that is closed to Virgil. It is hard not to see Dante's ascent into Heaven as reflecting not just on his status as a Christian, but on his status as a poet. Dante presents himself as being in a position to see more and write of more than Virgil, precisely because he is a Christian and Virgil is not. And this, of course, is the poet's mission: as Matthew Arnold would put it, the poet must "see life steadily, and see it whole." On the Mount of Purgatory, it finally becomes clear to Dante that he can see a steady whole that his master cannot. The saved Dante may continue his quest upwards, while the damned Virgil must trek back to his home in Limbo. This description makes it clear that Dante's work is a subtle, literary form of propaganda: It pushes one value system or ideology on the reader by way of inference, allusion, and tendentious logic. This, then, seems at least as important a heroic undertaking than the poetic accomplishment of the work: to score a victory for Christianity. The most important contest in the *Commedia* is therefore not between Dante and any of the creatures he encounters in Hell, but rather between Dante and the Roman poet who is his guide and master. Their journey together called on them to evade one mythological threat after another, but on the Mount of Purgatory Dante finds that he now must move beyond Virgil himself.

Dante's election of himself as hero of his own epic is therefore a remarkably bold decision. As the poet takes the place of the warrior as epic hero, the value system of the epic tradition itself undergoes a seismic shift. Dante and Virgil's confrontations with a series of monsters from the classical tradition call on the reader to compare their actions with those of the heroes of Greek and Roman mythology and literature. Whereas the heroes of the classical world entered into combat with these monsters, the poets use words and wiles to evade them. The success of Dante and Virgil in journeying across Hell, as well as the punishment of so many of the men whom the classical world took as heroes, suggests that the poet is equal or superior to the warrior as a heroic figure. The great accomplishment of Dante's poem is to present poetry itself as a heroic undertaking and hence to license future poets to write of their own experience of the world rather than that of a warrior–hero. Whereas Homer and Virgil wrote poetry of heroism, Dante writes of the heroism of poetry.

Works Cited

Alighieri, Dante. *Dante's Inferno: The Indiana Critical Edition*. Ed. and trans. Mark Musa. Bloomington: Indiana UP, 1995.

_____. *Dante's Inferno: Translations by Twenty Contemporary Poets*. Ed. Daniel Halpern. Hopewell, NJ: Ecco, 1993.

_____. *La Divina Commedia: Testo Critico della Società Dantesca Italiana*. Ed. Giuseppe Vandelli. Milan: Ulrico Hoepli, 1987.

Homer. *The Odyssey*. Trans. Robert Fagles. New York: Penguin, 1996.

Raffa, Guy P. "Dante's Beloved yet Damned Virgil." *Dante's Inferno: The Indiana Critical Edition*. Ed. and trans. Mark Musa. Bloomington: Indiana UP, 1995. 266–85.

Shakespeare, William. *Hamlet. The Riverside Shakespeare*. Ed. G. Blakemore Evans. Boston: Houghton, 1974.

Vergil. *Aeneid*. Latin Edition. Ed. Clyde Pharr. Wauconda, IL: Bolchazy, 1999.

The Bildungsroman as Quest Narrative:
Great Expectations and *Jane Eyre* _____

Victoria Williams

The bildungsroman is a genre of literary fiction that takes its name from the German words *roman* meaning "novel" and *bildung* meaning "education" or "formation." In short, the bildungsroman is a coming-of-age tale that investigates the tensions experienced by an individual as he or she tries to balance the desire for personal freedom with the demands of social constraints.

The bildungsroman is at its core a quest narrative in that it charts the spiritual, social, moral, and psychological development of the story's protagonist from childhood through a variety of adventures and trials until the eventual establishment of the character in a secure adult role within a certain social order (Case and Shaw 75). Quest narratives involve a subject seeking an object (Knutson 38) that requires a great deal of effort—physical, mental, and emotional—to attain and to retain. In the case of the bildungsroman, the quest undertaken by the focal character is the quest for self-realization.

The bildungsroman novel was particularly popular during the Victorian era despite psychological theories of child development suggesting that children should be taught self-control and that self-discipline was crucial to a child's development (Brantlinger and Thesing 72). Victorian writing about childhood often went against such theories, which resulted in novels that were sympathetic to children and sometimes even sentimental. The bildungsroman novels of the Victorian age tell of the complex emotions and psychological development of children by following a child as he or she navigates a path to adulthood.

Bildungsromans also emphasize intense emotions and psychological turmoil, which suggests a link between the past and the present, and that "the powerful feelings and experiences of childhood shape the adult character" (Brantlinger and Thesing 74). Further to this, the bildungsroman implies that the "haunting power of memory (whether traumatic or pleasurable) provides the link between childhood and adulthood" (Brantlinger and Thesing 74) as it is the remembrance of past feelings and events that help to construct the core of an individual's identity. By examining the relationship between the experiences of childhood and the shaping of the adult self and by investigating the function of memory in constructing the human psyche, it could be argued that Victorian writers of the bildungsroman contributed to the field of childhood psychology (Brantlinger and Thesing 75).

Victorian bildungsroman novels such Charlotte Brontë's *Jane Eyre* and Charles Dickens's *Great Expectations* focus on characters who prove to be heroic as they embark on journeys of self-discovery from childhood to adulthood and manage to achieve self-knowledge, while retaining their true natures, in the face of physical and psychological tests, emotional upsets, and social pressures.

The ideas of becoming and of self-discovery, which are inherent in the bildungsroman, tie the genre to Romanticism, which was flourishing in the first half of the nineteenth-century. Romanticism celebrated introspection, creativity, and self-knowledge (Amigoni 55). In *Jane Eyre*, Charlotte Brontë reveals an affinity with the followers of Romanticism, who celebrated passion and treasured experience.

Jane Eyre adheres to the bildungsroman structure particularly closely: The novel follows Jane from her traumatic childhood—first at her Aunt Reed's Gateshead home where she is psychologically tortured and bullied by her relatives and then later at Lowood school where the schoolgirls are starved and beaten—through to her troubled romance with Mr. Rochester, her self-imposed exile at Moor House, and her eventual marriage. Though she is very unhappy living at Gateshead and then at Lowood, Jane needs to experience these hardships because bildungsroman require conflicts to be of interest. The first-person narrative voice, which is so important in *Jane Eyre*, makes the reader acutely aware of Jane's feelings as she experiences her childhood hardships and fosters the reader's identification with her suffering. This form of narration places the emphasis on youthful feelings and experiences and casts *Jane Eyre* as a novel concerned primarily with Jane's process of maturation from an alienated and willful orphan to an educated, wealthy mother, with Jane narrating her own autobiographical bildungsroman (Amigoni 61).

Since the story of *Jane Eyre* is told by a narrator–autobiographer, it means that at times there almost seems to be two Janes in the novel: the youthful Jane who describes events at the time of their occurrence and, occasionally, an older Jane who adds judgments or knowledge from hindsight. This is exemplified in a passage in which Jane recounts her childhood love for a doll noting, "It puzzles me now to remember with what absurd sincerity I doated on this little toy, half fancying it alive and capable of sensation. I could not sleep unless it was folded in my night-gown; and when it lay there safe and warm, I was comparatively happy, believing it to be happy likewise" (Brontë 22). The inclusion of the word *now* highlights the historical distance between the narrator–Jane and the Jane who experienced happiness with her doll, for the narrator–Jane is looking back on her childhood. This doubling allows Brontë to reveal both the immediate feelings the younger Jane experienced as well as how the older Jane feels about the experience with the benefit of hindsight. This double-voiced narration shows how Jane has matured through the experiences of her younger self; Jane's clear-headedness is one of the proofs of her having developed and achieved her quest to grow up successfully.

When *Jane Eyre* was first published, some reviewers were shocked by what they perceived as the angry defiance exhibited by the central character on her quest to adulthood (Case and Shaw 69). However, feminist critics have praised the anger and pride exhibited by Jane, viewing them as positive attributes. Such critics argue that Jane is the first in a long line of female characters that question authority and that represent a character whose determination, heroism, and deep thinking allow her to deal with the difficult situations she encounters along her route from childhood to adulthood. Indeed, it can be argued that Jane's journey is a movement toward self-knowledge, or, as feminist critics have described, "a dialogue of self and soul" (Gilbert and Gubar 336).

Literary critics have paid special attention to *Jane Eyre* as a rare example of a bildungsroman centering upon a female character. The Victorian bildungsroman is sometimes thought of as an especially male genre of literature because female characters, like Victorian women in real life, faced restricted mobility in terms of travel and in opportunities for adventure from which to learn. However, the heroine of *Jane Eyre* travels across England—from Gateshead to Lowood, from Lowood to Thornfield Hall, from Thornfield Hall to Moor House, from Moor House to Ferndean—and is able to encounter a variety of situations and people so that *Jane Eyre* is now "unequivocally regarded as an archetypal female Bildungsroman or novel of female development" (Rubik and Mettinger-Schartmann 27). Though Jane is unable to leave home and travel to a large city in search of an independent life, which is the preserve of the male protagonist of the bildungsroman, she does reach maturity successfully and becomes one with the society in which she exists with her triumphant transition to adulthood marked by her union with Mr. Rochester.

The quest structure is also the usual narrative structure of the fairy tale, a genre that underpins the bildungsroman since both the fairy tale and the bildungsroman see the heroic protagonist acquire the skills necessary to achieve their goals in life. The quest is both historically and structurally related to the fairy tale, and as *Great Expectations* makes clear, the patterns of behavior and events found in fairy tales, as investigated by theorists such as Vladimir Propp in *The Morphology of the Folktale*, form the original model for the bildungsroman (Knutson 38). As the bildungsroman is essentially a story that focuses on a character's journey to adulthood, it is quite common to find elements of fairy tales in bildungsroman novels. Indeed, it has been noted that the bildungsroman tends to be set in a "fairy-tale-like closed world" (Moretti 28) that allows the extraordinary and the mundane to coexist. Fairy tale elements are often employed in bildungsroman novels because fairy tales tend to deal with the psychological processes of growing up, allowing internal conflicts to become understandable via the characters and events found in these tales (Bettelheim 25). Unlike religious stories or classical myths, fairy tales are not overtly didactic: They do not teach the correct way to behave. Instead, they help individuals to work out for themselves the best way to solve their inner problems (Bettelheim 25). Fairy tales, like myths, appeal to both our unconscious and conscious minds, speaking to the reader (or listener) through symbols that express the hidden meanings of the stories; while these symbols are often fantastical, they represent ordinary problems faced by most individuals as they grow up. It is for this reason that Sigmund Freud and Carl Jung used fairy tales to try to understand the mind. Jung in particular focused on fairy tales in his development of the concept of "collective unconscious," a deeply embedded, collective repository of images and characters shared by all individuals and appearing frequently in fairy tales. According to Jung, the symbolic language of fairy tales, dreams, and myths is composed of timeless forms that he termed *archetypes*. These archetypes, argued Jung, act as universal symbols that show the way to transformation and development.

Although myth and fairy tale both feature fanciful figures and extraordinary events, the way these characters and occurrences are portrayed differs greatly. Myths revolve around gods, demigods, and legendary figures that are so removed from the everyday that their lives do not seem to bear any relation to the lives of ordinary people. In contrast, the extraordinary events of fairy tales are presented in a way that suggests that such things are commonplace, and it is far easier to relate to the heroes and heroines of fairy tales than it is to the heroes and heroines of myth. Fairy tale heros or heroines are never divine. Rather, they may be defined by their parentage (the miller's son), by social status (the prince or princess), by their relationship with their siblings (the little brother or little sister), by their intelligence (the clever tailor), or by their physical appearance (Snow White or Thickasathumb) (Tatar 181). This makes the fairy tale hero or heroine particularly easy to identify with. This is true, too, of bildungsroman novels, which focus on Everyman/Everywoman characters and exhibit a wealth of fairy tale elements, thereby reflecting the bildungsroman's evolution from folktales concerned with a young hero's quest. In *Great Expectations*, for example, the main character, Pip, sets out on an episodic quest of self-development that explores Pip's psychological and moral evolution as he journeys from childhood to adulthood, experiencing trials and adventures on the way to maturity. It is only after Pip battles through the conflict between his social aspirations and personal morality that he acquires a sense of himself and is able to function as a fully formed adult. Pip's story closely resembles the structure of the fairy tale quest as suggested by Propp: that for a hero to exist, other characters, including the helper, the giver, the princess, and the antagonist, must interact with the hero because the basic fairy tale plot depends on the hero leaving home, meeting both helpers and enemies, going through trials, and returning home after having gained some form of wealth. While Propp's pattern focuses upon males who become kings after having undergone a series of encounters and experiences, the classic bildungsroman plot "posits 'happiness' as the highest value" (Moretti 8) so that the form of wealth that the protagonists of the Victorian bildungsroman seek to attain is generally happiness, especially romantic fulfilment, rather than riches or power. This can be seen in *Great Expectations* in which Pip meets helpers, exemplified by Magwitch, and adversaries, such as Miss Havisham, as he travels in a cycle beginning and ending at home.

At the beginning of *Great Expectations*, Pip is physically absent from home and is visiting the tombs of his relatives, yet he is at home in his dependence on his guardians with whom he lives. It is among the graves that Pip meets Magwitch, the escaped convict who will set Pip on his quest of self-discovery by acting as a fairy-godmother figure.

The next stage of Pip's journey to maturity is marked by his visit to Satis House where he meets the disturbed Miss Havisham and her ward Estella. Miss Havisham is a corpse-like horror who wishes to destroy

Pip by making him fall in love with Estella, a girl who has been taught to be a cruel temptress. Eventually, Pip escapes Miss Havisham's destructive grasp and becomes a gentleman, using the money lent to him by an unknown benefactor, who is in actuality Magwitch. Pip's social mobility highlights the novel's affinity with fairy tales in its motif of a poor boy becoming a prince through the interventions of a mysterious helper. Pip, however, becomes warped by his new gentility, and he begins to feel ashamed of his old friends such as his warm-hearted guardian Joe. It is only when Magwitch reenters the novel that Pip begins to recover his old self and is able to move on toward full adulthood. Pip learns that Magwitch is his benefactor and publicly supports Magwitch when the old convict is imprisoned, and just as Pip makes peace with Magwitch, so he also reaffirms his relationship with Joe.

Dickens wrote two ends to Pip's quest to maturity. In the original ending, Pip encounters Estella on a city street. She is still aloof, yet she has suffered at the hands of her husband and, as a result of this suffering, is now much mellower. There is, however, no hint that Pip and Estella will form a romantic union. In the second, more often published ending, Dickens strongly hints that Pip and Estella will marry. In this later ending, Pip finds himself back at Satis House where he encounters Estella once again. This time, Pip and Estella are older and wiser, and it seems that destiny will unite the two in marriage when Pip recalls, "I saw no shadow of another parting from her" (Dickens 492). In this second version, it appears that Pip has achieved a sense of peace with the world, and both Pip and Estella seem to have reconciled themselves with their shared past and attained a rueful contentment. While the original ending is in keeping with the melancholy tone of the novel, the alternative, happy, ending adheres to the fairy-tale qualities that are evident throughout *Great Expectations*. The second ending continues the pattern of unions, separations, and reconciliations found in the novel, and it unites Pip's past, present, and future. The adult versions of Pip and Estella differ greatly from their childhood selves as they have both been changed by suffering, and both deserve to experience some happiness after having suffered so much. It is particularly apt that Pip finds his happiness with Estella, for it is revealed that she is the daughter of Magwitch, another character whom Pip loved and who brought Pip happiness. It is Pip's ability to experience transformations in his character and still be able to recognize his true self, together with his ability to experience great emotional turmoil yet retain an inner goodness, that mark Pip as heroic.

Another protagonist of the bildungsroman who finds romantic happiness as the reward for successfully completing the quest to adulthood is Jane Eyre. Jane's female character makes for a bildungsroman that differs from that of a male character such as Pip, though both are imbued with many fairy-tale qualities. Fairy-tale elements appear repeatedly in *Jane Eyre* since Jane is likened to fantastical beings such as a fairy, elf, imp, witch, and mermaid. Indeed, when Jane's eventual husband, Rochester, sees Jane for the first time, he thinks "unaccountably of fairytales" (Brontë 106). As is the case with many female fairy-tale figures such as Snow White and Little Red-Riding Hood, Jane finds herself repeatedly trapped in forest-like surroundings. (In fact, throughout her quest to adulthood she travels from one entrapping institution to another.) However, she is able to escape her various imprisonments in order to ultimately triumph and achieve fulfillment and maturity. The fairy-tale wish-fulfillment elements of *Jane Eyre* parallel the bildungsroman structure in which personal development is accompanied by the capacity for greater self-expression.

Jane Eyre begins with the title character, a traditional down-trodden Cinderella figure, and follows the heroine as she embarks on a journey toward emotional and sexual maturity, a path that is marked by the transition from one fairy tale situation to another. Through the course of her trials and adventures, Jane is able to amalgamate her morality, mind, and instincts to form her distinct adult persona. The opening chapters of the novel establish Jane as an orphan living with unloving relatives and who wonders "Why was I always suffering, always browbeaten, always accused, for ever condemned?" (Brontë 10). These first few chapters also see the first instance of Jane as a prisoner. Jane is trapped by necessity to live with the Reed family and suffers constant bullying at the hands of her selfish aunt's son, John Reed, who takes on the role of evil step-sibling to Jane's Cinderella. Indeed in one particular instance, John indirectly imprisons Jane. When he discovers Jane hiding from him he throws a book at her head, which causes her to bleed, and when she retaliates, Jane's punishment is to be locked in the reputedly haunted red-room. Imprisoned in the room in which her kindly uncle died, Jane believes that she will be visited by his ghost and she becomes sick with fear. The red-room incident has been interpreted as a manifestation of Jane's complex love for her uncle, the only man to have ever loved her (Maynard 101), and it has been suggested that Jane's fainting is a manifestation of her youthful fear of sexual emotions. However, as Jane progresses towards adulthood through the course of her encounters and adventures, she learns to understand and accept her sexuality.

The debilitating imprisonment Jane experiences at Gateshead prefigures the treatment that she and others will receive from Mr. Brocklehurst when they are trapped by him in Lowood Institution's harsh regime. When Jane first sees Mr. Brocklehurst, she remarks to herself, "What a great nose! and what a mouth! and what large prominent teeth!" (Brontë 25), a description that echoes Little Red Riding Hood when she looks at the disguised wolf and that signals to the reader that beneath Mr. Brocklehurst's image as a benevolent headmaster lies a man dangerous to young girls. At Lowood, Jane is singled out by Mr. Brocklehurst for particularly unwarranted punishment, which highlights Jane's loneliness in the world by denouncing her as a "little castaway: not a member of the true flock, but an interloper and an alien" (Brontë 56). It is arguable that Mr. Brocklehurst represents the worst aspects of patriarchy and that he is particularly cruel to Jane because she possesses an especially spirited resilience that he aims to subdue through cruelty. That Jane's spirit is not broken by her treatment but rather grows stronger through withstanding punishment not only marks Jane as heroic, but it aids Jane in her future dealings with Rochester, another man with the potential to misuse his position of power. Jane's strength of character is such that she survives Lowood and is able to continue on her journey to adulthood. Throughout her quest towards self-determination, Jane encounters several female characters that may be viewed either as personifications of the trials she must overcome in order to reach maturity or as options she may take on her journey. Just as Rochester and Mr. Brocklehurst can be interpreted as personifications of patriarchal authority, so can the female characters, such as Jane's best-friend Helen Burns, be seen as an expression of female resignation. Unlike Jane, Helen never leaves childhood because she renounces the world, which she views as a world of earthly pain, and instead opts to enter a spiritual realm in which she will be free from tyranny and hardship. However, it seems as if Helen decides to die rather than exist in a patriarchal society. In order to find her own identity, Jane must resist destructive extremes, such as Helen's religion-fueled self-renunciation, just as later in the novel Jane must refuse to yield to sexual temptation in the form of Rochester's bigamous proposal. Instead, in order to reach the goal of her quest, maturity, Jane must learn to reconcile the conflicting impulses of morality and desire. Jane does this when she refuses to become Rochester's mistress and also when she turns down St. John Rivers, whose proposal of marriage stands for extreme morality and self-destructive self-denial. While in the male bildungsroman it is deemed beneficial to the protagonist's moral and emotional development to experience a love affair, however unwise, for the female protagonist such an experience would result in punishment in the form of societal ostracism. Thus when Jane rebuffs Rochester's suggestion that she love him despite his existing wife—a love that would go against both religious and social conventions—Jane acts heroically and remains true to herself without diluting her own personal morality in the face of temptation.

The Thornfield Hall section of *Jane Eyre* sees Brontë combine multiple fairy tales: Jane is simultaneously an imprisoned Cinderella trapped within Bluebeard's castle and a Little Red Riding Hood in love with Mr. Rochester's wolf. Brontë calls attention to the fairy-tale allusions when, on being shown around Thornfield Hall for the first time, Jane admits that she feels she has entered "some Bluebeard's castle" (Brontë 92), suggesting that Rochester might have secrets he wishes to hide, especially from a naïve girl. In the "Bluebeard" fairy tale, a young bride discovers that her new husband has murdered her predecessors and locked their corpses in a forbidden room. The description of Thornfield Hall as a "Bluebeard's castle" is apt because, like the fairy-tale castle, the house does indeed hide its master's matrimonial secrets—namely, his mad wife, Bertha. Also as in "Bluebeard," the heroine is restricted from an area of the house, for Jane notes, "I chanced to see the third-storey staircase door (which of late had always been kept locked)" (Brontë 143). This exclusion pricks Jane's curiosity, just as it did that of Bluebeard's unfortunate new wife. Jane concludes "that there was a mystery at Thornfield; and that from participation in that mystery I was purposely excluded" (Brontë 144), and so Jane is tempted to learn the mysteries of Thornfield Hall and along the way experiences temptation in the shape of Rochester.

Many critics read the Thornfield Hall/Bluebeard's castle scenario in a feminist light. As Anne Williams argues, "Bluebeard's secret is the foundation upon which patriarchal culture rests: control of the subversively, curious 'female' personified in his wives" (41), and Jane expresses this curiosity about the wider world, yearning for liberty and equality when, standing on the battlements of Thornfield Hall, she reveals, "I longed for a power of vision which might overpass that limit; which might reach the busy world, towns, regions full of life I had heard of but never seen" (Brontë 94). Jane takes on the role of Bluebeard's new wife, imprisoned by patriarchal society. Patriarchy is represented by both the Bluebeard's castle of Thornfield Hall and by Rochester's proposal to enter into a marriage that, unknown to Jane, would prove bigamous. Unlike the extremely naïve Little Red Riding Hood, who fails to understand her situation and pays for her ignorance with her life, Jane is able to save herself. When Bertha's presence is revealed and Jane makes it clear that she will not willingly become Rochester's mistress, Jane's stoicism softens Rochester's temper. This represents a turning point in the novel. From this point on, Jane's Little Red Riding Hood has power over Rochester's wolf, something Jane notices when she reveals, "I was not afraid: not in the least. I felt an inward power; a sense of influence" (Brontë 267) and suggests that Jane has taken a large step towards attaining her quest's aim of maturity.

Jane's new-found mastery of Rochester has its roots in their first meeting when Rochester falls at her feet from his horse, and, although Jane says she "obeyed him" (Brontë 98) in assisting her stricken employer, it is he who needs her help in order to stand. The delicate balance of power between Jane and her employer is also questioned when Jane acts as the decisive rescuer saving Rochester from his bed after Bertha had set it alight, an act of importance recognized by Rochester when he tells Jane, "Why, you have saved my life!—saved me from a horrible and excruciating death!" (Brontë 132). Such incidents are prescient because they suggest that Rochester could never and will never have total power over Jane and will ultimately need her help as he does when living at Ferndean after he is maimed trying to save Bertha from a burning Thornfield Hall.

In the bildungsroman novel, the culmination of the main character's journey to maturity is often marked by a marriage that acts as a reward for reaching adulthood and that contrasts with an unsuccessful love affair experienced by the protagonist on the way to maturity. The marriage also acts as a contrast to the emotional discontent that compels the protagonist to undertake the journey to maturity. In *Jane Eyre*, Jane's marriage to Rochester seems to be the proof of her reaching adulthood because society will no longer regard her as an orphaned child but instead as a woman who is wealthy in her own right. However, many critics, especially feminist literary critics, find the ending of *Jane Eyre* problematic. Some suggest that having marriage as Jane's reward moves *Jane Eyre* away from the bildungsroman genre and posits the novel in another genre altogether—the courtship novel in which the primary goal of a young woman is marriage with her own individuality almost erased when she weds her husband. In the courtship novel, the heroine develops and is educated but by her husband rather than by acquiring self-knowledge and maturity through her own endeavors. However, this is only partly true of *Jane Eyre*. While Jane does participate in a courtship with Rochester, large sections of the novel see her learning about life and progressing through phases of self-development, and it is Jane who ultimately chooses to be with Rochester out of love rather than financial necessity, having already matured into her adult-self (Case and Shaw 75). Other critics argue that the relationship between the two can never be equal despite Jane's new inheritance and Rochester's fall from grace and disfigurement, with the troublesome nature of the relationship symbolized by Ferndean's dank appearance and atmosphere of decay. It has been suggested that "(u)nanimously, the feminist critics maintained that Jane's fulfilment is ultimately impossible" (Rubik and Mettinger-Schartmann 152) as they feel that for Jane to have a truly happy ending, she would have to exist in an alternative realm, free of patriarchal forces—a world that they believe Brontë, as a Victorian woman, was unable to imagine. Indeed Jane seems to participate in the classic trajectory for female protagonists of the bildungsroman: traditionally, the female focus of the bildungsroman begins her journey from the parental home (or in Jane's case, from the home of her guardian) and travels to the home of the man she marries. The male protagonist, on the other hand, leaves home in search of an independent existence (Brandström 8).

It is arguable that at this stage of the novel, Jane and Rochester begin to resemble another fairy tale couple, Beauty and the Beast, as much as they have invoked Bluebeard and his wife or the wolf and Little Red Riding Hood earlier in the novel. Jane even acknowledges Rochester's Beast-like appearance when, on meeting him again at Ferndean, she notes his long mane of hair and says, "I see you are being metamorphosed into a lion, or something of the sort" (Bronte 386), while "your hair reminds me of eagles' feathers; whether your nails are grown like birds' claws or not, I have not yet noticed" (Bronte 386). This description conjures up the image of Rochester as a Beast-human hybrid. In the "Beauty and the Beast" fairy tale, the Beast becomes more human when Beauty enters his castle and this is mirrored in *Jane Eyre*. Rochester is able to "rehumanise" (Brontë 386) through Jane's presence at Ferndean. Jane, meanwhile, resembles Beauty by loving Rochester despite his disfigurement and is able to look beyond appearances.

The author of the "Beauty and the Beast" fairy tale reveals that Beauty and her prince/beast are "perfectly happy" (Lang 118) and "lived happily ever after" (119). It is not mentioned whether Beast's being a prince while Beauty has a lower social standing becomes a problem for the couple. The same is partly true of *Jane Eyre*. However, some see their equality as problematic. Maynard suggests that Jane is able to approach Rochester at Ferndean "because his injuries make him," as she notes, "dependent, just when she has become independent" (Maynard 140), having inherited a fortune from her uncle. Jane's fortune thus allows Jane to approach her former employer minus the fears of a poor governess. In this way, according to Maynard, Brontë presents the disparity between Jane and her lover as "evened out or even somewhat reversed" (Maynard 140). However, it could be argued that Ferndean is a pared down paradise so remote from society, it seems that Brontë is suggesting such unions of equality are almost impossible in a patriarchal society. Either way, the new form of equality in the relationship allows Jane to adjust to loving Rochester, to come to Ferndean as a mature woman with an adult's perspective on Rochester and an adult sexual desire for him. Through her various encounters with temptation, Jane has conquered her earlier fear of sexual emotions and has achieved the goal of her quest—sexual maturity, a target that is so often the prize for fairy-tale heroines who progress to adulthood. Jane's acceptance of herself as a sexual being is shown when she fails to flinch from Rochester's passionate embrace.

Indeed, Jane's newly found sexual confidence is highlighted when she recalls gladly, "The muscular hand broke from my custody; my arm was seized, my shoulder—neck—waist—I was entwined and gathered to him" (Brontë 384), and it is further reflected in the descriptions of Ferndean and its surroundings that change gradually from dull and dingy to lush and fertile. The foreboding forest that greeted Jane on her arrival at Ferndean gives way to "brilliantly green" (Brontë 389) fields, full of flowers and hedges that Jane describes for her unseeing lover. Instead of an unhealthy, unwelcoming lodge that Rochester deems unsuitable even for Bertha, Ferndean is now the fairy tale forest of sanctuary and protection as in "Snow White" and "Sleeping Beauty." The natural goodness inherent in Ferndean also affects Rochester who reawakens both mentally and physically, as Jane notes when she tells him, "Plants will grow about your roots, whether you ask them to or not, because they take delight in your bountiful shadow" (Brontë 394). Ferndean's greenness marks it out as a place of fertility and productiveness, and this is apt as the closeness grows between the lovers until Jane feels, "No woman was ever nearer to her mate than I am: ever more absolutely bone of his bone and flesh of his flesh" (Brontë 399). That this love produces a child is the ultimate symbol of Jane's total attainment of adulthood. Jane is no longer the penniless orphaned Cinderella dependent on others. Instead, she is now an independently wealthy mother and wife.

The ending of *Jane Eyre* sees Jane complete her journey to adulthood for she is now fully matured, her persona having been shaped by the many experiences and characters she has met along the way. The process of maturity Jane undergoes is long and painful as she finds that her wishes and desires clash with the society in which she lives, thus mirroring the experiences of other protagonists found in the bildungsroman. The conclusion to Jane's story fits well with the traditional bildungsroman genre because it demonstrates that the varied incidents of Jane's life are linked, meaningful, and necessary (Melville Logan 94) for Jane to become a well-rounded individual and productive

member of society. Jane has undergone the transformation traditionally associated with the protagonist of the female bildungsroman: self-
realization, religious and philosophical conflict, inner turmoil, education, love, and marriage. Although there are common themes between
the male and female bildungsroman—the need to foster relationships
with friends and family, education in love and sexuality, and the goal
of self-development—the pattern of *Jane Eyre* reveals that the female
protagonist must undergo a much more convoluted path to maturity
than the male hero. Further, while the male protagonist has to contend
with social hierarchies in order to raise his social standing, the female
protagonist must repudiate this same society since it is male dominated, and she must rebel to a certain extent in order to escape inherent
social injustices.

Ultimately Jane, like Pip, is able to reach a happy conclusion to
her quest, a journey that is marked by events and experiences through
which she has grown from a child to an adult. This journey mirrors the
quest narratives of fairy tales in which the goal of characters is to attain
happiness. Both Dickens and Brontë employed the prevalent fairy tale
motifs in their bildungsroman as they recognized the inherent similarities between that genre and the fairy tale quest. The fairy tale elements
of *Jane Eyre* and *Great Expectations* function to strengthen the quest
aspects of the narratives and highlight the heroic qualities of Jane and
Pip.

Works Cited

Amigoni, David. *The English Novel and Prose Narrative*. Edinburgh: Edinburgh UP,
    2000.
Bettelheim, Bruno. *The Uses of Enchantment: The Meaning and Importance of Fairy
    Tales.* New York: Knopf, 1976.
Brändström, Camilla. "Gender and Genre": A Feminist Exploration of the Bildung-
    sroman in *A Portrait of the Artist As a Young Man* and *Martha Quest*. Diss. Swed.:
    U of Gävle, 2009.
Brantlinger, Patrick, and William B. Thesing, eds. *A Companion to the Victorian Nov-
    el*. Oxford: Blackwell, 2002.
Brontë, Charlotte. *Jane Eyre*. Hertfordshire: Wordsworth, 1992.

Case, Alison A., and Harry E. Shaw. *Reading the Nineteenth-Century Novel: Austen to Eliot*. Oxford: Blackwell, 2008.

Dickens, Charles. *Great Expectations*. Middlesex: Penguin, 1973.

Gilbert, Sandra M., and Susan Gubar. *The Madwoman in the Attic: The Woman Writer and the Nineteenth-Century Literary Imagination*. New Haven: Yale UP, 1979.

Knutson, Susan Lynne. *Narrative in the Feminine: Daphne Marlatt and Nicole Brossard*. Ontario: Wilfrid Laurier UP, 2000.

Lang, Andrew, ed. *The Blue Fairy Book*. New York: Dover, 1965.

Maynard, John. *Charlotte Brontë and Sexuality*. London: Cambridge UP, 1984.

Melville Logan, Peter, ed. *The Encyclopedia of the Novel*. Oxford: Blackwell, 2011.

Moretti, Franco. *The Way of the World: The* Bildungsroman *in European Culture*. London: Verso, 2000.

Propp, Vladimir. *Morphology of the Folktale*. 2nd ed. Trans. Laurence Scott. Austin: U of Texas P, 1968.

Rubik, Margarete, and Elke Mettinger-Schartmann, eds. *A Breath of Fresh Eyre: Intertextual and Intermedial Reworkings of Jane Eyre*. Amsterdam: Rodopi, 2007.

Tatar, Maria. *The Hard Facts of the Grimms' Fairy Tales*. Princeton: Princeton UP, 1987.

Williams, Anne. *The Art of Darkness: A Poetics of Gothic*. Chicago: U of Chicago P, 1995.

Varied and Conflicting Quests in Melville's
Moby-Dick: The Nine "Gams" _____

Robert C. Evans

I. Varied "Quests" in *Moby-Dick*: A Brief Overview

Nearly every reader of Herman Melville's *Moby-Dick* would agree that
it is a "quest novel," although a more accurate designation might be
"a novel of varied quests." Although the word *quest* appears only six
times in the book itself, the same word appears extremely frequently in
writing *about* the work. In fact, "questing" in *Moby-Dick* has been defined in an extraordinary number of ways—ways that can be reviewed
only briefly here.

Often the various quests discussed by interpreters of *Moby-Dick*
have focused on Ahab's quest(s). Henry Alonzo Meyer, for instance,
sees the novel as the captain's "quest for certainty" (Parker and
Hayford 184); Sophie Hollis, in a particularly suggestive remark that
represents a very widespread and generally persuasive view of Ahab,
regards him as pursuing "the hand of God" in order "to destroy it"
(Parker and Hayford 187); and Edward H. Rosenberry sees Ahab's
voyage as "a struggle for a definitive death" (Hayford and Parker 685).
Lowry Nelson Jr. sees it as "both a search for significant evil and for
[Ahab's] own identity" (Parker and Hayford 297); Alan Heimert links
it to American "imperial aspirations" (Parker and Hayford 307); while
Harry Levin thinks Ahab's questing makes him "a culture hero, a
dragon-slayer and therefore a liberator" (Gross 140).

Alfred Kazin mentions the word *quest* repeatedly while claiming that
"*Moby-Dick* is not so much a book *about* Captain Ahab's quest for the
whale as it is an experience *of* that quest" (Bloom, *Moby Dick* 8), which
is a view that admirably focuses on the aesthetic impact of the novel.
David S. Reynolds sees the "object of Ahab's quest" as a kind of "dark
reform" relevant to nineteenth-century politics (Bloom, *Moby Dick*
102), while Sanford E. Marovitz sees it as a "quest for ultimate Real-

ity beyond time" (Bloom, *Herman Melville* 42). For Philip Armstrong, Ahab's quest is "an allegory of that attempt to master nature which characterized industrial capitalism" (1042), a particularly intriguing suggestion. Similarly thought-provoking is Richard Brodhead's claim that the book depicts "a quest for absolute potency, a quest in which the aggressive assertion of masculine strength calls up a fantastically enlarged version of that strength as its imagined nemesis" (9–10). In other words, Brodhead thinks that aggressive men, such as Ahab, seek (or imagine) enormously strong opponents. Charles Feidelson Jr., however, thinks Ahab pursues a "symbolic voyage to the utmost . . . realizing at the same time its ineffectuality" (Hayford and Parker 673).

Often, though, questing in *Moby-Dick* is treated in wider terms in relation to the novel as a whole. Thus, E. K. Grant Watson calls Melville's text an adventure-book dealing with "the highest plane of spiritual daring" (Parker and Hayford 137), while James D. Koerner sees it as a story of "man's search for the meaning of life" (Parker and Hayford 250). Bernard DeVoto calls it a quest "through eternity after the infinite" (Hayford and Parker 633), while Newton Arvin calls it "a quest or pilgrimage . . . downward and, so to say, inward to the primordial world" (Bloom, *Herman Melville* 112). Martin Leonard Pops emphasizes the novel's "quest for the Sacred" (Hayashi 88); Ronald James Black highlights its "quest for spiritual truth" (Hayashi 382–83); and Nancy Fredricks notes that the book has long been used to discuss ideas about "the romantic quest into the wilderness away from home and mother" (Bloom, *Herman Melville* 113). Finally, D. H. Lawrence, famously proclaimed that the white whale "is hunted, hunted, hunted by the maniacal fanaticism of our white mental consciousness" (Bloom, *Herman Melville* 133), a view that has all the limits of any ethnic generalization.

In an especially useful book, Christopher Sten defines *Moby-Dick* as a "quest epic" (vii) involving multiple quests: "for the soul" (2), for "individuation" (that is, the process of becoming an individual), and for "spiritual awakening" (3). Meanwhile, Bert Bender, in a typical example of his consistently valuable work, argues that "*Moby-Dick* is not so much 'a quest for a knowledge of the universe'" (as J. A. Ward had claimed) as it is "a quest for the language that might most fully and beautifully *celebrate* the knowledge that Melville affirms at the outset of the voyage. . . . As a quest for knowledge." Bender suggests "*Moby-Dick* ends where, from Melville's point of view, any such voyage of mind must end: where it begins, in his belief that we can never 'grasp' the mystery of life" (32). Certainly this view does justice to the memorable impact that the final chapters of *Moby-Dick* have on many readers.

Some commentators have seen *Moby-Dick* as a quest narrative highly relevant to Melville's own life and thoughts. Willard Thorp, in a particularly provocative comment, suggests that it might reflect Melville's own "quest for the Ultimate," a "quest perhaps dangerous to [his] sanity" (Hayford and Parker 635). Charles Feidelson Jr. regards both Melville and Ishmael as representatives of "the voyaging mind" and argues that Melville himself "discovers that he is potentially an Ahab, the devil's partisan, the nihilist" who believes in nothing (Hayford and Parker, 671, 673, 676). Frank Clark Griffith treats the novel in terms of Melville's "Quest for God" (Hayashi 23), while Stanley R. Beharriell emphasizes the author's "Search for Community" and "the violation of community by the intense individualism of [Melville's] age, represented by Ahab" (Hayashi 34).

For present purposes, however, perhaps the most helpful recent discussion of questing in *Moby-Dick* is by James I. McIntosh, who writes that "*Moby-Dick* fits the traditional literary form of the quest-romance." McIntosh also convincingly argues that the book is "virtually unique in romantic literature in that it is a multiple, not a singular, quest" (29).[1]

II. Questing and the "Gams"

What is a "quest"? As the preceding shows, the term can be defined in an enormous number of ways. Often a quest is defined as a journey (literal or symbolic) involving some kind of heroism. Frequently the journey is in pursuit of some larger objective, some ultimate goal that can only be reached by expending energies that imply heroic efforts and that, in the process, might deeply transform the quester himself.

Are there, one might ask, lesser and greater quests? Also, is a quest an individual or a collective undertaking, and if collective, how big can the group be? These are just two of the questions raised by the idea of questing, especially in *Moby-Dick*. For present purposes, this chapter will adopt a fairly broad definition of questing—one that allows us to see the *Pequod*'s quest as both individual (on the part of Ahab) and collective (on the part of the men Ahab entices and coerces to share his personal quest). For Ahab, the quest is not merely literal; it is also figurative. It is a quest after some larger metaphysical or even spiritual objective. For Ahab, the white whale is not simply a beast of the sea, nor is it even simply a monster he seeks to punish for the loss of his leg.

For Ahab, the whale is—what? This question has been answered in an extraordinary variety of ways, ways that would require a far more extensive survey than the survey already given of "questing" in Melville criticism. To pretend that the whale represents just one thing to Ahab, or that what it represents can be easily defined in ways that would satisfy every reader (or even most of them), would be to simplify radically the experience of the book. Melville's novel seems designed more to raise questions than to answer them, more to stimulate thoughts than to settle interpretive disputes. The one thing that almost all interpreters of *Moby-Dick* can agree on, however, is that Ahab does indeed pursue a personal quest for vengeance. That is the aspect of his questing that this chapter will focus on.

It is easy—perhaps too easy—to see Ahab's quest as heroic, and certainly his quest demands great courage, determination, and effort. Yet if Ahab is a hero, his heroism is of a particularly dark and disturbing sort, a sort that exacts an enormous spiritual cost from Ahab and a highly destructive practical cost from his crew. No wonder that so many readers of the novel have been tempted to see Ahab as a kind of Hitlerian figure: obsessed with his own "lofty" dreams of vengeance, gifted with extraordinary rhetorical power, followed loyally to their own destruction by people partly cowed by him and partly in the grip of his charisma, and initially seen as a heroic quester by many intelligent people of his time. Of course, the analogy with Hitler is too extreme (although it recurs often in comment on the novel). Napoleon might be a better and less anachronistic parallel. Regarded at first (and even today) by many as a Romantic hero, he was the source of much ultimate disappointment to many of his first admirers. One thinks of Beethoven angrily rejecting his original decision to write his "Heroic" symphony in Napoleon's honor. Instead, he finally obliterated Napoleon's name from the title page, putting in its place the following explanation: "composed to celebrate *the memory* of a great man" (emphasis added).

For Ahab's crew, the quest after Moby-Dick is, for the most part, something much simpler and less grand than it is for Ahab: It is a quest to profit financially by satisfying their captain's strange obsession. Heroism (in the sense of strength and determination under circumstances of great personal risk) is required both from Ahab and from his crew. Yet Melville also shows that such heroism was required of practically all the whale-men at sea, often for years at a time, in the early nineteenth century. Indeed, Melville himself makes a special point of emphasizing the dangers of whaling, particularly the dangers of dying at sea. All whale-men risked death almost as soon as they left port, perhaps never to return. This, of course, is the special burden of Chapter 7 ("The Chapel"), which Melville is careful to place very early in the novel.

One might argue that whale-men, even more than other sailors of the time, were particularly at risk. Merchant ships and slave ships undertook voyages that were relatively short and relatively direct; certainly few merchant ships were at sea as continuously long as most whale ships were. The object of quests by merchant ships and slave ships was mostly to get to the next port, and the sailors aboard such ships faced few of the personal risks endured by whale-men, particularly the whale-men who descended down into small boats, armed merely with harpoons, to pursue gigantic beasts. Sailors on war ships obviously faced real risks of death but only when their nations were at war. During the time of the *Pequod*'s voyage, and for decades earlier, the United States Navy had mainly been at peace. The men on whale ships, by contrast, risked life and limb all throughout their voyages. (Perhaps only pirates were more widely and consistently at personal risk, but they assaulted other people not gigantic wild creatures.) Whale-men had to display heroism, determination, and bravery even more, and more consistently, than practically any other men at sea.

This claim is significant, for during the course of its own lengthy voyage, the *Pequod* encountered nine other whaling vessels engaged in varied quests of their own. Some of these ships, as will be seen, had already faced and/or suffered enormous risks. Each encounter helps highlight, through similarity or contrast, the *Pequod*'s own quest. Each encounter also leads to a "gam," a word whose meaning Ishmael carefully explains:

> GAM. NOUN—A social meeting of two (or more) Whale-ships, generally on a cruising-ground; when, after exchanging hails, they exchange visits by boats' crews: the two captains remaining, for the time, on board one ship, and the two chief mates on the other. (Melville 1050)[2]

As so often in *Moby-Dick,* this phrasing proves highly ironic. Most of the "gams" the novel describes fail to fit this definition very well at all, mainly because Ahab is so obsessed with pursuing his own single-minded quest that he takes little time for any "*social meeting[s]*," let alone for any "*exchange [of] visits.*" Only once, in fact, does Ahab go aboard another ship, nor do any "*chief mates*" exchange visits during the *Pequod*'s voyage. Ahab is too busy pursuing his own egocentric, monomaniacal quest to take any real interest in the purposes, aspirations, or achievements of others. Isolated from his own crew, he is even more isolated from any other crews he meets. His fanatical quest leaves him little time or inclination to engage in the idle chit-chat of an ordinary gam. To Ahab, the varied ships he encounters are merely potential sources of information about the white whale.

Ishmael comments that Ahab "cared not to consort, even for five minutes, with any stranger captain, except he could contribute some of that information he [Ahab] so absorbingly sought" (1047). The words *stranger captain* are used repeatedly in describing the various "gams," but it is Ahab who deliberately turns *himself* into a stranger. In pursuing his obsession, he neglects tradition, common courtesy, and the needs and concerns of others. Just as he cares little about his own crew, so he cares even less about the crews of other whalers. Paradoxically, the gams that should help temporarily alleviate the *Pequod*'s isolation only help emphasize it all the more.

The traditional purpose of "gams" was to suspend, temporarily, the specific quest of each participating ship. Whaleships inevitably competed, but gams allowed them to suspend competition, at least briefly, in order to engage in what Ishmael calls "closer, more friendly and sociable contact" (1047). Whaleships meeting in gams often exchanged news about home, especially if they had sailed from the same original port, but Ahab's compulsive quest makes him impatient with such "dear domestic things" (1047). Almost by definition, most quests involve (at least initially) movement away from home, from the "domestic." Certainly Ahab's quest involves both leaving and losing home, never to return.

Ishmael, explaining the purposes and value of gams, notes that outward-bound ships often gave letters from home to the ships they encountered, and that "in return for that courtesy, the outward-bound ship would receive the latest whaling intelligence from the cruising-ground" (1048). But Ahab, of course, is not really interested in "the latest whaling intelligence"; all he really cares about is Moby-Dick's location, and in each of the *Pequod*'s nine gams with other ships, the first and almost the only question Ahab or his officers ask concerns the white whale's whereabouts. The nine "gams," then, help emphasize again and again the single-minded narrowness of Ahab's personal, obsessive quest. He has no time for "agreeable chat"; he has no interest in "a common pursuit"; he is unconcerned with "mutually shared privations and perils" (1048). Having chosen to isolate himself on his own ship, Ahab chooses to isolate himself (and his crew) even more from the other ships they encounter.

Commenting on meetings between English and American whalers, Ishmael notes that each ship tends to suffer, at first, from "a sort of shyness" (1048), although shyness, of course, is the last trait Ahab is ever likely to exhibit. He is too full of pride to be shy. Sometimes (Ishmael notes) "English whalers . . . affect a kind of metropolitan superiority" (1048), but such affectations are nothing compared to Ahab's supreme egotism. The typical American whale-hunter, Ishmael notes, is not really bothered by superior English attitudes, "probably . . . because he knows that he has a few foibles himself" (1048). Ahab, however, seems generally incapable of such modesty and self-criticism. His personal quest has so possessed his mind and temperament that he, unlike a normal whale-man, cannot perceive his own flaws.

Ishmael next notes that "of all ships separately sailing the sea, the whalers have most reason to be sociable—and they are so" (1048), words that make the behavior of Ahab and the *Pequod* seem all the more abnormal. Merchant ships, "crossing each other's wake in the mid-Atlantic, will oftentimes pass on without so much as a single word of recognition" (1048). These ships, obsessed with earning profits, have little time for each other. The *Pequod* is not a merchant ship, but Ahab's obsessive quest makes it act like one. The *Pequod* behaves like a merchant ship, but Ahab's quest is not to make money but to impose punishment.

Another kind of ship mentioned in the chapter on gams is the warship, a vessel designed to fight (or at least to deter fighting) and therefore engaged in an entirely different kind of quest than the *Pequod*'s. When warships "chance to meet at sea," Ishmael reports, "they first go through such a string of silly bowings and scrapings, such a ducking of ensigns, that there does not seem to be much right-down hearty good-will and brotherly love about it at all" (1049). Like Ahab, these ships, in pursuing their narrow quests, display pride and pomposity and an absence of much capacity for real friendship. Yet they at least communicate, which is more than Ahab usually does. He has turned the *Pequod* into a kind of warship, pursuing and combating the white whale but failing to display the common courtesies that even men-of-war exhibit.

Ironically, the next kinds of vessels Ishmael mentions are those transporting slaves: "As touching Slave-ships meeting, why, they are in such a prodigious hurry, they run away from each other as soon as possible" (1049). In this sense, they resemble both the merchant ships already mentioned and the *Pequod* itself. Indeed, in some respects Ahab has turned the *Pequod* into an odd amalgam of the worst aspects of merchant ships, warships, and slave ships. The *Pequod*'s behavior, in a sense, encompasses the behaviors of all the other three kinds of vessels combined, and the *Pequod* also resembles the next kind of ship Ishmael describes—the pirate ship:

> And as for Pirates, when they chance to cross each other's cross-bones, the first hail is—'How many skulls?'—the same way that whalers hail—'How many barrels?' And that question once answered, pirates straightway steer apart, for they are infernal villains on both sides, and don't like to see overmuch of each other's villanous [*sic*] likenesses. (1049)

Thus, of the four other kinds of ships Ishmael describes (warships, merchant ships, slave ships, and pirate ships), the *Pequod*, under Ahab, most resembles the final three just mentioned. Each of these ships is on a particular kind of quest, but the *Pequod*'s quest under Ahab in some ways encapsulates them all. Ishmael contrasts the behavior of these other ships with the ideal behavior of a whaling ship ("But look at the godly, honest, unostentatious, hospitable, sociable, free-and-easy whaler!" [1049]). Yet under Ahab, of course, the *Pequod*'s conduct is neither godly, honest, unostentatious, hospitable, sociable, nor free-

and-easy. In this chapter of the book, then, as often later, Ishmael's descriptions of other ships help highlight in various ways the peculiarly dark and perverted quest of the *Pequod* under Ahab.[3]

III. Questing and the *Pequod*'s Encounter with the *Goney*

The first other whaleship the *Pequod* encounters is the *Goney*, or *Albatross*. Ishmael's description of this ship (returning home after four years at sea) is full of ominous details, already suggesting, perhaps, the fate awaiting the *Pequod* as it moves ever farther from Nantucket: ". . . this craft was bleached like the *skeleton* of a stranded walrus. All down her sides, this *spectral* appearance was traced with long channels of reddened *rust*, while all her spars and her rigging were like the thick branches of trees furred over with *hoar-frost*" (1045; italics added). This phrasing emphasizes death and decay, suggesting, if nothing else, that quests for whales can be both wearing and wearying. Indeed, the *Goney*'s crew seems as worn down and worn out as their ship:

> A wild sight it was to see her *long-bearded look-outs* at those three mast-heads. They seemed clad in the skins of beasts, so *torn and bepatched* the raiment that had *survived* nearly four years of cruising. Standing in *iron hoops nailed* to the mast, they swayed and swung over *a fathomless sea*; and though, when the ship slowly glided close under our stern, we six men in the air came so nigh to each other that we might almost have leaped from the mast-heads of one ship to those of the other; yet, those *forlorn-looking* fishermen, mildly eyeing us as they passed, *said not one word* to our own look-outs. . . . (1045; italics added)

Any naïve illusions that Ishmael (a self-described "tyro" [1045]—that is, a beginner or novice) may have once entertained about whaling are further undermined by this encounter, but at least the *Goney*'s men are nearing the final stage of their own quest. Exhausted and silent though they are, they have at least survived, which is more, of course, than will be true of almost everyone aboard the *Pequod*. The sailors aboard the *Goney* can justly be called heroes and questers, as indeed could most whale-men. They have shown bravery and faced great risks in pursuit of their specific goals, and Melville emphasizes the awful toll their quest has taken.

The grim silence of the *Goney*'s crew helps contribute to our sense of the *Pequod*'s ever-increasing isolation. The only words successfully exchanged between the two ships emerge from the *Pequod*: "Ship ahoy! Have ye seen the White Whale?" (1045). Each time the *Pequod* meets another whaler, this will be the only inevitable question—a reiterated reminder of the stunning narrowness of Ahab's quest.

Ishmael goes out of his way to suggest the significance of the *Pequod*'s odd encounter (or nonencounter) with the *Goney*. The first of the *Pequod*'s "gams" is in fact hardly a gam at all:

> But as the *strange* captain, leaning over the *pallid* bulwarks, was in the act of putting his trumpet to his mouth, it *somehow fell* from his hand into the sea; and the wind now rising amain, *he in vain strove to make himself heard* without it. . . . Meanwhile, in various silent ways the seamen of the *Pequod* were evincing their observance of *this ominous incident at the first mere mention of the White Whale's name* to another ship. . . . (1045; italics added)

Ishmael reinforces the symbolic significance of this "strange" encounter by noting another odd event: a school of small fish, previously following the *Pequod*, now deserts Ahab's vessel to follow the *Goney*. "'Swim away from me, do ye?' murmured Ahab, gazing over into the water" (1046), significantly using "me" rather than "us." Ahab's quest for the white whale is essentially, and will always remain, *Ahab's* quest—a quest he could easily end at any time but chooses not to. The small fish deserting the *Pequod* have no larger quest in mind; they are free to move as they wish, unlike Ahab's crew.

In the meantime, Ahab proclaims that he is "bound round the world." He instructs the *Goney* to tell Nantucketers "to address all future letters to the Pacific ocean! and this time three years, if I am not at home, tell them to address them to—" (1046). Again, Ahab does not say "if *we* are not at home" but instead refers only to himself. His quest is egocentric; his men are mere useful appendages. His proclamation here shows his pride, his cockiness, and, in the reference to "—" (that is, to "hell"), perhaps an ironic foreshadowing of his ultimate eventual fate. Indeed, in this chapter's final paragraph, Ishmael intriguingly suggests that nearly all human quests may be doomed in one sense or another. He comments that when humans pursue "those far mysteries we dream of, or in tormented chase of that demon phantom that, some time or other, swims before all human hearts; while chasing such over this round globe, [such mysteries or phantoms] either lead us on in barren mazes or midway leave us whelmed" (1046). The *Pequod*'s initial "gam" thus sets an ominous precedent for those that follow.

IV. The *Pequod*'s Quest and "The *Town-Ho*'s Story"

If the *Pequod*'s first encounter with another whaleship pursuing another quest is highly symbolic, so too are all its later gams. The next, with the *Town-Ho*, results in a chapter so long and independently significant that it almost epitomizes the novel as a whole. Indeed, "The *Town-Ho*'s Story" was even separately published several times before *Moby-Dick*. This is not the place to comment on all its rich implications, but one point worth emphasizing is how often this chapter, like the novel itself, presents diverse quests prompted by diverse motives, almost all of them requiring real heroism in pursuit of frequently dangerous goals.

Briefly, "The *Town-Ho*'s Story" describes conflict between the first mate (Radney) and a popular sailor (Steelkilt). When Steelkilt mocks Radney, Radney orders him to swab a filthy deck. When Steelkilt refuses, Radney physically threatens him with a hammer. Steelkilt, in response, seriously injures Radney and leads an abrupt revolt, but he and his angry sympathizers—a third of the crew—are eventually locked in

---

the ship's hold. However, as conditions worsen there, he is deserted by all but two followers. Eventually the three are strung up, whipped, and then released, but before Steelkilt can vengefully kill Radney, Radney pursues the white whale, who grabs and drowns him. Ultimately, Steelkilt and many others desert the *Town Ho* when it reaches port. Later, having stolen some native war canoes, Steelkilt encounters a small boat commanded by the *Town Ho*'s captain. Steelkilt forces the captain to delay any pursuit, so all the deserters can safely escape.

One striking aspect of this chapter is simply how many *different* kinds of quests it describes, making it resemble the larger novel. These quests include the following (not all of them equally impressive):

1. The *Town-Ho*'s "homeward-bound" quest when it first encounters the *Pequod* (1052).

2. The *Town-Ho*'s initial quest when, with its first crew, it was "cruising" for whales (1053).

3. The *Town-Ho*'s quest for "the nearest harbor among the islands" (1053) when it springs a serious leak.

4. Radney's earlier quests throughout the "austere Atlantic and [the] contemplative Pacific" (1055).

5. The quests of other captains who, facing leaks, "think little of pumping their whole way across" the Atlantic (1055).

6. The quest of Steelkilt and most of his crewmates who originally signed onto the *Town-Ho* merely "for the cruise" (1062) and who thus can legally depart whenever they desire.

7. The *Town-Ho*'s quest after Moby-Dick—a quest that leads to the death of Radney (who strongly resembles Ahab).

8. The quest, by the *Town-Ho*'s captain, toward Tahiti to replace the deserters (1070).

9. Steelkilt's own quest for Tahiti as he flees the potentially vengeful captain (1070).

10. The quest by the deserters away from Tahiti (1070–71).

11. The quest by the *Town-Ho*'s captain aboard a small boat back to his whaleship where he "again resumed his cruisings" (1071).

Not all these quests, of course, involved the same degrees of danger or required the same degrees of personal heroism. Yet, as stressed above, all of them, almost by definition, involved *some* degree of danger and required determination and personal bravery. This is particularly true of the third, the fifth, and the seventh through eleventh voyages listed, some of which are described in quite harrowing terms.

Thus, whether by accident or by design, "The *Town-Ho*'s Story" presents in miniature a structure resembling the structure of the whole novel—a structure juxtaposing one large quest with many smaller ones undertaken by different people for various, often conflicting, purposes. Melville thus emphasizes questing as a major theme: Ahab's is by no means the only quest he depicts. Questing, Melville implies, is in some ways the natural human condition, as all the varied quests inevitably suggest.

In *Moby-Dick*'s remaining pages, Ishmael describes many different encounters between the *Pequod* and other questing vessels. Each quest illuminates, in distinctive ways, the quest of the *Pequod* itself.

V. The *Pequod*'s Quest and Seven More Gams

The *Pequod* next encounters the *Jeroboam*, also from Nantucket. Initially she is seen "shooting by" in an apparent quest of her own so that "the *Pequod* could not hope to reach her" (1128). But eventually the *Jeroboam* approaches. "It turned out," Ishmael reports, "that the *Jeroboam* had a malignant epidemic on board, and that Mayhew, her captain, was fearful of infecting the *Pequod*'s company" (1128). Mayhew's quest requires bravery and determination on his part as well as on the part of his entire crew, especially since many of them are ill.

The ironies of the encounter with the *Jeroboam* are various, especially since the *Pequod* has already been infected by Ahab with a figurative sickness ultimately more dangerous than the literal sickness afflicting the *Jeroboam*. Equally ironic is the fact that Mayhew seems more genuinely concerned about the well-being of Ahab's crew than Ahab is. In some ways, Mayhew is far more truly a hero than is Ahab.

The *Jeroboam* is under the domineering influence of one crewman, a wild-eyed religious prophet nick-named Gabriel, who variously resembles Ahab. Thus, Ishmael reports of Gabriel that a "deep, settled, fanatic delirium was in his eyes" and that he had "gained a wonderful ascendency over almost everybody" (1129). He exhibits the "cunning peculiar to craziness" (1129), and the crew is actually "afraid of him" (1130). He displays "the measureless self-deception of the fanatic himself, as [well as] his measureless power of deceiving and bedevilling . . . many others" (1130). In all these ways and others, Gabriel resembles Ahab.

Like Gabriel, Ahab is both proud and self-assured, as when, displaying his machismo, he tells the *Jeroboam*'s captain, "'I fear not thy epidemic, man, . . . come on board'" (1130), thus risking his entire crew's health. Mayhew never boards the *Pequod*, but when Ahab inevitably asks about the white whale, Gabriel shouts, "'Think, think of thy whale-boat, stoven and sunk! Beware of the horrible tail'" (1131). This obviously crazy man thus seems saner than Ahab and is a truer prophet than Ahab realizes. The *Jeroboam* has already pursued Moby-Dick, despite Gabriel's warnings. Ishmael reports that "Macey, the chief mate, [had] burned with ardor to encounter [the white whale] (1131)." Yet Macey's quest had ended, ominously, in his own destruction. Ironically, it was Gabriel, not the *Jeroboam*'s captain, who had "called off the terror-stricken crew from the further hunting of the whale" (1132). Nevertheless, Ahab refuses to abandon his own quest, which seems increasingly doomed. The encounter with the *Jeroboam* presents Melville's readers with a ship, like the *Pequod*, whose originally simple quest had first been abandoned in favor of the fanatical quest of Gabriel and then briefly superseded by Macey's self-destructive desire to pursue Moby-Dick. Thus the *Jeroboam* has already suffered from the conflicting quests (at least three of them) that will later afflict the

---

Pequod. Moby-Dick is not only a novel of varied quests but also (as in the case of the *Jeroboam* and the *Town-Ho*) of quests that genuinely conflict.

Conflicting quests are again important in the next gam. When the *Pequod* encounters the *Jungfrau* (that is, the *Virgin*), she seems variously virginal. She hasn't yet encountered a whale and may even be on her maiden voyage. Ironically, she has run out of even enough oil to light her lamps. Her captain, Derick De Deer, approaches the *Pequod* asking for oil and is generously given some. Just as the oil is handed over, however, whales are sighted, and the *Jungfrau*'s boats immediately pursue them, ignoring the *Pequod*'s generosity. Ishmael then describes the spirited competition between the Germans and Americans, a competition that puts men from both ships (including De Deer himself) at great personal danger and that therefore requires real bravery. Melville describes both the danger and the bravery in detail. "At first," he reports, "Derick's boat still led the chase, though every moment neared by his foreign rivals" (1171). Later, when Derick jeeringly flaunts his brimming oil can, the Americans are especially aroused. Eventually Derick even flings the can at the approaching Yankees. Ultimately, though, the Yanks succeed not only in harpooning the whale but in spilling the Germans into the sea. The *Jungfrau*, when last sighted, is pursuing a speedy Fin-Back, a whale the Yankees realize she will never catch. Her quest (like the *Pequod*'s) is doomed to fail, but for very different reasons. Ishmael ultimately draws the obvious lesson about questing in general: "Oh! many are the Fin-Backs, and many are the Dericks, my friend" (1179).

The next gam, with the *Rosebud*, a French ship, provides great comic relief and shows how variously Melville could employ these "gamming" chapters. Indeed, perhaps of all the whale-men encountered in the chapters on "gamming," the men of the *Rosebud* seem to be exposed to the least amount of personal risk; they seem the least involved in a quest and seem almost uniquely ridiculous. The *Rosebud*, the only ship the *Pequod* meets that is not actually moving, has attached itself to two decaying, stinking whales, not realizing that one contains highly valuable ambergris. Yet Stubb (one of the *Pequod*'s crewmen) realizes the whale's value and eventually tricks the French out of their unrecognized prized possession. They are only too willing to cut loose from the putrid, rotting carcasses, and so it might be said that Stubb succeeds in his own small quest. His men share his happiness about the quest for ambergris: They are "in high excitement" and look "as anxious as gold-hunters" (1229). As in their own quests for Moby-Dick, the profit motive chiefly spurs them. They do not really understand or share Ahab's own peculiar quest. The chapter about the *Rosebud*, overtly comic, is indeed very funny. The French vessel is the one whaleship the *Pequod* encounters that seems to be going nowhere.

A more serious meeting next occurs with an English whaler, the *Samuel Enderby*. Its hearty, good-humored captain, Boomer, has himself lost an arm by pursuing Moby-Dick. He now wears an artificial arm, carved from whale bone, resembling Ahab's artificial leg. Boomer, unlike Ahab, has now abandoned further quests for the white whale. He has already proven his bravery, his determination, and his ability to suffer great pain (and to recover from it, both mentally and physically). Clearly he is a sensible foil to the *Pequod*'s maniacal captain. He cares about the welfare of his men, and in that sense he is far more a true hero than Ahab is. (Readers of *Moby-Dick* often over-glamorize the "heroic" Ahab in the ways that readers of *Paradise Lost* often over-glamorize the "heroic" Satan.) At first, after meeting the cheerful, good-natured Boomer, even Ahab momentarily seems somewhat sociable. Thus, hearing of Boomer's encounter with the white whale, Ahab says, "'Spin me the yarn . . . how was it?'" (1261). Indeed, this chapter is one of the most obviously funny and cheerful in the book, especially when Boomer begins swapping pointed jokes with Dr. Bunger, the ship's surgeon. Even their names are comic, and Boomer illustrates how entirely differently, in contrast to Ahab, a person might respond to Moby-Dick taking a limb.

As Ahab listens to the Englishmen's back-and-forth joshing, he quickly becomes exasperated: "'What became of the White Whale?' now cried Ahab, who thus far had been impatiently listening" (1264). Bunger, noticing Ahab's growing frustration, says "'this man's blood—bring the thermometer;—it's at the boiling point!—his pulse makes these planks beat!—Sir!'—taking a lancet from his pocket, and drawing near to Ahab's arm." But Ahab is not amused: "'Avast!' roared Ahab, dashing him against the bulwarks —'Man the boat! Which way heading?'" (1265). Instead of profiting from this chance encounter with the one man from whom he might actually learn something, Ahab quickly returns to his own narrow quest, a quest that indeed seems all the narrower now that he has encountered the good-natured Boomer.

Meanwhile, the fact that Ahab physically attacks Bunger makes his quest's sheer violence now seem plainly literal. Boomer, shocked, exclaims, "'Good God! . . . Is your Captain crazy?'" (1265). The fact that Boomer (unlike Ahab) can still consider God good is significant, while his sense that Ahab may actually be insane is just the latest in a string of ominous details. Yet Boomer gives Ahab the information Ahab needs to continue his quest. Referring to Moby-Dick, Boomer says, "'He was heading east, I think'" (1265). That final qualification, *I think* is telling: It implies that Boomer, unlike Ahab, doesn't really care any longer about the whale's precise position. Any questing by Boomer after Moby Dick has now definitely ended.

The *Pequod*'s next encounter, with the *Bachelor*, further illuminates Ahab's quest. The *Bachelor*, highly successful in questing for oil, is joyfully headed home. Not all quests need be gloomy or sullen, although all quests by whale-men during this period were inherently dangerous and required bravery and determination in pursuing risky and often unattainable goals. Apparently the *Bachelor*'s men have been bravely doing something right, for Ishmael remarks that "the two ships crossed each other's wakes—one all jubilations for things past, the other all forebodings as to things to come" (1320). Ahab angrily rejects an invitation, by the *Bachelor*'s happy captain, to come aboard and celebrate: "'Thou are too damned jolly,'" Ahab says. "'Sail on'" (1320). Ironically, Ahab (so foolish himself) considers the other captain a "fool" and tells him, "'So go thy ways, and I will mine'" (1321). Again Melville reiterates the theme of contrasting quests, and again (by using *I* and *mine* rather than *we* and *ours*), he subtly emphasizes Ahab's narcissism. More evidence of conflicting quests occurs later when the *Pequod* encounters the *Delight*. The relevant chapter opens with significant words: "The intense *Pequod* sailed on" (1370). Yet if the *Pequod* seems intensely questing, the ironically named *Delight* seems battered and beaten, having recently pursued Moby-Dick with self-destructive results. Ahab, of course, refuses to learn anything from this encounter, and so the briefest of all the "gams" soon ends.

Perhaps the most significant of all the gams is with the *Rachel*, whose captain quickly announces his own quest: He is looking for a whale boat that has disappeared during the *Rachel*'s very recent pursuit of Moby-Dick. This chapter, indeed, describes several quests by the *Rachel*: first the quest after Moby-Dick, then a quest after another separated boat, and then finally a quest after yet another small boat lost in the initial quest. The latter two quests—inevitably involving risks and bravery—are especially praiseworthy and might be called quests in a far more lofty sense than the one Ahab pursues. The captain pleads with Ahab—and even offers money—to persuade Ahab to briefly help the *Rachel* search for the missing boat. This is the first time any other ship has asked the *Pequod* to join it in a quest.

Yet Ahab refuses, even after the *Rachel*'s captain finally reveals that his own young son is aboard the errant boat. Having failed so far in its own quest (a noble quest if there ever was one) to find the boat, the *Rachel* now seeks Ahab's assistance, and the *Rachel*'s captain even begs Ahab's help "'[f]or God's sake'" (1360) and reminds Ahab that he too has a young son. Yet Ahab stubbornly refuses: "'Captain Gardiner, I will not do it. Even now I lose time. Good bye, good bye. God bless ye, man, and may I forgive myself, but I must go'" (1362). But, of course, Ahab in fact need *not* go; only his selfish monomania leads him to reject this plea from a desperate, grieving father. If Ahab is quest-ing at this point (and he is), Melville shows that not all quests are ad-mirable by any means. Ahab invokes what Milton, referring to Satan, once damningly called "necessity, / The tyrant's plea" (*Paradise Lost* 4.393–94). Significantly, Ahab doesn't even ask for God's forgiveness but instead narcissistically hopes that he may be able to forgive him-self. Nowhere else in the book is the immorality of Ahab's blind quest so painfully emphasized as it is here. There is cruelty, and then there is cruelty that victimizes children. Ahab is guilty of the latter. Nowhere else in the novel is the theme of *conflicting* quests so starkly empha-sized. The literal inhumanity of Ahab's quest is now made perfectly clear. Sadly, none of the *Pequod*'s officers or men insist that Ahab help the *Rachel*, even though Ishmael suggests that the men clearly sympa-thize with Gardiner's quest.

In the novel's final chapters, Ahab's single-minded quest for Moby-Dick leads not only to his own destruction but also to the destruction of his ship and almost his entire crew. As the *Pequod* sinks beneath swirling waters, Ishmael alone has survived, buoyed up by a sealed coffin constructed by his good friend Queequeg (an anti-Ahab, and one of the genuine heroes of the novel). Now Ishmael finds himself in a kind of anti-quest that is pulled in a direction he dreads and by forces over which he has entirely no control: "*when the half-spent suction of the ship reached me, I was then, but slowly, drawn towards the clos-ing vortex*" (1408; italics in original). But this, of course, is in a sense the same situation in which he has found himself throughout the book. Only the surprising rise of the buoyant sealed coffin gives him some-thing literally to hang on to, and only the unexpected arrival of one more questing ship saves his life: "*It was the devious-cruising Rachel, that in her retracing search after her missing children, only found an-other orphan*" (1408). The novel's final sentence, then, emphasizes one last time the theme of questing, and it also implies how much the *Rachel*'s quest contrasts with the quest of the *Pequod*. Significantly, we never see the *Rachel* pause to pick up Ishamel; instead, the final sentence of the chapter (and of the entire book) meaningfully depicts the ship in mid-quest. Similarly, the epigraph to this chapter ("And I only am escaped alone to tell thee," from the biblical book of Job) implies Ishmael's determined quest to share his knowledge with his readers—a quest that has resulted in the richly complex book we have just completed.

Part of the richness and complexity of *Moby-Dick* results from the comparisons and contrasts made possible by the *Pequod*'s encounters with the nine other ships discussed in this chapter. Each of those ships is, by definition, on its own quest, if only in the sense of being involved in the inevitably dangerous and demanding quest for whales—a kind of questing that required unusual determination and bravery from everyone involved. Of course, the captains of these ships were, even more than the other men on board, questers in the sense that each captain had to make fateful decisions every day that might put the lives of his men at risk or that might prevent them from facing dangers even more life-threatening than they inevitably faced on a voyage. When Ahab is set beside most of these other captains, he obviously emerges as a quester in the most darkly "Romantic" sense of the term. He is certainly a truer "quester" in this sense than Captain Vere in Melville's *Billy Budd*, a figure often condemned by critics for hanging a single sailor (a sailor who does actually commit a crime). Ahab may indeed have a deeper mind and greater heroic potential than Vere does, but what he actually does with that mind and that potential is part of the special and hugely unfortunate tragedy presented in *Moby-Dick*.

Notes

1. Further valuable discussions of questing in *Moby-Dick* appear, for instance, in works by Ausband, Boone, Boren, Foulke, Frye, Gupta, Otter, Rogers, Selby, Slochower, Thomson, Todd, Walcutt, and especially Grenberg—a list that might easily be greatly extended. See also pages 221–22 and 237–38 in Williams; pages 188–90 and 205 in Wright; and the following volumes and pages (covering 1954–1994) in the four-volume *Critical Bibliography of American Literature Studies*: 1: 37, 166, 393, and especially 589–90; 2: 544; and 3: 15. By now,

however, the point is clear: *Moby-Dick* is a book about questing in ways almost too numerous to mention.

2. Quotes from *Moby-Dick* are taken from Melville. See list of Works Cited.

3. For valuable discussions of the "gams" in *Moby-Dick*, see especially the articles by Granger, Stone, and Young.

Works Cited

A Critical Bibliography of American Literature Studies. 4 vols. Oxford: Blackwell, 1998.

Armstrong, Philip. " 'Leviathan Is a Skein of Networks': Translations of Nature and Culture in Moby-Dick." *ELH* 71.4 (2004): 1039–63.

Ausband, Stephen C. "The Whale and the Machine: An Approach to *Moby-Dick*." *American Literature* 47.2 (1975): 197–211.

Bender, Bert. *Sea-Brothers: The Tradition of American Sea Fiction from* Moby-Dick *to the Present*. Philadelphia: U of Pennsylvania P, 1988.

Bloom, Harold, ed. *Herman Melville*. New York: Chelsea House, 2008. Bloom's Modern Critical Views.

_____. *Herman Melville's* Moby-Dick. New York: Chelsea House, 2007. Bloom's Modern Critical Interpretations.

Boone, Joseph A. "Male Independence and the American Quest Genre: Hidden Sexual Politics in the All-Male Worlds of Melville, Twain, and London." *Gender Studies: New Directions in Feminist Criticism*. Ed. Judith Spector. Bowling Green, OH: Bowling Green State U Popular P, 1986. 187–217.

Boren, Mark Edelman. "What's Eating Ahab? The Logic of Ingestion and the Performance of Meaning in *Moby-Dick*." *Style* 34.1 (2000): 1–24.

Brodhead, Richard H. "Trying All Things: An Introduction to *Moby-Dick*." *New Essays on* Moby-Dick. Ed. Richard Brodhead. Cambridge: Cambridge UP, 1986. 1–22.

Foulke, Robert. *The Sea Voyage Narrative*. New York: Routledge, 2002.

Frye, Northrop, and Michael Dolzani. *Words with Power: Being a Second Study of "The Bible and Literature."* Toronto: U of Toronto P, 2008.

Granger, Bruce Ingham. "The Gams in *Moby-Dick*." *Western Humanities Review* 8 (1954), 41–47.

Grenberg, Bruce Leonard. *Some Other World to Find: Quest and Negation in the Works of Herman Melville*. Urbana: U of Illinois P, 1989.

Gross, Theodore L. "Melville." *Hawthorne, Melville, Stephen Crane: A Critical Bibliography*. Ed. Theodore L. Gross and Stanley Wertheim. New York, Free, 1971. 101–201.

Gupta, R. K. "*Moby-Dick* and Schopenhauer." *International Fiction Review* 31.1–2 (2004): 1–12.

Hayashi, Tetsumaro, ed. *Herman Melville: Research Opportunities and Dissertation Abstracts*. Jefferson, NC: McFarland, 1987.

Hayford, Harrison, and Hershel Parker, eds. Moby-Dick: *An Authoritative Text*. New York: Norton, 1967. Norton Critical Edition.

Long, Kim. "Ahab's Narcissistic Quest: The Failure of the Masculine American Dream in *Moby-Dick*." *Conference of College Teachers of English Studies* 57 (1992): 42–50.

McIntosh, James. "The Mariner's Multiple Quest," *New Essays on* Moby-Dick. Ed. Richard Brodhead. Cambridge: Cambridge UP, 1986. 23–52.

Melville, Herman. *Redburn, White-Jacket, Moby-Dick*. Ed. G. Thomas Tanselle. New York: Viking, 1983.

Otter, Samuel. *Melville's Anatomies*. Berkeley: U of California P, 1999.

Parker, Hershel, and Harrison Hayford. Moby-Dick *as Doubloon: Essays and Extracts (1851–1970)*. New York: Norton, 1970.

Rogers, Robert. "Down in the Whole World's Books: The Humanism of *Moby Dick*." *The Humanist* 68.6 (2008): 33–37.

Selby, Nick, ed. *Herman Melville:* Moby-Dick. New York: Columbia UP, 1998. Columbia Critical Guides.

Slochower, Harry. *Mythopoesis: Mythic Patterns in the Literary Classics*. Detroit: Wayne State UP, 1970.

Sten, Christopher. *Sounding the Whale:* Moby-Dick *as Epic Novel*. Kent, OH: Kent State UP, 1996.

Stone, Edward. "The Function of the Gams in *Moby-Dick*." *College Literature* 10.3 (1983): 268–78.

Thomson, Shawn. *The Romantic Architecture of Herman Melville's* Moby-Dick. Madison, NJ: Fairleigh Dickinson UP, 2001.

Todd, Jeff. "Ahab and the Glamour of Evil: A Burkean Reading of Ritual in *Moby Dick*." *Papers on Language and Literature* 33.1 (1997): 3–8.

Walcutt, Charles Child. *Man's Changing Mask: Modes and Methods of Characterization in Fiction*. Minneapolis: U of Minnesota P, 1966.

Williams, Stanley T. "Melville." *Eight American Authors: A Review of Research and Criticism*. New York: Norton, 1963. 207–70. Norton Library.

Wright, Nathalia. "Herman Melville." *Eight American Authors: A Review of Research and Criticism*. Rev. ed. Ed. James Woodress. New York: Norton, 1971. 173–224. Norton Library.

Young, James Dean. "The Nine Gams of the *Pequod*." *American Literature* 25.4 (1954): 449–63.

One for All: The Fantasy Quest in *The Hobbit, The Wizard of Oz*, and *His Dark Materials*_____

Stephen W. Potts

Although "the fantastic," as Eric S. Rabkin calls narratives of myth and magic, goes back to the very origins of story-telling, there is widespread agreement that the genre we know as "fantasy" is relatively modern. It derives from a tradition in world literature generally referred to as "romance," not to be confused with today's popular genre of the same name. Romances were originally medieval stories, often of knights and kings and ladies, told in vernacular language such as French, then called *romanz*.

Of these, the most familiar are the Arthurian romances, especially the quest for the Grail. Later, twentieth-century scholars, such as Jessie L. Weston in her 1920 study *From Ritual to Romance*, would interpret the Grail Quest as a relic of ancient initiation rituals built on symbolic death and resurrection, often identified with "the Fisher King," a wounded figure whose health is tied to his land. As a result, the romance quest is "traditionally associated with rites of passage, particularly initiation rites, which represent in ritual the transformation of the quester into a new state of being and symbolize his rebirth" (Mathews, *Fantasy* 49). This *rite de passage* represents the transition during which the "emerging adult successfully casts off childhood, frees himself or herself from parents, proves his capacity to stand on his own feet," and then "is fully integrated into adult society" (Brewer 11). Pursuant to the Grail tradition, "an identity between individual and social quests has always been latent in romance" (Frye 58). Since "[f]airy tales and most medieval romances are essentially stories of the successful *rite de passage*" (Brewer 11), typically the hero or heroine eventually acquires autonomy and authority by placing the needs of the greater community ahead of his or her own needs. Thus, the initiation quest tracks a passage from childish self-absorption to mature social engagement.

Despite the dominance of literary realism in the nineteenth century, a sophisticated fantasy quest tradition emerged in the hands of authors such as George MacDonald and William Morris. By the beginning of the twentieth century, quest fantasy had followed fairy tales into the children's corner where it grew up in the decades before World War II. The two authors most credited with this evolution are L. Frank Baum, creator of the Oz books, and J. R. R. Tolkien, the Master of Middle-earth. When Baum published *The Wonderful Wizard of Oz* in 1900, he proclaimed it a "modernized fairy-tale." Tolkien's *The Hobbit* (1937), although linked to his broader Middle-earth *mythos*, sets out as a straightforward children's tale before waxing more serious. In most respects these are two very different fantasies from two very different authors; however, they both embody the basic pattern of the fantasy quest.

First of all, neither fantasy has a hero that qualifies as either mythic or romantic, that is, "superior to other men—often in rank but more significantly in personal qualities" (Barron 67). As a farm girl from Kansas, Dorothy comes directly from the real world, without unusual abilities; as such, she is a "mimetic" protagonist who even identifies herself as "the Small and Meek" when she first confronts the Wizard (107). In *The Hobbit*, Tolkien intentionally avoids a hero in the romance mode, since he found most classic heroes subject to a vice he called by the Anglo-Saxon word *ofermod*, defined as "overmastering pride" (Clark 49). Bilbo, on the other hand, is anything but overly proud. Although middle-aged for a hobbit, he comes across as a child in many respects: obsessed with food and comfort, leery of participating in adventures— in short, a little guy content to remain wrapped up in his own little world. Both, typical for fairy tale protagonists, are orphans. Max Lüthi, a modern scholar of the fairy tale, observes, "The first thing that is apparent in the fairy tale . . . is that it portrays its hero as *isolated* . . . often an only 'child' or a stepchild, and therefore 'easily detachable' from home and society" (*Fairytale* 135, 136). This fairy tale hero tends to be "the insignificant, the neglected, the helpless. But he unexpectedly proves to be strong, noble, and blessed" (*Once Upon a Time* 145).

Fortunately, "being neither tied down by personal characteristics nor limited by specific talents or training," such heroes "are potentially always open to entering into new relationships"; thus, Dorothy "is capable of making contact with helpers, of accepting their gifts and advice" (*Fairytale* 138, 139). Such magical assistance is an essential part of the fantasy quest. Immediately after accidentally killing the Wicked Witch of the East, Dorothy receives magic tokens in the shoes (silver in the book) and the Good Witch's blessing, a kiss that leaves a mark on her forehead. She soon accumulates the magical companions with whom she will share mutual aid on the quest: the Scarecrow, the Tin Man, the Lion. Bilbo begins with magical helpers, especially the wizard Gandalf, but will acquire significant magic tokens on the way: the elvish sword he eventually names Sting, and more importantly the Ring that will mark the turning point in his transformation from "baggage" to successful burglar.

Each quest begins with passage through a portal, which symbolically marks transition out of a child-like state. Farah Mendlesohn draws a close equivalence between "quest fantasy" and "portal fantasy"; in both the "protagonist goes from a mundane life, in which the fantastic, if she is aware of it, is very distant and unknown (or at least unavailable to the protagonist) to direct contact with the fantastic." Mendlesohn views *The Wonderful Wizard of Oz* as a classic example, although she observes that even in Tolkien's tales, the hobbit heroes venture "from a small, safe, and *understood* world into the wild, unfamiliar world of Middle-earth" (2). Both Dorothy and Bilbo are ejected forcefully from home: Dorothy by the irresistible force of the tornado, Bilbo by the irresistible authority of Gandalf. Both set out on quests in the form "There and Back Again"— the literal subtitle of *The Hobbit*—a pattern inherited from both the romance and the fairy tale.

The Wicked Witch of the West suggests another feature of the fairy tale that finds its way into modern fantasy: the presence of symbolic parental figures, both good and bad. Bruno Bettelheim views this characteristic psychologically as the "Fantasy of the Wicked Stepmother"

(66), observing how many fairy tales balance good fairies with wicked witches, or present a father figure in the form of king, ogre, or "ferocious giant [that] can always be outwitted by the clever little man— somebody seemingly as powerless as the child feels himself to be" (68). Such figures, ubiquitous in fantasy, symbolize "the family drama": "Parents are seen in many different guises, helping and hindering. Parental attitudes, at first needed and desired by the growing child for his or her protection, come to be felt as unduly constrictive. The womb becomes a tomb if it is not left behind" (Brewer 8). The childlike hero must conquer or break free from the parent to complete the initiation quest.

For Dorothy, good mother and wicked stepmother are embodied in the Witches, Good and Wicked. She follows without question the advice of the former (one in the movie, two in the book), though they provide her no other material assistance. The one fatherly figure in Oz, the Wizard, first proves threatening, then false, then helpful at least in intent. In revealing him as a fake and then serving as the reason he vacates the Emerald City, Dorothy unwittingly overturns his authority, as she has ended the power of both Wicked Witches. Bilbo likewise changes his relationship to authority in the course of his quest. Though there are no maternal surrogates in *The Hobbit*—because there are no female figures of any kind—Bilbo is initially under the power of two fathers. Gandalf advises and protects, while Thorin criticizes and demands. When Gandalf exits the quest at the borders of Mirkwood, Bilbo is left on his own and must grow into his role. He does so in the dark forest by using his talents and magic tokens first to free the Dwarves from the spiders and then to free them from the Wood Elves.

As a traditional part of the quest, the hero must endure passage through the Underworld, that is, a confrontation with death. Alluding to Mircea Eliade's studies of initiation rites, Lüthi sees this "process of death and resuscitation, . . . the journeys to hell and to heaven" as part of the "pattern of initiation which is reflected in the fairy tale . . ." (*Fairytale* 160). Arguably, Dorothy experiences this brush with death during her captivity by the Wicked Witch of the West, more clearly in the movie version. Bilbo traverses a literal, deadly underworld while fleeing the goblins under the mountains and especially when competing in Gollum's cave for the Ring. Both protagonists are symbolically reborn thereafter: Dorothy in killing the Witch and exposing the Wizard and Bilbo in escaping with the Ring.

Each quest climaxes with a moment of moral clarity. When Dorothy first asks her companions to join her, "each is so bound up in his or her own quest that at first none really thinks of the others. The Scarecrow, Tin Man, and Lion are all absorbed in their own problems, and each sets out with Dorothy from a motive of self-interest" (McLachan 148). In learning how to work together and help one another, however, they earn the recognition of their innate abilities that they receive from the otherwise phony Wizard. His role as Confidence Man is to give them confidence: "by seeking the Wizard—and subsequently the Witch's broom—and helping Dorothy, they become worthy of receiving these brains, hearts, and courage as gifts from the Wizard. The only gift that they received, however, is the public recognition of who they are— that is, of who they have become . . ." (Altamura 42). In the novel, Dorothy's three companions graduate to kingships, a traditional fairy tale symbol of self-mastery and achievement. Dorothy gets merely a return flight to her aunt and uncle in Kansas. However, when Glinda informs her that the Silver Shoes could have taken her home at any time, Dorothy embraces the idea that her quest has served "the moral growth of those she influences" (Mendlesohn 5).

The original pretext for Bilbo's quest concludes when he tricks Smaug into revealing his weak spot, which leads to the dragon's death at the hands of Bard. At this point, Tolkien steers the plot into the moral realm, and it is here that Bilbo achieves true heroism, not as a burglar but as an individual. We see Thorin mastered by *ofermod* as he refuses to negotiate with the Men and Elves over division of the recovered treasure. Bilbo, meanwhile, has spirited away the Arkenstone, the one piece of treasure most coveted by Thorin, and handed it over to Bard as a bargaining chip, even volunteering to sacrifice it as his promised fourteenth of the treasure and thus placing the needs of the whole ahead of his own. That he has made the correct choice is underlined by Gandalf, who suddenly reappears to praise him with " 'Well done, Mr. Baggins!' " (284). As noted by one critic,

> Bilbo has acted with physical courage, altruism, and loyalty to his comrades even as he attempts to stave off the war Thorin's desire for the dragon's whole hoard has made likely. Bilbo has grown thinner, stronger, braver in the long march from the comfortable Shire to the Lonely Mountain; danger makes a new hobbit of him, or rather, brings out the latent quality Gandalf had perceived in Bilbo long before (Clark 43).

Unlike Dorothy, Bilbo does come home with more than just self-awareness; Tolkien grants him a fairy tale treasure as well, although he returns to a shattered home and suspicion from his fellow hobbits, who will forever regard him as "queer." The triumph of the little guy, in this case, results in no honor in his own land and certainly not in a fairy tale marriage or throne. Virtue is its own reward: His quest has been a rite of passage into mature responsibility.

The Hobbit was a warm-up exercise for Tolkien's mid-century masterpiece, *The Lord of the Rings,* in which he set the "classic quest fantasy . . . into its final form" (Mendlesohn 30). He restored elements of romance and myth to the fairy tale pattern we have seen so far: the humble hero, the crossing of the portal, the assistance of magical helpers and tokens, the separation from the symbolic parent, the passage through the underworld, and the moral triumph. Tolkien's mythic battle against evil features an exceptional romance hero in Aragorn; a fairy tale hero in Sam, who begins as a gardener and ends up founding a dynasty in the Shire; and in Frodo, a quest hero who sacrifices everything for the salvation of Middle-earth. One author who acknowledges the influence of this work is Philip Pullman, who found *The Lord of the Rings* "full of the most tremendous excitement, with a narrative that left me breathless, and which continues to teach some very interesting things about the quest story" (Pullman, Interview with Brown 285).

Exactly one hundred years separate *The Wonderful Wizard of Oz* and *The Amber Spyglass,* the final book of Philip Pullman's trilogy *His Dark Materials*. Despite his praise for Tolkien's narrative, Pullman sets himself starkly against Tolkien's conservative worldview; he is even more adamant about Tolkien's friend and fellow fantasist C. S. Lewis, whose *Narnia Chronicles* Pullman regards as "an invaluable guide to what is wrong and cruel and selfish" ("Republic of Heaven," 58). Although raised in the same Church of England to which Lewis belonged, Pullman calls himself a "Christian atheist" (Pullman, Interview with Odean 50) who argues that "we are not subservient creatures dependent on the whim of some celestial monarch, but free citizens of the republic of Heaven" ("Republic of Heaven" 57).

His Dark Materials boldly argues this belief, relying on a number of works in an alternative Judeo-Christian tradition: the non-canonical Enochist and Gnostic scriptures; *Paradise Lost,* the epic verse version of the fall of Satan, Adam, and Eve by Puritan poet John Milton; and the writings of eighteenth-century author, artist, and religious mystic William Blake. Kathryn Patricia Smith adds such sources as "the Bible, northern mythology, Greek mythology, classic fairy tales, and William Shakespeare" (137). By reinvesting his fantasy with romantic and mythic elements, much in the tradition of Tolkien and Lewis, he transforms the modern quest, rooted in adolescent initiation, into a new testament for the twenty-first century.

The first book of the trilogy, *The Golden Compass* (published in the UK as *Northern Lights*) introduces us to Lyra Belacqua, a girl Michael Chabon describes as "headstrong, cheerful, forthright, loyal, and articulate, rather in the Dorothy Gale style of female fantasy heroines" (25). She lives on an alternate Earth where every human being has a "daemon," an animal version of the soul, as a constant companion. In children like Lyra, the daemon—Lyra's is named Pantalaimon, usually shortened to "Pan"—constantly changes form to suit the moment.

The daemons of adults, on the other hand, are "settled" into single animal forms that embody the personality and status of their humans. Daemons are connected to another ingenious invention of Pullman's: Dust. As we learn in the first chapter, Dust consists of subatomic particles that appear to collect around adults but not children. Dust becomes central to the plot because of another significant difference between the world of *The Golden Compass* and ours: its history. Lyra's Europe is dominated by a powerful Church and its ubiquitous bureaucracy, the Magisterium, who have come to regard Dust as "the physical evidence for original sin" (*Golden Compass* 371).

Like many a hero in the fantasy quest tradition, Lyra has been raised as an orphan. Now eleven years old and on the verge of adolescence, she has grown up running untamed around the grounds of her Oxford home, Jordan College, under the absentee patronage of Lord Asriel, whom she believes is her uncle. Although Lyra seems to have a talent for mischief, for inventiveness, and for leadership of the local children, we are told that she is otherwise perfectly average, even "a coarse and greedy little savage" (*Golden Compass* 36). Pullman has emphasized that Lyra is "a very ordinary little girl," and that he is wary of the romantic tradition "in which somebody's born to a particular destiny or is gifted by nature with supreme, divine gifts" (Pullman, Interview with Brown 284). Thus, she shares with her fantasy predecessors Dorothy and Bilbo a "little guy" status.

Like them she is soon called to her quest. In an echo of *The Lion, the Witch, and the Wardrobe,* Lyra's adventure begins while she is hiding inside a wardrobe, hearing Lord Asriel challenge Church orthodoxy by proposing to pursue the source of Dust through the *aurora borealis* or "northern lights," which he claims, heretically, is a gateway between worlds. When she begs Asriel to take her along on his expedition to the North, however, he refuses. Her next call northward comes from the elegant, seductive Mrs. Coulter, who shows up to spirit Lyra away to a life that promises glamour and adventure. Characteristically, upon crossing that portal she receives a magic token in the form of the alethiometer, the "golden compass" of the title: a truth-telling device that will allow Lyra, once she learns how to use it, to see into other times and places. Having a truth device as her magic amulet carries a certain irony given that Lyra's other chief talent is telling convincing lies. Indeed, when she is "lying, she felt a sort of mastery . . . the same sense of complexity and control that the alethiometer gave her" (*Golden Compass* 281). Lyra does not actually begin her quest to the North until, realizing that she is a virtual prisoner and that Coulter is intent on getting the alethiometer herself, she and Pan flee their gilded cage. By this time she has also learned that Coulter is behind the kidnapping of children by "Gobblers," that is, by the Magisterium's General Oblation Board over which Coulter has control; one of the kidnapped children is Lyra's friend Roger. Lyra's quest in *The Golden Compass* is thus a result of the triangulation that Pullman sets up between Lyra, Asriel, and Coulter.

This triangle becomes especially significant once we learn that Lyra is in fact the product of an adulterous relationship between the two adults. With pointed significance, Pullman thus turns the symbolic parental figures characteristic of the fantasy quest into the protagonist's actual parents. For most of the trilogy, Coulter functions as "a kind of wicked witch" (Hines 41). Her role as "bad mother" is epitomized at her arctic laboratory at Bolvangar, where instead of shoving children into an oven like a fairy tale witch, she is severing them from their daemons, and thus from sexuality and free will; in short, this "intercision" will prevent them from becoming autonomous adults. Although Mrs. Coulter saves Lyra from this fate at the last possible second, proving she is not completely without maternal qualities, her overall agenda is central to Pullman's theme. As a villain allied with the Church, "she *is* the Oblation Board" (*Golden Compass* 89), and we are told that *oblation* is a medieval term meaning "sacrifice," applied originally to children whose parents handed them to the Church to be made monks or nuns.

Lyra's relationship with her father is more complicated, matching Asriel's role in the trilogy. Cold and arrogant, he never comes across as a sympathetic character; he treats Lyra with contempt or at best bemusement. Lyra shares with him a natural leadership ability, seen as she gathers a number of helpers during her quest, magical and otherwise, such as the witch Serafina Pekkala, the armored bear Iorek Byrnison, and the balloonist Lee Scoresby. Her father is the one character who remains blind to her charisma; as late as *The Amber Spyglass,* he calls her a "wretched child . . . not intellectual; impulsive, dishonest, greedy" (199). Nevertheless, throughout *The Golden Compass,* Lyra hero-worships Asriel, no doubt because his contempt for authority, especially the authority of the Church, resonates in her. In fact, she regards her quest northward as motivated not only by the desire to free the kidnapped children but to deliver the alethiometer to her father to help in his own quest.

Lyra experiences her first major disillusionment—and confronts her own fallibility—when she witnesses Asriel severing her friend Roger from his daemon to power his portal through the aurora. Although his motivations could not be further from Mrs. Coulter's, since he is bent on destroying the Church and thus "sin," he is capable of the same evil act. As a Byronic antihero who "owes much to Milton's Satan [. . .,] in rebellion against the forces that claim to represent God," Asriel is "a kind of Nietzschean *übermensch,* willing to go beyond good and evil in quest of his goals" (Hatlen 87, 88). When Lyra pointedly renounces both her father and mother at the conclusion of *The Golden Compass,* she takes a major step in her rite of passage. Her next major step immediately follows, literally in her father's footsteps, through the portal to another world. She has completed only the first lap of her larger quest.

The quest in *The Subtle Knife* embraces the other young hero of the trilogy, who also confronts parental issues. Twelve-year-old Will Parry lives in Oxford in our Earth, where he takes care of a psychologically troubled mother in the absence of his long-lost adventurer father. He shows his incredible strength of will—like Lyra, his name suggests his chief ability—when he saves his mother from a pair of intruders, inadvertently killing one. Despite his skill, Will perfectly fulfills Lüthi's image of "the fairy tale hero" who, "even if he is a dragon-slayer, is time and again shown . . . as one who is helpless, who sits down on the ground and weeps because he has no ideas what to do" (*Fairytale* 137). His way out is a literal portal, a mysterious window into yet another Earth, a dying post-Renaissance world. Here adults are preyed upon by ghostly Spectres who feed off their souls, robbing them of the will to act or live, leaving the unsupervised children roaming in violent gangs. When Will comes across a nearly helpless Lyra in the forsaken city Cittàgazze, they end up joining forces for mutual protection. Lyra decides to trust Will when the alethiometer tells her that he is a murderer, and he is to take her father's place in giving direction to her quest. That her male counterpart is now a peer instead of a parent underlines that she is growing psychologically.

While helping Lyra recover her alethiometer from the villainous Lord Boreal, Will advances in his rite of passage, crystallizing his heroic role, when he fights to win the subtle knife, a blade of great power that cuts anything including space itself. In the process, he loses two fingers, leaving a wound that will bleed continuously throughout the rest of the novel. This wounding marks Will as Chosen by the knife and links him to the tradition of the Grail Quest and the Fisher King: the weapon, whether sword or lance, that produces an unhealable wound must also be used to heal the land. Indeed, we eventually learn that the wasteland of Cittàgazze was created by use of the knife to open portals between worlds, which allowed the Specters to invade this one. By the end of the trilogy it will become clear that the entire universe is threatened with the death of consciousness because the open portals have allowed Dust, the substance of consciousness, to leak away.

Reminiscent as well of the Grail quest, in *The Amber Spyglass* Will accidentally breaks the subtle knife in a scene pregnant with meaning: in a cave that suggests the womb as tomb, where Lyra is being held drugged and helpless by Mrs. Coulter. At the very moment Will is using the knife to open an escape route for Lyra, his eyes drift to Mrs. Coulter, "and for a moment it wasn't her face at all; it was his own mother's face, reproaching him, and his heart quailed from sorrow;

and then as he thrust with the knife, his mind left the point, and with a wrench and a crack, the knife fell in pieces to the ground" (*Subtle Knife* 153). Significantly, as a maternal symbol Coulter disempowers the young hero. As Will once confesses to Lyra, his greatest fear "is getting stuck somewhere and never seeing my mother again" (184). Will's role in the quest can only be successful if, as Iorek warns him while reforging the knife, he is able to "put her aside" (*Amber Spyglass* 194).

For Will to perform as hero, he must come to terms with both parents. An important stage of Will's initiation occurs at the conclusion of *The Subtle Knife,* when he suddenly recognizes his lost father John Parry in the shaman Stanislaus Grumman, just at the moment Grumman is killed by a witch. It is Will's father who manages to stop the bleeding of Will's wound and begin his healing process. As his final act in this scene, Will takes on his father's mantle, as his mother predicted he should—literally his father's cloak, figuratively his role as intercessor between worlds. With the death of his father, Will becomes his own embodiment of masculine authority. Throughout *The Amber Spyglass* he exercises command over such beings as Iorek, the angels Balthamos and Baruch, and the small but lethal Gallivespians.

Once emancipated from parental bonds, Will and Lyra together proceed to the climactic stage of their conjoined quest. Their confrontation with death is an actual descent into the Underworld of the Dead. Lyra is determined to keep her promise to find Roger; Will hopes to locate his dead father and achieve some closure. The subtle knife opens their way to Underworld, a dreary place much like the mythic Greek Hades; like Hades it can only be entered by crossing a waterway via ferry. For the living to enter the land of the dead, however, they must leave behind their daemons, an oblation Lyra naturally finds wrenching. Lyra and Will confront the possibility that they may not emerge from the Underworld again.

Once more Pullman transforms a typically symbolic aspect of the initiation quest into a literal passage for his characters. In bargaining with the harpies who guard the land of the dead, Lyra must learn to tell them the truth about life, in other words to give up her childish facility with fiction. In return, the harpies will show the children the way out, allowing Lyra and Will to guide the dead to an emancipation of dissolution and becoming one with Dust. This particular conquest of death may mean individual oblivion, but ultimately it means the rebirth of the story's cosmos. During this passage, Lyra and Will actually take power over their respective fathers. John Parry's ghost helps guide Will toward the place where he can create a portal exit while sharing his knowledge about the connections between worlds. Once Lyra and Will emerge back into life, we are informed they are "no-longer-quite-children" (*Subtle Knife* 391).

Even more astounding, when Asriel learns of Lyra's underworld journey, he finally accepts her leadership role in the battle against Heaven. With Coulter, they do a far, far better thing than they have ever done before; they sacrifice themselves to overcome the tyrannical angel Metatron (a figure that combines Enochist and Gnostic scriptural traditions) and drag him into the abyss, essentially ending the Kingdom of Heaven. Lyra and Will next encounter the ultimate father figure, the Authority or "Ancient of Days," the angel who originally set himself up as God. They find him incredibly old, "[d]emented and powerless" (*Subtle Knife* 410). With pity and compassion, they help him out of his crystal litter, only to have him dissolve with "a sigh of the most profound and exhausted relief" (411). As with the triumphs of Dorothy and Bilbo, this consummation is due to the selflessness of the heroes, signifying a major turning point for the world.

After the death of the Authority, only one quasi-parental figure remains in the story. Dr. Mary Malone was introduced in *The Subtle Knife* as a former nun turned physicist in Will's Oxford. The alethiometer sends Lyra to her because Malone is researching consciousness in a form we recognize as Dust. By the end of that volume, she has slipped through the portal into Cittàgazze, and thence to a new world inhabited by the *mulefa*, sentient beasts who live in harmony with their environment but who are threatened by the disappearance of Dust, which they call *sraf*. After leaving the Underworld, this appropriately Edenic land is where Lyra and Will discover their love for one another as they wait for their daemons to find them; as one critic notes, "[a]rguably, the deficiency this produces in each of their subjectivities enables them to conjoin" (Shohet 33). In short, each finally recognizes in the other a soulmate.

Malone functions as Temptress, telling Lyra her own story of abandoning holy orders after her sexual awakening. Soon thereafter, as the new Eve foretold throughout the trilogy Lyra lifts a piece of fruit to Will's mouth, and he responds with excitement and joy. In a moment they are declaring their love for one another, kissing with newly aroused feelings. As Dust settles on "these children-no-longer-children, saturated with love," it stops leaking out of the *mulefa*'s world (*Subtle Knife* 470). Pullman emphasizes that their sexual awakening is psychological: "They don't have to do anything else; the kiss is the revelation" (Pullman, Interview with Cooper 54). Pullman presents this Fall from innocence as a "fall" into liberated consciousness and "as a coming of age for the human race" (Pinsent 202)—the dawn of the Republic of Heaven.

Having learned from Mary about the leakage of Dust through the open portals, Will must use his knife to seal them, making the cosmos whole for universal consciousness. Only one portal can be left open, the one that will allow the dead to escape the Underworld. However, this choice requires a very adult sacrifice on the part of the two adolescents: Due to a hitch in the rules Pullman has devised, one cannot live long in a world one was not born to, as Will learned from his dead shaman father. Thus, Will and Lyra must withdraw to their separate worlds, closing the portals between them. Their only consolation will be to sit on the same bench in their respective Oxfords once a year and think of each other. In making this oblation for the sake of humanity and conscious beings everywhere, they are making the choice of the hero, the choice of the adult. What both Lyra and Will have gained in growing up is greater wisdom, an enriched life of experience beyond innocence.

Pullman shows us that "fantasies of escape to an alternate world are foreclosed: We must live in this one and make it as much like 'heaven' as humanly possible" (Lenz 9). Furthermore, he "reminds us that each moral choice changes the universe and that each one of us carries the future of the cosmos on our shoulders" (Hatlen 91). As Pullman himself says, "Our purpose is to understand and to help others to understand, to explore, to speculate, to imagine. And that purpose has a moral force" ("Republic of Heaven" 60). His great achievement in *His Dark Materials* has been to map his message upon the traditional fantasy quest. In so doing he makes manifest what underlies its patterns: its roots in initiation romances and the psychological symbolism of the fairy tale. Not least, he has produced a narrative rich in inventiveness and adventure that can be enjoyed simply as a great story—not only by adolescents but by everyone. Philip Pullman has transformed the fantasy quest for the twenty-first century.

Works Cited

Altamura, Gina, and J. M. Fritzman. "Very Good, but Not So Mysterious: Hegel, Rushdie, and the Dialectics of Oz." *The Wizard of Oz and Philosophy.* Eds. Randall E. Auxier and Phillip S. Seng. Chicago: Open Court, 2008. 33–48.

Barron, W. R. J. "Arthurian Romance." *A Companion to Romance: From Classical to Contemporary.* Ed. Corinne Saunders. Oxford: Blackwell, 2004. 65–84.

Baum, L. Frank. *The Wonderful Wizard of Oz.* New York: Ballantine, 1956

Bettelheim, Bruno. *The Uses of Enchantment: The Meaning and Importance of Fairy Tales.* New York: Vintage, 1989.

Brewer, Derek. *Symbolic Stories: Traditional Narratives of the Family Drama in English Literature.* Totowa, NJ: Rowman, 1980.

Chabon, Michael. "Dust & Daemons." *The New York Review* 25 Mar. 2004: 25–28.

Clark, George. "J. R. R. Tolkien and the True Hero." *J. R. R. Tolkien and His Literary Resonances: Views of Middle-earth.* Eds. George Clark and Daniel Timmons. Westport, CT: Greenwood, 2000. 39–51.

Frye, Northrop. *The Secular Scripture: A Study of the Structure of Romance.* Cambridge, MA: Harvard UP, 1976.

Hatlen, Burton. "Pullman's *His Dark Materials,* a Challenge to the Fantasies of J. R. R. Tolkien and C. S. Lewis, with an Epilogue on Pullman's Neo-Romantic Reading of *Paradise Lost.* " His Dark Materials *Illuminated: Critical Essays on Philip Pullman's Trilogy.* Eds. Millicent Lenz and Carole Scott. Detroit: Wayne State UP, 2005. 75–94.

Hines, Maude. "Second Nature: Daemons and Ideology in *The Golden Compass*." His Dark Materials *Illuminated: Critical Essays on Philip Pullman's Trilogy.* Eds. Millicent Lenz and Carole Scott. Detroit: Wayne State UP, 2005. 37–47.

Lenz, Millicent. "Awakening to the Twenty-first Century: The Evolution of Human Consciousness in Pullman's *His Dark Materials.*" His Dark Materials *Illuminated: Critical Essays on Philip Pullman's Trilogy.* Eds. Millicent Lenz and Carole Scott. Detroit: Wayne State UP, 2005. 1–15.

Lüthi, Max. *The Fairytale as Art Form and Portrait of Man.* Trans. Jon Erickson. Bloomington: Indiana UP, 1984.

_____. *Once Upon a Time: On the Nature of Fairy Tales.* Trans Leed Chadeayne and Paul Gottwald. Intro. and notes by Francis Lee Utley. Bloomington: Indiana UP, 1970.

Mathews, Richard. *Fantasy: The Liberation of Imagination.* New York: Twayne, 1997.

_____. "Romance in Fantasy Through the Twentieth Century." *A Companion to Romance: From Classical to Contemporary.* Ed. Corinne Saunders. Oxford: Blackwell, 2004. 472–87.

McLachan, James. "Off to See the Wizard: The Romantic Eschatology of *The Wizard of Oz.*" *The Wizard of Oz and Philosophy.* Eds. Randall E. Auxier and Phillip S. Seng. Chicago: Open Court, 2008. 133–48.

Mendlesohn, Farah. *Rhetorics of Fantasy.* Middletown, CT: Wesleyan UP, 2008.

Pinsent, Pat. "Unexpected Allies? Pullman and the Feminist Theologians." His Dark Materials *Illuminated: Critical Essays on Philip Pullman's Trilogy.* Eds. Millicent Lenz and Carole Scott. Detroit: Wayne State UP, 2005. 199–211.

Pullman, Philip. *The Amber Spyglass.* New York: Knopf, 2000.

_____. *The Golden Compass.* New York: Knopf, 1995.

_____. Interview with Ilene Cooper. *Booklist* 97.3 (2001): 354.

_____. Interview with Kathleen Odean. "The Story Master." *School Library Journal* 46.10 (2000): 50.

_____. Interview with Tanya Brown. "Philip Pullman: Storming Heaven." *Locus* 45.6 (2000): 8, 80–82.

_____. "The Republic of Heaven." *Horn Book* 77.6 (2001): 655–67.

_____. *The Subtle Knife.* New York: Knopf, 1997.

Rabkin, Eric S. *The Fantastic in Literature.* Princeton, NJ: Princeton UP, 1976.

Shohet, Lauren. "Reading Dark Materials." His Dark Materials *Illuminated: Critical Essays on Philip Pullman's Trilogy.* Eds. Millicent Lenz and Carole Scott. Detroit: Wayne State UP, 2005. 22–36.

Smith, Karen Patricia. "Tradition, Transformation, and the Bold Emergence: Fantastic Legacy and Pullman's *His Dark Materials.*" His Dark Materials *Illuminated: Critical Essays on Philip Pullman's Trilogy.* Eds. Millicent Lenz and Carole Scott. Detroit: Wayne State UP, 2005. 135–51.

Tolkien, J. R. R. *The Hobbit.* Boston: Houghton, 1966.

_____. *The Lord of the Rings.* Boston: Houghton, 1954–1955.

Weston, Jessie L. *From Ritual to Romance.* Garden City, NY: Doubleday, 1957.

Chatwin's Postmodern Quest: *In Patagonia*_____

Simon Cooke

When the English author Bruce Chatwin (1940-1989) published his debut, *In Patagonia*, in 1977, it was greeted with widespread acclaim, winning the Hawthornden Prize and the E. M. Forster Award and attracting the admiring attention of such literary luminaries as Graham Greene, who pronounced it "one of my favourite travel books" (Shakespeare, *Chatwin* 309). The book tells of a journey in the region of Argentina and Chile known as Patagonia to a cave at Last Hope Sound. The author is in search of a patch of hairy skin from the extinct Giant Sloth, which is a replacement for the lost scrap that Chatwin describes having marveled at in his grandmother's cabinet of curiosities when he was a child, when he believed it to have been "a piece of brontosaurus" (*Patagonia* 1). But the account of this journey, which already skirts the borders of fact and fiction in its marvelous unlikelihood, is far from straightforward: the ninety-seven short chapters make explicit reference to the object of the journey, offering little by way of description of travel from one point on the itinerary to the next, sometimes flashing back and forth in time, and incorporating an eclectic range of stories, episodes, and forms of writing from investigative reportage on historical figures such as Butch Cassidy and the Sundance Kid (42–50) to a literary critical interpretation of Shakespeare's *The Tempest* (95–97) to philological analyses of the indigenous Yaghan language (121–33). In literary-aesthetic terms, *In Patagonia* is exemplary of "the postmodernization of the travelogue" (Pfister), and as the work that, through its popular appeal and influence on fellow authors, decisively heralds a "renaissance of the travel book" (Graves) in the late 1970s and 1980s.

Chatwin's response to this (predominantly appreciative) critical reception was to write a series of letters. Ahead of U.S. publication, he requested that his book be removed from the Travel category (Shakespeare, "Introduction" xiv), which was a move that may have as much to do with perceptions about the literary status of travel writing as with a resistance to generic pigeonholing. More unusually, Chatwin also emphatically downplayed the novelty of *In Patagonia*, choosing instead to stress its links to what he considered the oldest of literary traditions: "the hunt for a strange animal in a remote land" (Shakespeare xiv). In other words, as he put it in a letter to a friend, Chatwin regarded the book—essentially, if not exclusively—as a quest:

> the FORM of the book seems to have puzzled them (as I expect it did the publisher). There's a lot of talk of 'unclassifiable prose', a 'mosaic', a 'tapestry', a 'jigsaw', a 'collage' etc. but no one has seen that it is a modern WONDER VOYAGE: the Piece of Brontosaurus is the essential ingredient of the quest. (Shakespeare, *Chatwin* 310)

As the proliferation of terms above already indicates, one of the fascinating features of *In Patagonia* is the way it mixes so many different forms, thereby resisting final or exclusive generic classification. But it will be argued here that there is much to be said, more than has been the case in most critical commentary, for reading *In Patagonia* as a work in the tradition of the hero's quest. This is to say, *In Patagonia* can be placed in a tradition that, as Christopher Booker has argued in *The Seven Basic Plots* (2004), may be seen to bind such diverse tales as Homer's *Odyssey*, Bunyan's *Pilgrim's Progress*, and Steven Spielberg's *Indiana Jones and the Lost Ark* (69). As Booker puts it: "Far away . . . there is some priceless goal, worth any effort to achieve: a treasure; a promised land; something of infinite value. From the moment the hero learns of this prize, the need to set out on the long hazardous journey to reach it becomes the most important thing to him in the world. Whatever perils and diversions lie in wait on the way, the story is shaped by one overriding imperative; and the story remains unresolved until the objective has been finally, triumphantly secured" (69). To read *In Patagonia* as a heroic quest, then, is to suggest at the broadest level that it is an account of a hazardous journey to Patagonia

---

in pursuit of a great prize: a "piece of brontosaurus" that is really a piece of Mylodon.

Expressed so matter-of-factly, it can easily be imagined why some of the most influential and insightful commentaries on the book have regarded the idea of *In Patagonia* as a heroic quest with profound scepticism. Simply put: Why would anyone go all the way from England to Patagonia to find a little piece of hairy skin from an extinct animal? Surely, we might suspect, the object must be a MacGuffin (an arbitrary object without any significance in itself that merely provides an excuse for the journey). And even if the *quest* were accepted as genuine for the traveler, could anyone regard the undertaking of such a quest as being in any way *heroic*? Readers familiar with one of the most famous of hero's quests—Jason's hunt for the Golden Fleece in the ancient Greek epic the *Argonautica*—may recognize an allusion in Chatwin's journey and agree with Manfred Pfister that there is a "marked-downgrading from the mythical heights of the Golden Fleece to a brontosaurus skin," from there to "that of a mylodon," and from there to the lump of "turd" that Chatwin eventually finds, and *In Patagonia* is thus a travel account in which the "topos of questing" is "ironically deflated and emptied" (256). Holland and Huggan see the skin as an "object lesson" in the salience of "hoaxes" in contemporary travel writing, suggesting it is "of doubtful authenticity; it seems much more than likely that it is an utter fake" (13). And indeed, within the text itself, upon reaching his goal, Chatwin writes of accomplishing the object of what he calls a "ridiculous journey" (93) just as, looking back in *Patagonia Revisited*, he describes the hunt for the piece of skin as "spurious quest" (16). Thus, according to a prevalent current in critical readings supported by some of the author's statements, *In Patagonia* emerges not so much as a heroic quest than as a mock-heroic parody of questing, a spoof.

The argument to be made here takes account of all this, but attempts to make the case that we should entertain as genuine Chatwin's claim, noted earlier, that "the Piece of Brontosaurus is the essential ingredient of the quest" (Shakespeare, *Chatwin* 310). This is not to deny

Chatwin's self-effacement and reflexivity regarding the peculiarity of the quest; nor is it to say that we can or should read *In Patagonia* to find out whether the man, Bruce Chatwin, really did lust after the relic as a child or go in search of (or find) a replacement as an adult. Rather, it is to claim that the text itself lives most fully if we consider the "piece of brontosaurus" to be the object of a quest. Although not quite a Golden Fleece, it is also not simply a red herring. What, then, is the point of this quest, and what is heroic about it? Chatwin's "piece of brontosaurus" is obviously unlike Jason's Golden Fleece in that its objective value is questionable: Jason wants the Fleece as it will enable him to take his place on the throne; Chatwin writes only, "Never in my life have I wanted anything as I wanted that piece of skin" (*Patagonia* 2). Part of the appeal of *In Patagonia* is precisely the way it begs, rather than bluntly answers, the question of *why* this might be: fascination? the forbidden? a fetish? The concern of this chapter is less to try to plumb the psychological depths of the author's childhood desire than it is to propose that *In Patagonia*, in questing after an object associated with a childhood longing, validates the personal and the idiosyncratic and celebrates the endurance of fascination, imagination, and memory. Furthermore, the specific object itself *does* have a range of symbolic and historical significances wider than the purely personal association for the traveler: Above all, as a relic of an extinct creature that reminds us of the worlds that preceded us, the quest can be seen as an attempt to recover and pay tribute to lost worlds and hidden histories including those oppressed by the European conquest of the New World of the Americas.

The question of whether such a quest is heroic is twofold: On one level, the question is whether we consider the text to have been *presented* as heroic. How does Chatwin fashion himself in the narrative: as hero or as antihero or mock-hero? *In Patagonia*, for all that the quest appears markedly mock- or antiheroic, in fact enacts a complex, not entirely parodying, negotiation with the model of the hero, something in which Chatwin was deeply interested. On a second level, the question is somewhat different: To be heroic, rather than delusional, one has to be *somebody else's* hero. There is no doubt that Chatwin himself is something of a hero-figure as he is famed for his looks and style, his restless traveling, and his storytelling in person (see Clapp 3–24) as well as for his work: "Nearly every writer of my generation in England," wrote Andrew Harvey reviewing Chatwin's later, more fictionalized travel account of Australia, *The Songlines* (1987), "has wanted, at some point, to be Bruce Chatwin; wanted, like him, to talk of Fez and Firdausi, Nigeria and Nuristan, with equal authority; wanted to be talked about, as he is, with raucous envy; wanted, above all, to have written his books" (29). But the more personal argument as to why the traveler's quest in *In Patagonia* should be seen as heroic (exemplary, noble, admirable) is rather through the ways in which it adopts and adapts the model of the quest: its celebration of the idiosyncratic over the purposive; its not seeking to overcome a monster, but to rediscover it; its quest not for power but to recall vanquished pasts.

Some general remarks are necessary about the place of *In Patagonia* as a travel book in the tradition of the hero's quest. The first and most fundamental distinction to stress is that, unlike other examples of the genre, *In Patagonia* is basically a first-person, nonfictional, autobiographical narrative in which the author, narrator, and traveler share in a single identity. We should immediately voice the general qualifications that author, narrator, and traveler should not be crassly conflated: The narrator and traveler are to a degree stylized productions by the author, and any "nonfictional" narrative is inevitably shaped by subjective and culturally inflected processes of selection, arrangement, and omission (and is thus "fictional" to a degree). And there are specific qualifications in Chatwin's case: for one thing, his writing is far from personally confessional (beyond the initial reminiscence of the enduring childhood longing for the "piece of brontosaurus," *In Patagonia* reveals very little of its narrator's autobiography). Additionally, his work as a whole often blurs the distinction between fact and fiction (the question of whether Chatwin ever actually found a scrap of Giant Sloth skin, for example, is an area of critical contention). With these general and specific provisos in mind, however, it is clear that *In Patagonia* can be distinguished from classical quests such as Homer's *Odyssey* because the book, however imaginatively rendered, is an account of a journey made by Chatwin himself. Though traveler, narrator, and author cannot be assumed to be simplistically one and the same, nor can they be neatly delineated from one another. (It thus seems justifiable, as well as less cumbersome, to refer to "Chatwin," rather than "Chatwin's narrator" or "Chatwin's persona.")

If, then, we are to consider a first-person travel account as a heroic quest (however parodic), the author will automatically occupy the position of the hero (or mock-hero): Chatwin is both author of and character in *In Patagonia*, both Homer and Odysseus (or Cervantes and Don Quixote) at the same time, so to speak. In figuring his own journey as a quest, Chatwin draws on a long tradition of interactions between overtly fictional quest romances and ostensibly factual travel accounts in which "heroic self-fashioning" (Thompson 174) is a central feature. In a sense, travel accounts and quest romances cannot help but share some common ground: the quest implies a journey, figuratively if not literally (in that even a philosophical quest for truth can be understood as a mental journey) while, conversely, any journey has the potential to be experienced in relation to the paradigm of the quest. The poet W. H. Auden went so far as to suggest that "[i]t is impossible to take a train or an airplane without having a fantasy of oneself as a Quest Hero setting off in search of an enchanted princess or the Waters of Life" (11) and Paul Fussell has suggested, by extension, that all travel books can be described as being, among other things, "displaced quest romances" (209). There are also more concrete historical links. Just as travel accounts often provide material as well as inspiration for transformation into fictional quests, so the accounts of travelers have often been fashioned in accordance with the conventions of the fictional quest. Medieval and Renaissance travelers such as Walter Raleigh, Francis Drake, and Christopher Columbus, for example, often presented their explorations of the New World of the Americas in the language of the quest romance (see Greenblatt 132–33) while many texts, most notoriously the *Travels of John Mandeville*, were apparently presented and received by contemporary readerships as documents of fact yet were in fact composite fictions. *In Patagonia*, with its tale of a fabled beast in a far-off land, thus evokes a contentious terrain in which travelers' reports teeter between the factual and the fabulous, in a mutual exchange (and sometimes confusion) between fictional quest romances and actual journeys. Indeed, the author Edmund White once remarked that Chatwin "really was a bit like the fourteenth-century John Mandeville telling stories of the fabulous monsters he'd encountered and any scepticism might have spoiled the fun" (124–25).

Chatwin's self-presentation in *In Patagonia*, however, is far from self-aggrandizing: As already noted, advertising one's attempt to find a hairy fossil makes no self-evident claim to heroism, and there are few occasions when the traveler is presented as being especially admired or brave: Chatwin lets us know that, when visiting one family, the young boy Nicky "asked if he could hold the visitor's hand," which surprises the mother: "Usually he hates visitors" (11); and at one point, when visiting the Bahai Institute of Trevelin, a Persian named Ali, apparently jealous of a rapport between Chatwin and the man Ali calls pointedly "*my friend*," wields a machete declaring "IIa! I kill the ungodly," to which Chatwin's coolly unflappable response—"Put that thing down"—is enough to quell any threat (14). Such scenes, in which Chatwin lets us witness him as likeable, calm under pressure, laconically authoritative, are rare and tempered by the far more pervasive sense of self-deprecation infused in the peculiarity of the quest.

Yet this is not a simple ousting of the idea of heroism and the hero's quest. Nor is it a journey without any hope at all of absorbing the qualities of the classical hero. Indeed, one of the reasons it is difficult to dismiss the idea of *In Patagonia* as at least an attempt at a heroic quest is that Chatwin had a long-standing fascination with the form and its place in literature and life. This interest finds expression very early on in his writing in his ambitious unpublished first book: the anthropological cum cultural-historical thesis provisionally entitled "The Nomadic Alternative," where Chatwin outlines what he calls the "Myth of the Archetypal Journey, that of the Hero and His Road of Trials" ("Nomadic" 36) as follows:

> A young man, bursting with vigour and often credited with superhuman audacity in childhood, leaves home on a long journey. After a sequence of adventures in remote and fabulous lands, he faces the Jaws of Death. A fire-breathing monster menaces with fangs and claws and, jealously hoarding a treasure, threatens the inhabitants of the land with total destruction unless they cringe before it and appease its bloodthirstiness with sacrificial victims. The hero fights and kills the monster, rewards himself with the treasure and a bride, returns home to the jubilant acclamations of his proud parents and people and they all live happily ever after. ("Nomadic" 36–37)

This idea recurs persistently in Chatwin's writings and interviews. In *The Songlines*—Chatwin's later, more fictional account of a journey he made to Australia to explore the Aboriginal dreaming tracks—Chatwin recites in almost identical terms to those above the idea of the "Hero and His Road of Trials" and adds to this the idea of a second journey that—at least within his terms—makes up the second stage in the hero's career. The first journey involves winning treasure, a bride, prestige, which the hero "enjoys into late middle age, when the clouds darken again. Again, restlessness stirs in him. Again, he leaves: either like Beowulf to die in combat, or, as the blind Tiresius prophesies for Odysseus, to set off for some mysterious destination, and vanish" (*Songlines* 215–16).

What is quite remarkable about Chatwin's life and work is the degree to which they display an investment in the idea that the hero represents "an idealized programme for the human life cycle" (Chatwin, "Interview" 27–28). Indeed, it is notable in this regard that Chatwin's two travel narratives might be mapped out in accordance with the second of his claims above, that the hero tends to make two principal journeys: *In Patagonia* might be seen as the first journey in which the "young man receives a 'call,' . . . travels to a distant country where some giant or monster threatens to overcome the population . . . [and] overcomes the Power of Darkness" (Chatwin, *Songlines* 215), while *The Songlines*—published in 1987, two years before Chatwin's early death of AIDS-related illness—bears consideration as representative of the second journey, in "late middle age when the clouds darken again" (*Songlines* 215). It is not so fanciful, then, to propose that *In Patagonia* can be seen as the literary work that resulted, in part, from Chatwin's sense that the hero's quest is an essential component of ideal human development. The "ideal" is important here, in that Chatwin need not necessarily believe, or express the conviction in his work, that such an ideal has been or can be achieved: It is clear on which side of heroism Chatwin sees himself when he writes that "Most of us, not being heroes, dawdle through life, mis-time our cues, and end up in our various emotional messes" (*Songlines* 216). But we might say that one dimension of the quest in *In Patagonia* involves an attempt to learn from the example of the classical hero, an attempt to live out the myth in life.

Chatwin does not simply emulate what he refers to as "an unchangeable paradigm" (*Songlines* 216) in adopting the hero's quest. *In Patagonia* also represents a substantial revision, as well as a recurrence, of the form. Having established that Chatwin certainly drew inspiration from a clear and long-standing fascination with the paradigm, we can now look more closely at the ways in which *In Patagonia* enacts a response to it—drawing on Chatwin's outline above.

The overarching narrative structure of *In Patagonia* involves departure on a long journey to a far-off land, the reaching of a goal and the retrieval of an object, and a return, thus framing the journey as a quest, but with important qualifications. The first chapter sets the scene for the departure: the loss of the "piece of brontosaurus" and the discovery that had been found "in a cave on Last Hope Sound in

Chilean Patagonia" (*Patagonia* 2) represents the "call," and the initial idea of the "piece of brontosaurus"—that it is a "shaggy lumbering creature with claws and fangs and a malicious green light in its eyes" (1)—is clearly a version of the terrifying monster in a far-off land. However, in most quests the object of the journey is made explicit, even if the question of what that object represents or symbolizes in the text is debatable. But *In Patagonia* shows that the quest element is almost exclusively implicit. Though the "piece of brontosaurus" allusively signals a quest motif, it is not stated overtly at the outset that Chatwin plans to recover a replacement. From the opening chapter we know only that our narrator had longed to possess a "piece of brontosaurus" that had been kept in his grandmother's cabinet ("Never in my life have I wanted anything as I wanted that piece of skin" [2]) but that had eluded him, as it was thrown away when his grandmother died (2). The hero-figure of Chatwin's grandmother's cousin, Charley Milward, suggests another possible reason for travel to Patagonia: that of a kind of ancestral pilgrimage; and Chatwin's childhood was in the 1940s when "the Cannibal of the Kremlin"—that is, the Soviet dictator Josef Stalin—"shadowed our lives" (3) provides yet another potential motivation: "[T]he Cold War woke in me a passion for geography," Chatwin writes, recalling that fears of atomic war led him and his peers to fixate on Patagonia—at the far end of the world from Europe—"as the safest place on earth, . . . somewhere to live when the rest of the world blew up" (3). But none of these memories equates to a statement of why the adult remembering this childhood period should wish to go to Patagonia. And the implication that the Mylodon Cave with its family associations is the object of a planned journey is extremely oblique: "Then Stalin died and we sang hymns of praise in chapel, but I continued to hold Patagonia in reserve" (3). The actual decision to travel to Patagonia, then, is not overtly stated. Any potential reasons for the traveler having gone to Patagonia—to replace the skin, to follow the footsteps of the hero-figure ancestor—are not explicit in the text and must be inferred. That the traveler intends to replace the "piece of brontosaurus" is not mentioned until Chapter 87 and then indirectly, in an understated way as if it were one among other things: "I had one more thing to do in Patagonia: to find a replacement for the lost piece of skin" (178). It is only upon consummation of the quest—with the sentence: "I had accomplished the object of this ridiculous journey" (194)—that the skin is explicitly referred to as the quarry.

Just as the motivation for the quest is left largely unstated, so Chatwin's physical travel is rarely described. The quest form often involves an arduous journey, full of challenges and dangers, but Chatwin's journey and experiences are hardly presented as the trials of an Odysseus. The longest part of the journey, across the Atlantic from England to Argentina, is not described at all: We read a childhood reminiscence about wartime and Cold War England in the first chapter; then the second chapter transports us instantly to Buenos Aires. And throughout *In Patagonia*, the actual traveling is almost always described with a single sentence, with very little ornament, and with barely any descriptions of the journey itself. The following are typical: "I took the train to La Plata to see the best natural history museum in the world" (5); "In the evening Bill drove me to Bahía Blanca" (12); "I took the nightbus to Chubut Valley" (22). The Patagonian desert may well fit the role of a wild, inhospitable, and daunting prospect, but, as noted earlier, Chatwin rarely presents himself as a traveler facing or overcoming great dangers or enduring great hardships: As we have seen, the machete-wielding Ali at the Bahai Institute of Trevelin posed no great threat (14), Chatwin seems to be greeted with hospitality by strangers throughout, and the sufferings and difficulties overtly described are those of others, not the traveling narrator. The most crucial way in which *In Patagonia* departs from the model in which the journey involves frequent triumphs over adversity is, of course, in the nature of its "monster"—the piece of brontosaurus—which can hardly be thought of as posing a mortal threat either to the inhabitants of Patagonia or the traveler himself. What is the significance of this quarry? As W. G. Sebald has suggested, "there is no mistaking the fetishistic character of the sloth relic. Entirely without value in itself, it inflamed and satisfied the lover's illicit fantasy" (184). That Chatwin's "fleece" has indeed a fetish-like quality was something he himself, in his first draft of the book, had considered including, as is suggested in the following edited passage:

> I cannot say if my impulse to cling to a piece of antediluvian fluff was an atavistic ~~memory~~ nostalgia ~~to cling to~~ for the pelt of a hairy ancestor. And it is unclear if my mother was present when I first saw the piece of brontosaurus. But throughout my childhood I ~~longed~~ yearned for it with a persistent longing. (*Songlines* Box 4: 6)

A little further in, Chatwin notes that the "Viennese doctor" (the famous pioneer of psychoanalysis, Sigmund Freud) would likely "point to an atavistic impulse, in an insecure child" (6). Chatwin here refers to the theory that (simply put) we form attachments to objects as substitutes for security, and—in that remark about it being "unclear" if his "mother was present" (*Songlines* Box 4: 6)—that attachment to objects can relate to the libidinal relationship of a child with the mother. There is even an element of sexual innuendo about the almost genital quality of a small patch of hairy skin—a sexual dimension echoed in *The Songlines*, when Chatwin recalls that his "most treasured possession" as a child was a "conch shell called Mona[:] . . . I would ram my face against her sheeny pink vulva [and pray that] a beautiful blond young lady would suddenly spew forth" (7). And if one psychoanalytical scenario is that sexual fulfilment may be impeded by a problematic relationship with the mother, it is worth noting that, upon reaching the object of his quest in *In Patagonia*, the Mylodon Cave in Last Hope Sound, and finding the object of his quest, the narrator considers spending the night in the cave but hears the singing of a troop of nuns and is removed by none other than a Mother Superior (93).

It is notable that Chatwin omits such speculations and direct interpretations from the published text, choosing to leave this question open—and it seems wise similarly to refrain from too explicit a psychological interpretation of the credibility or significance of Chatwin's personal desire for the skin in his own life. But we can perhaps go further into what features of the object might prompt such a journey and make it significant as the object of a quest rendered in literary form. It is, first of all, an object that is experienced as something it is not in fact. Just as it is the "brontosaurus" that comes crashing through the wall at night in the boy's dreams, so it is a piece of brontosaurus of which Chatwin writes: "Never in my life have I wanted anything as I wanted that piece of skin" (*In Patagonia* 1). When the Mylodon Cave at Last Hope Sound is reached, "I tried to picture the cave with sloths in it, but I could not erase the fanged monster I associate with a blacked-out bedroom in wartime England" (93). The factual, physical quest may be to find a replacement scrap of Mylodon skin, but the desire on which the quest is premised—that is, to replace and possess the lost "piece of brontosaurus"—remains teetering on the brink between fact and fiction, and the traveler's own quest is thus readable either as an endurance of this desire, or as a desire to reawaken that childlike sense of fascination. It is a fragment: This too means that the object invites imagination (the piece of skin demands that the creature must be imagined in its wholeness) and the actual object, the scrap of skin from the extinct Giant Sloth, captures the imagination of the child as a piece of brontosaurus. When Robert Taylor wrote in the *Boston Globe* that the book "celebrates the recovery of something inspiring memory, as if Proust could in fact taste his Madeleine," Chatwin responded: "*ENFIN* somebody's got the point" (Shakespeare, *Chatwin* 353).

Perhaps the most radical difference and important clarification between *In Patagonia* and other quests in which the "hero fights and kills the monster" (Chatwin, "Nomadic" 36), is that in this traveler's quest, the "monster" poses no threat to anyone, and the object of the journey is not to kill or overcome the beast. On the contrary, Chatwin's quest is for a fossil—a remnant of a beast that not only died long ago, but that belongs to an extinct species—and the quest is not to find and kill a monster, but to find and recover a souvenir of its life. The distinction is described well in the natural historian George Gaylord Simpson's observation, in *Attending Marvels*, which is listed in Chatwin's bibliography at the end of the book as his source for prehistoric animals in Patagonia: "The fossil hunter does not kill; he resurrects" (82). In both its fictional and factual form, the scrap of skin is thus a reminder that the world was once a very different place and that entire species and ecosystems have risen and fallen. Chatwin's quest is thus in part to remind us of the vastness of the past: the object inspires memory not only of the traveler's own past, but of the past that precedes his own life.

It could be argued that one of the aims in the narrative may thus be to undermine a colonial, conqueror's perspective that is often associated—sometimes too indiscriminately—with travel writing generally (see Holland and Huggan; Lisle). One of the key critical studies that contributed to academic interest in travel writing is Edward Said's *Orientalism*, published in 1978, one year after *In Patagonia*. Said scrutinized the travel writing of nineteenth-century European authors, along with novels, poetry, and scholarly writing, to demonstrate their role in systematically "producing" rather than objectively representing the Orient as the projection of an exotic cultural "other" necessary to confirm the centrality (and tacitly justify the hegemony) of European power. Mary Louise Pratt has done most to extend Said's analysis into travel writing more generally, showing in *Imperial Eyes* (1992) the extent to which travel writing has employed a rhetoric of colonial vision. With such contexts in mind, it is notable that *In Patagonia* is not a quest for power or victory, but for the recovery of what has been lost, defeated. The object itself is highly charged in its historical significance. As Peter Hulme has observed, at the height of imperialist science in the Victorian era, the giant sloth

> was *the* emblem of Patagonia, congruent with its surviving indigenous population in that both offered keys to the prehistoric past, but also symbolic of that population's lumbering slowness: behind the times, at the

back of history, the last in the human race. That population's subsequent genocide owed much to the scientific picture of Patagonia which had that sloth as its central image. (226; emphasis in original)

This lends historical resonance to the object of Chatwin's quest; and indeed, one of the notable aspects of *In Patagonia* is the attention it affords to the Yaghan language—the Yaghan being among those tribes to be all but obliterated by European colonialism in South America. Of a piece with this is the self-reflexive way in which Chatwin places his own quest amid what might be described as a gallery of portraits of would-be questing heroes, in which lunacy, megalomania, and folly are often salient features. There is the iconic South American revolutionary, Ernesto (Che) Guevara, described by a "lady novelist" who recalls him in his youth as "at that time an untidy young man pushing for a place in society" (5); there is Orélie-Antoine de Tounens, the nineteenth-century French lawyer who established himself as the King of Patagonia (16–21); there is the Patagonian Polymath who persists in and pursues a conviction that the unicorn is a real animal (71–75). Chatwin's quest is thus placed within a context of many other quests, with a high degree of reflexivity regarding the potential for his own quest to be regarded in a similar light, but also marking a contrast in that his own journey is acknowledged as idiosyncratic and involves no quest for power.

Chatwin gives us no instructional guidelines as to what we should make of any potential comparisons here, and this lack of authorial didactics is evident too in the way that one of the stock elements of the quest pattern is conspicuous by its absence: that in which the hero "rewards himself with the treasure and a bride, returns home to the jubilant acclamations of his proud parents and people and they all live happily ever after" (Chatwin, "Nomadic" 36–37). After the consummation of the quest—which achieves for the traveler an understated sense of being "immensely pleased" (194)—there remain four short chapters (two of which are only half a page or so): a brief portrait of a dying man

(195); an encounter with a lingerie salesman from Santiago who also has a prehistoric relic and is described by a hotel manager as "*loco*" (195–97); a rumination on Walter Rauff, a Nazi who had been involved in the Holocaust and who is in exile in Punta Arenas (198). And then there is a departure: Chatwin waits for a week in Punta Arenas for the ship, boards, and we assume sets sails for England—but just as the journey to Patagonia is not described at the outset, so is no destination specified at the end. Though the "return" is, like the departure, implicit, the quest draws to a close with a "hero" unmoored into an unspecified future, which feels rather more like a departure than a return. In a sense, it is as if the accomplishment of the quest has not caused any great change or transformation in the traveler. But more importantly, in its open-endedness and in its immediate attention to stories peripheral to the quest, *In Patagonia* suggests a kind of questing that remains conscious of its own relativity, embedded within many other narratives and concerns.

The open-endedness of *In Patagonia* might be taken as a cautionary note against attempting to draw too final a conclusion about the book, and critical controversy is likely to remain over how seriously we should interpret the quest for the piece of brontosaurus. At one end of the spectrum, *In Patagonia* has become something of a travel guide for many: It has been described as the Patagonian tourist's "Bible" (Shakespeare, "Introduction" xxiv), and many followers have themselves been writers who have set about tracking Chatwin's footsteps as precisely as possible as the basis for their own books. In a sense Chatwin invites such followers (he himself indicates that he follows the footsteps of others in his travels), but nothing in *In Patagonia* requires that we follow the author to Last Hope Sound: It invites us to marvel at the story rather than verify or falsify it, and such literal emulation is out of keeping with the spirit of the work.

The argument here has been that while Chatwin's "piece of brontosaurus" is indeed ridiculous, comical, pointless—with none of the purpose of Jason's quest to secure his inheritance as King of Iolkos, none of the violence or glory of the quest to find and kill a monster, nor the achievement of winning a bride and great fortune (at least, not within the story)—the quest is not simply a hoax or parody, without meaning in itself. We have seen that Chatwin drew on a deep and long-standing investment in the model of the hero's quest and that he modeled his own journey very much in accordance with it. Thus, while in a sense Chatwin presents himself as a traveler following the path of the hero, rather than assuming this mantle (thus splitting heroism away from the quest), Chatwin does suggest the power of the hero ideal as a model for human endeavor—for all that the traveler's quest is presented self-reflexively, ironically, and in such a way as to leave the question of purpose enigmatic, it is nevertheless more than a mere conceit. And there is also a certain kind of heroism in the apparent self-effacement and lack of heroics in the quest: If we see *In Patagonia* as parody, it is ideologies of power and conquest—the ideology of the Fleece, not that of the piece of brontosaurus—that are brought into question. The heroism of the quest is that it seeks to resurrect and remember rather than to kill or overcome. It invites us to think on the vastness of the past. Equally, it places the quest among such a rich and complex web of other stories, it suggests a kind of questing that remains conscious of its own subjectivity. It thus relativizes, rather than trivializes, the idea questing. In its idiosyncrasy, its openness, and its mystery, *In Patagonia* invites us not so much to test the documentary veracity of Chatwin's own quest, but to identify and think on whatever might be our own "piece of brontosaurus"—thus pointing towards the inexhaustible potential for reformulations of the hero's quest in literature and in life.

Works Cited

Auden, W. H. Introduction. *Italian Journey*. By Goethe. London: Penguin, 1970. 7–20.

Booker, Christopher. *The Seven Basic Plots: Why We Tell Stories*. London: Continuum, 2004.

Chatwin, Bruce. "An Interview with Bruce Chatwin." By Michael Ignatieff. *Granta 21: The Story-Teller*. Ed. Bill Buford. Harmondsworth: Penguin, 1987. 23–37.

_____. "The Nomadic Alternative." Unpublished manuscript. Box 12, Nomads TS and Notes. Modern Western Manuscripts, Bodleian Library, U of Oxford, England. n.d.

_____. *In Patagonia*. London: Penguin, 2003.

_____. *The Songlines*. London: Vintage, 2005.

_____. *What Am I Doing Here*. London: Penguin, 1996.

Chatwin, Bruce, and Paul Theroux. *Patagonia Revisited*. London: Jonathan Cape, 1992.

Clapp, Susannah. "What Am I Doing Here." *The Guardian*, 19 Jan. 1989: 37.

_____. *With Chatwin: Portrait of a Writer*. London: Jonathan Cape, 1997.

Clarke, Robert. "Star Traveller: Celebrity, Aboriginality, and Bruce Chatwin's *The Songlines*." *Postcolonial Studies: Culture, Politics, Economy* 12.2 (2009): 229–46. Web. 1 July 2011.

Fussell, Paul. *Abroad: British Literary Travelling Between the Wars*. New York: Oxford UP, 1980.

Graves, Matthew. "Nowhere Left to Go? The Death and Renaissance of the Travel Book." *World Literature Today* 3.3–4 (2003): 52–56.

Greenblatt, Stephen. *Marvelous Possessions: The Wonder of the New World*. Chicago: U of Chicago P, 1991.

Harvey, Andrew. "Footprints of the Ancestors." *New York Times*, 2 Aug. 1987. Web. 1 July 2011.

Holland, Patrick, and Graham Huggan. *Tourists with Typewriters: Critical Reflections on Contemporary Travel Writing*. Ann Arbor, MI: U of Michigan P, 1998.

Hulme, Peter. "Patagonian Cases: Travel Writing, Fiction, History." *Seuils et Traverses: Enjeux de l'écriture du voyage*. Vol. II. Ed. Jan Borm. Brest: Centre de Recherche Bretonne et Celtique, 2002. 223–37.

Hulme, Peter, and Tim Youngs, eds. *The Cambridge Companion to Travel Writing*. Cambridge: Cambridge University Press, 2002. 87–101.

Lisle, Debbie. *The Global Politics of Contemporary Travel Writing*. Cambridge: Cambridge UP, 2006.

Murray, Nicholas. *Bruce Chatwin*. Mid Glamorgan: Seren, 1993.

Pfister, Manfred. "Bruce Chatwin and the Postmodernization of the Travelogue." *Literature, Interpretation, Theory* 7 (1996): 253–67.

Porter, Eleanor. "Mother Earth and the Wandering Hero: Mapping Gender in Bruce Chatwin's *The Songlines* and Robyn Davidson's *Tracks*." *The Journal of Commonwealth Literature* 32.1 (1997): 35–46. Web. 1 July 2011.

Propp, Vladimir. *Morphology of the Folktale*. 2nd ed. Trans. Laurence Scott. Austin: U of Texas P, 1968.

Raithel, Jürgen. *Der Gott der Wanderer: Bruce Chatwins postmoderne Reisebeschreibungen* In Patagonia *und* The Songlines. Trier: WVT Wiss. Verl. Trier, 1999.

Rushdie, Salman. *Imaginary Homelands: Essays and Criticism 1981–1991*. London: Granta, 1991.

Said, Edward. *Orientalism*. New York: Pantheon, 1978.

Sebald, W. G. "The Mystery of the Red-Brown Skin: An Approach to Bruce Chatwin." *Campo Santo*. Trans. Anthea Bell. London: Hamish Hamilton, 2005. 173–79.

Shakespeare, Nicholas. *Bruce Chatwin*. London: Vintage, 2000.

_____. "*In Patagonia*: An Introduction, by Nicholas Shakespeare." *In Patagonia*. Bruce Chatwin. London: Penguin, 2003. vii–xxiv.

Simpson, George Gaylord. *Attending Marvels: A Patagonian Journal*. Alexandria, Virginia: Time-Life, 1982.

Taylor, David. "Bruce Chatwin: Connoisseur of Exile, Exile as Connoisseur." *Travel Writing and Empire: Postcolonial Theory in Transit*. Ed. Steve Clark. London: Zed, 1999. 195–211.

Thompson, Carl. *Travel Writing: The New Critical Idiom*. Abingdon: Routledge, 2011.

White, Edmund. "Bruce Chatwin." *Arts and Letters*. San Francisco: Cleis, 2004. 123–127.

Youngs, Tim. "Punctuating Travel: Paul Theroux and Bruce Chatwin." *Literature and History*. 6.2 (1997): 73–88.

RESOURCES

Additional Works on The Hero's Quest _____

Drama

Everyman, late fifteenth century
Hamlet by William Shakespeare, 1604
A Doll's House by Henrik Ibsen, 1879
The Ascent of F6: A Tragedy in Two Acts by W. H. Auden and Christopher
    Isherwood, 1936

Long Fiction

Le Morte d'Arthur by Sir Thomas Malory, 1485
The Interior Castle by St. Teresa of Ávila 1577
Don Quixote by Miguel des Cervantes, 1605, 1615
The Pilgrim's Progress by John Bunyan, 1678
The History of Tom Jones by Henry Fielding, 1749
Candide by Voltaire, 1759
David Copperfield by Charles Dickens, 1850
Treasure Island by Robert Louis Stevenson, 1883
The Adventures of Huckleberry Finn by Mark Twain, 1884
The Castle by Franz Kafka, 1926
Lost Horizon by James Hilton, 1933
The Fountain Overflows by Rebecca West, 1956
2001: A Space Odyssey by Arthur C. Clarke, 1968
Martha Quest by Doris Lessing, 1964
Ceremony by Leslie Marmon Silko, 1977

Myths

"Argonautica" by Apollonius Rhodius, third century BCE
"Demeter and Persephone"
"Orpheus and Eurydice"
"Perseus"
"Tristan and Isolde"

Nonfiction

The Confessions by Saint Augustine, 398
The Road to Oxiana by Robert Byron, 1937
Black Lamb and Grey Falcon by Rebecca West, 1941
The Snow Leopard by Peter Matthiessen, 1978
Into the Wild by Jon Krakauer, 1996

Poetry

Das Nibelungenlied
The Song of Roland, c. 1150
La Gerusalemme Liberata by Torquato Tasso, 1581
The Rape of the Lock by Alexander Pope, 1712
Childe Harold's Pilgrimage by Lord Byron, 1812–1818

Bibliography

Ackerman, Robert. *The Myth and Ritual School: J. G. Frazer and the Cambridge Ritualists*. New York: Routeledge, 2002.

Allums, Larry, and Louise Cowan, eds. *The Epic Cosmos*. Dallas, TX: Dallas Institute Publications, 2000.

Arkinstall, Christine. *Literature and Quest*. Amsterdam: Rodopi, 1993.

Bentley, Eric. *A Century of Hero-Worship: A Study of the Idea of Heroism in Carlyle and Nietzsche*. 2nd ed. Boston: Beacon, 1957.

Campbell, Joseph. *The Hero with a Thousand Faces*. Princeton, NJ: Princeton UP, 1973.

_____. *The Masks of God: Occidental Mythology*. New York: Viking, 1964.

Carlyle, Thomas. *The Works of Thomas Carlyle: On Heroes, Hero-Worship, and the Heroic in History*. Ed. Henry Duff Traill. London: Chapman and Hall, 1897.

Clift, Jean D., and Wallace B. Clift. *The Hero Journey in Dreams*. New York: Crossroad, 1988.

Cooke, Victor. "Lord Raglan's Hero—A Cross Cultural Critique." *Florida Anthropologist* 18 (1965): 147–54.

Coupe, Laurence. *Myth*. New York: Routledge, 1997.

Covington, Coline. "In Search of the Heroine." *Journal of Analytical Psychology* 34.3 (1989): 243–54.

Doniger, Wendy. *The Implied Spider: Politics and Theology in Myth*. New York: Columbia UP, 1998.

Doty, William G. *Mythography: The Study of Myths and Rituals*. 2nd ed. Tuscaloosa, AL: U of Alabama P, 2000.

Eliade, Mircea. *The Myth of the Eternal Return: Or, Cosmos and History*. Trans. Willard R. Trask. Princeton: Princeton UP, 1971.

_____. *The Quest: History and Meaning in Religion*. Chicago: U of Chicago P, 1969.

Frazer, James George. *The Golden Bough: A Study in Magic and Religion*. Abr. ed. London: Macmillan, 1922.

Frye, Northrop. *Anatomy of Criticism: Four Essays*. Princeton: Princeton UP, 1957.

Frye, Northrop, and Jay Macpherson. *Biblical and Classical Myths: The Mythological Framework of Western Culture*. Toronto: U of Toronto P, 2004.

_____. "The Journey as Metaphor." *Myth and Metaphor: Selected Essays 1974–1988*. Ed. Robert D. Denham. Charlottesville: UP of Virginia, 1990. (212–26).

Giraud, Raymond. *The Unheroic Hero in the Novels of Stendahl, Balzac, and Flaubert*. New York: Octagon, 1979.

Golden, Kenneth L., ed. *Uses of Comparative Mythology: Essays on the Work of Joseph Campbell*. New York: Garland, 1992.

Hook, Sidney. *The Hero in History*. Boston: Beacon, 1955.

Jackson, W. T. H. *The Hero and the King: As Epic Theme.* New York: Columbia UP, 1982.

Jezewski, Mary Ann. "Traits of the Female Hero: The Application of Raglan's Concept of Hero Trait Patterning." *New York Folklore* 10.1–2 (1984): 55–73.

Jung, Carl Gustav. *The Essential Jung: Selected Writings.* Ed. Anthony Storr. Princeton: Princeton UP, 1983.

Jung, Carl Gustav, and Karl Kerenyi. *Essays on a Science of Mythology: The Myth of the Divine Child and the Mysteries of Eleusis.* Bollingen Series 22. New York: Princeton UP, 1973.

Kern, Edith. "The Modern Hero: Phoenix or Ashes?" *Comparative Literature* 10.4 (1958): 325–34.

Kirk, Geoffrey S. Myth: *Its Meaning and Functions in Ancient and Other Cultures.* Berkeley: U of California P, 1973.

Larson, Jennifer. *Greek Heroine Cults.* Madison: U of Wisconsin P, 1995.

Leeming, David A. *Myth: A Biography of Belief.* New York: Oxford UP, 2002.

_____. *Mythology: The Voyage of the Hero.* New York: Oxford UP, 1998.

Murray, Henry A., ed. *Myth and Mythmaking.* Boston: Beacon, 1960.

Noel, Daniel C., ed. *Paths to the Power of Myth: Joseph Campbell and the Study of Religion.* New York: Crossroad, 1990.

O'Faoláin, Seán. *The Vanishing Hero: Studies in Novelists of the Twenties.* London: Eyre & Spottiswoode, 1956.

Patton, Laurie, and Wendy Doniger. *Myth & Method.* Charlottesville: UP of Virginia, 1996.

Pearson, Carol. *The Hero Within: Six Archetypes We Live By.* San Francisco: Harper, 1989.

Pearson, Carol, and Katherine Pope. *The Female Hero in Amercian and British Literature.* New York: Bowker, 1981.

Propp, Vladimir. *Morphology of the Folktale.* 2nd ed. Trans. Laurence Scott. Austin, TX: U of Texas P, 1968.

Lord Raglan. *The Hero: A Study in Tradition, Myth, and Drama.* London: Methuen, 1936.

Rank, Otto. *The Myth of the Birth of the Hero and Other Writings.* Trans. F. Robbins and Smith E. Jelliffe. Ed. Philip Freund. New York: Vintage, 1959.

Rank, Otto, et al. *In Quest of the Hero.* Princeton, NJ: Princeton U Press, 1990.

Reed, Walter L. *Meditations on the Hero: A Study of the Romantic Hero in Nineteenth-Century Fiction.* New Haven, CT: Yale UP, 1974.

Segal, Robert A. *Hero Myths: A Reader.* Oxford: Blackwell, 2000.

_____. *Joseph Campbell: An Introduction.* New York: Penguin, 1990.

_____. *Myth: A Very Short Introduction.* New York: Oxford UP, 2004.

_____. *Theorizing about Myth.* Boston: U of Massachusetts P, 1999.

Smith, Evans L. *The Hero Journey in Literature: Parables of Poesis.* Lanham, MD: UP of America, 1987.

Vernant, Jean-Pierre. "The Reason of Myth." *Myth and Society in Ancient Greece.* Trans. Janet Lloyd. New York: Zone, 1990. (203–60).

Vickery, John B. *The Literary Impact of* The Golden Bough. Princeton: Princeton UP, 1973.

Whitman, Cedric H. *The Heroic Paradox: Essays on Homer, Sophocles, and Aristophanes.* Ed. Charles Segal. Ithaca, NY: Cornell UP, 1982.

CRITICAL
INSIGHTS

About the Volume Editors _____

Bernard Schweizer, a native of Switzerland, studied in the United States and received his doctorate in English from Duke University. He is now associate professor of English at Long Island University, Brooklyn campus. Schweizer's publications include three monographs: *Radicals on the Road: The Politics of English Travel Writing in the 1930s* (2001), *Rebecca West: Heroism, Rebellion, and the Female Epic* (2002), and *Hating God: The Untold Story of Misotheism* (2011). Schweizer has edited several essay collections in literary studies, including *Approaches to the Anglo and American Female Epic 1621–1982* (2006) and *Rebecca West Today: Contemporary Critical Approaches* (2006); he has also edited Rebecca West's posthumously published *Survivors in Mexico* (2003). Schweizer is currently president of the International Rebecca West Society.

Robert A. Segal is Sixth Century Chair in Religious Studies at the University of Aberdeen, Scotland. Born and raised in the United States, he relocated to the United Kingdom in 1994 to teach religious studies at Lancaster University, England. In 2006, he moved to the University of Aberdeen. His PhD from Princeton was on ancient gnosticism. Segal teaches and writes on theories, chiefly from the social science and of myth and of religion. He is the author or editor of, among other books, *The Poimandres as Myth: Scholarly Theory and Gnostic Meaning* (1986), *Joseph Campbell: An Introduction* (1990), *The Gnostic Jung* (1992), *Jung on Mythology* (1998), *The Myth and Ritual Theory: An Anthology* (1998), *Theorizing about Myth* (1999), *Hero Myths: A Reader* (2000), and *Myth: A Very Short Introduction* (2004).

Contributors _____

Bernard Schweizer is associate professor of English at Long Island University, Brooklyn campus. Schweizer's publications include *Rebecca West: Heroism, Rebellion, and the Female Epic* (2002), *Hating God: The Untold Story of Misotheism* (2011), and *Approaches to the Anglo and American Female Epic 1621–1982* (2006). Schweizer is currently president of the International Rebecca West Society.

Robert A. Segal is sixth century chair in Religious Studies at the University of Aberdeen, Scotland. He teaches and writes on theories, chiefly from the social sciences and of myth and of religion. He is the author or editor of, among other books, *Joseph Campbell: An Introduction* (1990), *Jung on Mythology* (1998), *The Myth and Ritual Theory: An Anthology* (1998), *Theorizing about Myth* (1999), *Hero Myths: A Reader* (2000), and *Myth: A Very Short Introduction* (2004).

Eric Ziolkowski, Charles A. Dana Professor of Religious Studies at Pennsylvania's Lafayette College, is the author of numerous books, articles, and reviews in religion and literature. His most recent monograph is titled *The Literary Kierkegaard* (2011). He is North American general editor of *Literature and Theology: An International Journal of Religion, Theory and Culture* (Oxford), one of the six main editors of the prospective 30-volume *Encyclopedia of the Bible and Its Reception* (2009–), and coeditor of the book series *Studies in Religion and the Arts*.

Jeremy M. Downes, professor of English at Auburn University in Alabama, received degrees from the University of Wisconsin–Madison and the University of Chicago. A specialist in epic (beginnings to the present), he is the author of *The Female Homer: An Exploration of Women's Epic Poetry* (2010), *Recursive Desire: Rereading Epic Tradition* (1997), and of three collections of poetry. He also manages the web directory *HyperEpos*, a substantial collection of links to epic texts, resources, and materials. He is currently at work on *Local Heroes*, a study of American local and regional epic.

Michael Bell has taught in France, Germany, Canada, and the United States. He is professor emeritus in the Department of English and Comparative Literary Studies at England's University of Warwick, where he is also an associate fellow and former director of the Centre for Research in Philosophy, Literature, and the Arts. His book-length publications include *Primitivism* (1972); *D. H. Lawrence: Language and Being* (1992); *Gabriel García Márquez: Solitude and Solidarity* (1994); *Literature, Modernism and Myth: Belief and Responsibility in the Twentieth Century* (1997); *Sentimentalism, Ethics and the Culture of Feeling* (2001); and *Open Secrets: Literature, Education, and Authority from J-J Rousseau to J. M. Coetzee* (2007).

Katherine Callen King received her PhD in Comparative Literature from Princeton University. For thirty years she has been a professor at the University of California, Los Angeles, in the departments of Classics and Comparative Literature. She specializes in epic, tragedy, the classical tradition (medieval, renaissance, and modern revisions of classical works), and gender studies. Her first two books, *Achilles: Paradigms of the War Hero from Homer to the Middle Ages* (1991) and *Homer* (1994), an edited collection about authors influenced by Homer's *The Iliad* and *The Odyssey*, reflect her scholarly interest in why and how a writer manipulates important cultural texts for ideological purposes. Her most recent book is *Ancient Epic* (2009).

Eric Sandberg completed his PhD in English literature at the University of Edinburgh. His research interests include literary modernism, hardboiled detective fiction, and literary characterization. He currently teaches English literature at Miyazaki International College in Miyazaki, Japan.

James B. Kelley holds an MA in German from the University of Wisconsin–Madison and a PhD in English from the University of Tulsa. He teaches courses in writing, literature, and theory and coordinates the English BA program at Mississippi State University–Meridian. Past accomplishments include a one-year Fulbright teaching appointment to Magdeburg, Germany, and receipt of the *Journal of Popular Culture's* Russel B. Nye award for outstanding article of the year for his piece on the song "Follow the Drinking Gourd."

Anthony Adams holds his PhD from the University of Toronto and is an assistant professor of English at Colby College in Maine. He specializes in medieval languages and literatures and has written on Old English and Carolingian poetry of war, Medieval Latin, Thomas Malory, the Middle English Charlemagne romances, Norse sagas, Chaucer, and *Beowulf.* He has coauthored (with A. G. Rigg) the first complete English translation and commentary of the ninth-century epic Latin poem *Bella Parisiacae urbis* in the *Journal for Medieval Latin* and is currently working on a book that examines sacrifice and violence in Middle English poetry.

Matthew Bolton earned his doctorate at the City University of New York Graduate Center, where he wrote his dissertation on T. S. Eliot's Victorian influences. The T. S. Eliot Society awarded him its annual Fathman Award for work related to his dissertation. Bolton's most recent publications include chapters in the books *Ernest Hemingway and the Geography of Memory* (2010) and *The Waste Land at 90* (2011). He lives and works in New York City.

Victoria Williams was awarded a PhD by King's College, London, for a thesis that examined the role of continental European fairytales in nineteenth-century British literature, art, and on film with special reference to the Brothers Grimm. This is an area on which she continues to focus. Another main research area is British and American cinema, especially the horror and the female Gothic genres, children on film, the works of Alfred Hitchcock, and Hollywood during the Studio Era of the first half of the twentieth century. She has worked as an editorial assistant on several academic projects linked to digital humanities, including *Nineteenth-Century Serials Edition* and the *Dictionary of Nineteenth-Century Journalism*, to which she also contributed entries.

Robert C. Evans is I. B. Young Professor of English at Auburn University at Montgomery. He is the author or editor of more than twenty books and two hundred essays, both in print and in online databases. Much of his writing focuses on close reading and critical pluralism. Evans is the recipient of grants from the National Endowment for the Humanities, the Folger Shakespeare Library, the Newberry Library, the Huntington Library, the American Philosophical Society, the Mellon Foundation, and the Center for Medieval and Renaissance Studies at the University of California, Los Angeles. Much of his recent work has dealt with American literature of the nineteenth and twentieth century.

Stephen W. Potts is on the faculty of the Department of Literature at the University of California, San Diego. A specialist in twentieth-century fiction and popular culture, he has published books on such authors as Joseph Heller and F. Scott Fitzgerald and articles on J. R. R. Tolkien, Ken Kesey, and a variety of topics in science fiction. He has been the recipient of a Fulbright Fellowship, a J. Lloyd Eaton Award for his monograph on Russian science fiction writers Arkady and Boris Strugatsky, and two teaching awards.

Simon Cooke is a research fellow in English at Wolfson College, Oxford. His research and teaching focuses on modern and contemporary literature, with particular interests in travel writing. He studied at Hull University and University College London, completing his doctorate in 2010 at Justus-Liebig-University Gießen, Germany, where he taught in the Department of English and American Studies and was a coordinator of the International PhD Program in Literary and Cultural Studies. Cooke is preparing his first monograph for publication—*Travellers' Tales of Wonder in Late Twentieth-Century Literature: Chatwin, Naipaul, Sebald*—and is a cofounder of "Travel Cultures: An Oxford Interdisciplinary Research Seminar."

Index

---

physical endurance and, 168, 201,
202, 207, 230
supernatural events and, 165

Rachel, the (*Moby-Dick*), 216–217
Raglan, Lord. *See* Lord Raglan
Rank, Otto
Freud and, 21, 23
heroic myths and, 21–23
Joseph Campbell and, 26–27
Lord Raglan and, 30–32
Oedipal wish in myths and, 22–23,
24
Religious quests
Christian ideals and, 48, 52, 149
versus worldly conquests, 39
See also Spiritual quests
Religious symbolism
Dante's *Divine Comedy* and, 66–67
written narratives and, 66–67, 82, 91,
92, 155
Restoration quests
Odyssey, The, and, 103
Return home quests, 62–63, 103, 104,
135, 186
Odyssey, The, and, 103–113
Rochester (*Jane Eyre*), 182
Romantic quests, 134
evolution of, 36, 149, 221
female role in, 188, 192
printed narratives and, 68
Rosebud, the (*Moby-Dick*), 213–14

Said, Edward
travel writing and colonialism, 250
Samuel Enderby, the (*Moby-Dick*),
214–15
Satan (*Divine Comedy*), 170–71
Sir Gawain and the Green Knight, 148
Arthurian romances and, 148, 151
chivalric quests and, 148

Christianity and, x, 155
Christmas game and, 153
Spencer, Herbert
criticism of Carlyle, 5
"Great Man" view of history, 5
theories compared to Sidney Hook, 5
Spiritual quests
Dante, 166
Moby-Dick and, 201
See also Religious quests
Supernatural, the
quests and, 103, 118, 135, 136

There-and-back-again quests. *See*
Return-home quests
"Town-Ho's Story, The" (*Moby-Dick*),
209–11
quests within, 209, 210–11
Tragic heroes, 102
Transformation of the hero, 139, 150,
182, 221
Beowulf and, 140–46
Joseph Campbell and, ix, 4
Travel writing
colonialism and, 250
In Patagonia and, 249
quest narratives and, xi, 237, 239,
242
similarities with romantic quests, 249
Trawpe. See Honor

Übermensch. *See* Overman, the
Underworld, the
Aeneid, The, and, 116, 119
His Dark Materials trilogy and, 232,
233, 234
Utnapishtim (*The Epic of Gilgamesh*),
100

Vengeance quests, 201
Venus (*The Aeneid*), 116, 118, 121–22